The Economics of Deforestation in the Amazon

The Economics of Deforestation in the Amazon

Dispelling the Myths

João S. Campari

Holds a Ph.D. in Economics and is Program Director at The Nature Conservancy

Edward Elgar

Cheltenham, UK • Northampton, MA, USA

Published by
Edward Elgar Publishing Limited
Glensanda House
Montpellier Parade
Cheltenham
Glos GL50 1UA
UK

Edward Elgar Publishing, Inc.
136 West Street
Suite 202
Northampton
Massachusetts 01060
USA

A catalogue record for this book
is available from the British Library

ISBN   1 84376 879 8

Printed and bound in Great Britain by MPG Books Ltd, Bodmin, Cornwall

In memory of
my friend and colleague Anna Luiza Ozório de Almeida

Contents

Preface

This book is the outcome of several years of research, field work, and policy advice concerned with the rapidly growing subject of deforestation in the Amazon. My initial intention was to test a leading hypothesis of deforestation, the 'turnover hypothesis', which holds that the migration of small farmers in the Amazon is one of the main causes of deforestation. Many authors, including myself, have assumed for a long time that this hypothesis provided a good theoretical framework to explain the relationships between migrations and deforestation in the Amazon. When I began working on this book, I expected that my main contribution to the deforestation debate would be to test and hopefully prove the validity of the turnover hypothesis. I never reached my initial goal because, in the course of my work, I found that the motives that cause migrations and deforestation proved not to be as simple as stated under that hypothesis. Most of the results of this study are unexpected and, therefore, require novel interpretation. I would hope that in challenging the turnover hypothesis using field evidence, I have been able to make a greater contribution to the current debate on deforestation than I intended originally. On a broad level, my findings are inconsistent with many other recent studies on the Amazon that regard deforestation as an artifact of distortionary government policies. I have found that although government policies have contributed to deforestation in the past, today it is the outcome of rational profit-maximizing local agents. This finding is as new to me as it must be for most authors who believe they have nailed the causes of deforestation. My findings show that deforestation continues today because current policies are based on old assumptions of regional development.

One of the main lessons I learned in writing this book is that a defining characteristic of a frontier settlement area – and the one feature analysts find most perplexing to contend with – is rapid change. Because history moves at high speed in such places, it has a persistent habit of leaping ahead of our analytical grasp, rendering obsolete hard-won conclusions that now seem to apply only to a previous period. It is no exaggeration to say that much of what we think we know about the Brazilian Amazon today is probably out of date, including the process of deforestation.

The empirical evidence presented in this study permits the observation of the changing character of human settlement and its association with deforestation in the region at the plot level. The data presented here provide the most current source of information on small farmer behavior in selected areas of the states of Pará and Mato Grosso. The first round of surveys was begun in 1981, and the second round of surveys was undertaken ten years later, in 1991. In this study, much new experience and information have been added since the last survey. The three-stage research design makes this one of the few studies that can lay legitimate claim to document the ways things have changed in newly settled areas of the Brazilian Amazon.

The ten-year frame that separates the first (1981) and second surveys (1991) encompasses a period of structural changes in the Brazilian economy that altered the impact of government policies on the Amazon region. This period marked a fundamental transformation in the character of migrations in the Amazon, and altered the structure of the local rural economies. The ability to track such changes at the level of the individual farm plots is therefore one of the things that makes this a truly unique study.

The argument presented here is a needed corrective to current thinking and policies that ignore small colonists or, worse, treat them as environmental pariahs. In the 1970s, small farmers were disregarded, as traditional policies favored cattle ranchers. Now that the emphasis has shifted towards conservation, small farmers still are considered hopeless deforesters, and the emphasis is on protected areas or, at best, indigenous groups presumed to be superior resource stewards. This study hopes to shift the focus to determinants of successful farming and to make convincing and compelling arguments for why this must be a key objective of current and future policies for containing deforestation in the Amazon.

The additional strength of this study is its methodological pluralism and its broad conceptual approach. Disregarding conventional classifications, it draws insights from macro and microeconomics, natural resource management and environmental economics, public finance, institutional analyses, political economy, demography and economic geography. The findings of the various methods are woven together using an interpretive framework that is sensitive to linkages between the transformations at the national level, and the effects such economic and political changes have had on the region and, ultimately, on the microeconomic factors that motivate land management and deforestation by colonists.

This study hopes to live up to its commitment to deliver specific policy recommendations regarding a subject that is ridden with contradictions. For example, the results of the analysis point to the rather daunting conclusion that deforestation is, ironically, the outcome (albeit for very different reasons) of both low productivity farming (and the itinerancy that results in deforestation of new areas) as well as high productivity farming (and the tendency to deforest where farmers are). On the basis of these, and similar results, this study goes beyond conventional income and pricing tools by proposing a set of policy recommendations uniquely tuned to local realities.

Most of the results presented in this study are quite definitive and lead to the rejection of much of what has been conjectured in the literature on the causes of deforestation in the Amazon. Many times, however, the connections made between multiple analytical levels are inevitably suggestive rather than definitive, in which case the interpretation of findings is open to criticism. At one end of the spectrum, a political economist might wish to see more attention given to, say, the restructuring that has taken place in Brazilian society since the early 1980s, and the way in which changes of this kind may have altered the course of deforestation in the Brazilian Amazon. At the opposite extreme, a microeconomist might wish to invoke more elaborate models of the decisions farmers make regarding land and resource use. But to heed either of these admonitions – legitimate though each may be in its respective domain – would undermine rather than enhance the study's main contribution: its willingness to offer an interpretation of frontier changes that culminate in deforestation, by plausibly integrating observations and data sources from multiple levels of economic and political organization. In contrast to a narrower approach, such a multileveled conceptualization is the only realistic way to come to grips with the complexities involved in the process of deforestation.

Acknowledgements

I am grateful to the Institute of Applied Economic Research (IPEA) for providing the data I used in this book. I am especially grateful to Adriana Alves, Gustavo Gontijo, Maria da Piedade Morais, and Ângela Moulin Penalva Santos for their hospitality, friendship and support.

Many of the ideas contained in this work were developed several years ago at the World Bank's Poverty and Social Policy Department (PSP). At PSP, Oey Astra-Meesook provided encouragement and institutional support for the development of important working papers which culminated in the publication of 'Sustainable settlement in the Brazilian Amazon' (Ozório de Almeida and Campari, 1996). 'Sustainable settlement' is an important precursor to this book. I am especially grateful to the contributions made by the Poverty Group.

Several colleagues in Brazil contributed in many different ways to this work. In Mato Grosso, I am especially grateful to Frederico Muller (Secretary of Environment), who welcomed me at the State Environmental Agency (FEMA), Edson Teixeira (Coordinator of FEMA's Geoprocessing Division) for providing digitized satellite images of the surveyed projects in Mato Grosso and Paulo Leite (Director of the Forest Department) for providing insights into most of the crucial questions I had on the dynamics of deforestation.

I would like to thank Gabriel de Lima Ferreira and Gina Valmórbida from the Ministry of the Environment for the helpful discussions about the institutional constraints involved in environmental management in the Amazon region. I am also grateful to the UNDP technical consultants who have always been willing to share their knowledge and experience on Amazonian issues.

I am grateful to Bernardo Mueller (University of Brasília), Philip Fearnside (INPA), and Robert Schneider (World Bank) who provided valuable reading material used in this study.

At the Department for International Development (DFID), I am grateful to Benedicte de la Brière for her thorough revision and comments on the empirical chapters, Marcel Viergever for his feedback on the policy chapter, Gail Marzetti for invaluable help in drafting the graphs and charts that illustrate this study, and to Jane Lovel for offering her comments on the final draft.

At the University of Texas, I am grateful to Vivian Goldman-Leffler for always being prompt to assist me with University matters, mainly after I returned to Brazil, and for her willingness to contribute to this work by carefully editing the first draft. I am also grateful to Mike Conroy, Gordon Hansen, and Chuck Wood, who have always been prompt to provide insightful comments in the early stages of this work.

In the Department of Economics, I am especially grateful to Peter Wilcoxen, my dissertation supervisor, who introduced me to the study of environmental and natural resources economics and always asked provocative questions that inspired my work. I truly appreciate his patience, his positive and critical feedback, as well as his willingness to spend many hours on the telephone discussing critical parts of this book. I am also grateful to Professor Don Fullerton, William Glade, Niles Hansen and Antonio Benjamin, for their insightful comments on the draft version of this manuscript.

I would like especially to thank David Pearce for his comments on the final manuscript, in particular for his recommendations on the policy chapter in this book.

Finally, I am very grateful to Nica, Mônica, Marcelo and Otavio who have always provided support and encouragement throughout these years.

Although Anna Luiza Ozório de Almeida – who was my mentor, co-author and good friend – is no longer among us, I dedicate this study to her, with all my respect and grateful thoughts.

1. Deforestation and its myths

1.1. INTRODUCTION

The Amazon Basin, most of which lies within Brazil, is one of the last large areas of the world currently undergoing frontier settlement. The expansion of demographic and economic frontiers into the Amazon is often seen as the movement of people and of new activities into unoccupied, empty spaces. In fact, these regions are rarely as clear of human inhabitants as is generally supposed. Rather, the existence of occupants who predate the expanding frontier is increasingly recognized.

The Amazon population today numbers more than 22 million people, of whom more than 8 million are farming the rain forest. The current migration of small farmers from old to new frontiers within the Amazon poses an important threat to the forest. These migrations are thought to be associated with the failure of agriculture in rain forest soils that are considered too poor to sustain production. In view of such failure, small farmers are prompted to sell their plots to other farmers who can invest in large-scale agriculture or cattle ranching. Although this is thought to be a widespread regional phenomenon, it is conjectured to be happening mostly in colonization projects established by the federal government during the 1970s, but also in projects sponsored by private colonization companies during the 1980s.

The movement of colonists from plot to plot, opening new frontiers and selling out to newcomers after a few years on the land, is called *turnover*. In the Amazon, high turnover on farming plots is thought to have strong implications for land re-concentration and deforestation. The literature on deforestation conjectures that since colonists do not have the means to sustain production without the heavy use of fertilizers and other soil correctives, they sell their small plots to newcomers, who are large entrepreneurs in agribusiness. Furthermore, individual plots are only as large as 100 hectares and, therefore, considered too small to undertake commercial agricultural activities. For this reason, deforestation analysts believe that, as frontiers mature, newcomers start buying small neighboring plots and transforming the areas which were originally destined for family farming into large agricultural holdings. The practice of extensive agriculture in the Amazon provokes an increase in the amount of land used for ranching and other large agricultural initiatives. This practice leads to an increase in the scale of deforestation since more land must be cleared for production.

The process described above is widely accepted in the literature on Amazon deforestation. This study formalizes this process and calls it the *Turnover Hypothesis of Amazon Deforestation*. The purpose here is to examine the claims that the literature has made for decades in favor of this hypothesis as a good theoretical framework to explain the process of demographic instability among the rural population (turnover), which is thought to have important implications for land re-concentration and deforestation in the region.

The current conjecture in the literature – one that has become the basis for the current views that attempt to inhibit the expansion of agriculture in the region – is that Amazonian agriculture leads to private as well as social losses, i.e., a *lose-lose* situation. From the point of view of public policies, the solid knowledge of the economics of deforestation seems fundamental to break with the mistaken premise that the 'by-product' of regional agriculture is an environmental disservice in terms of deforestation (externality) as well as a (private) economic 'bad'. If a *lose-lose* situation prevailed, the enforcement of stringent conservation policies would not yield high private economic losses. However, current policies are based on overly strict regulation that would lead to high private losses if they were enforced.

The analysis carried out in the forthcoming chapters provides field evidence to challenge the arguments of this hypothesis. It also provides evidence that supports an alternative explanation that dispels the myth of turnover being associated with deforestation and land re-concentration in the Amazon.

1.2.   DISPELLING OTHER MYTHS OF AMAZON DEFORESTATION

Contrary to what is usually conjectured, this study provides evidence that deforestation in the Amazon is a source of private economic gains, frequently substantial, at the same time as it imposes negative externalities, or social (environmental) costs associated with deforestation. This implies that deforestation leads to a *win-lose* scenario. The gains are generally associated with either relatively successful agriculture or speculation in land markets, in which case land is held as a hedge against inflation and later transacted so that its owner can reap capital gains. The first argument (successful agriculture) runs counter to the widespread belief that Amazonian soils are unsuitable for agriculture, even for small-scale farming. The second argument (speculation in Amazonian land markets) is much less considered in the deforestation literature.

By discussing this issue using empirical evidence, this book brings a new perspective to the literature on Amazonian deforestation. It shows that small itinerant farmers do not cause most deforestation, contrary to the conjectures of the turnover hypothesis; those successful ones who have stayed on their plots are the ones responsible for most of the land cleared in the Amazon. This is a historic trend that has been happening since the early days of colonization.

1.3. ORGANIZATION OF THE WORK

A common tendency in the literature on Amazon deforestation is to distinguish between the demographic and the economic frontiers. The literature treats the impact of the population and economic policies on deforestation as separate issues. This work does not follow that precedent. On the one hand, the demographic occupation of an inhospitable place – such as the Amazon in the 1970s – would have been impossible without some form of incentive for the development of economic activity. To ignore the former, or treat it separately, thus runs counter to the main goal of this work: to establish the relationships between the economic factors associated with the mobility of the rural population (turnover), land re-concentration, and deforestation.

This study is organized in ten chapters. Chapters 2 and 3 are background chapters. These chapters discuss policies and macro variables associated with regional occupation and deforestation. These variables can be thought of as the underlying causes of deforestation: policies that stimulated migrations to the region, government regimes, sectoral policies, domestic and international markets, tax and credit systems, and the rules of land allocation. Chapter 2 uses census data to reflect upon the environmental consequences of early occupation and changing migration patterns that have affected the Amazon for the past 30 years. Chapter 3 discusses the motives behind the federal government's initiatives to expand the agricultural frontier to the Amazon and induce regional occupation through large development programs during the 1960s and 1970s. It also explains why the government, after 20 years of promoting occupation, came to a complete halt in its support of Amazonian development during the 1980s. The impact that such incentives and omissions had on deforestation permeates the arguments of this chapter. These two chapters provide the foundations upon which the turnover hypothesis is conceptualized.

Chapters 4 through 8 are related to the turnover hypothesis itself. These chapters examine how turnover and land re-concentration are associated with deforestation. Chapter 4 discusses the inadequacy of standard models of land clearing and proposes an analytical framework to explain the behavior of Amazonian farmers. Chapter 5 develops a theoretical framework of the turnover hypothesis. Chapter 6 discusses the field work undertaken in colonization projects in the Amazon and the data (obtained from the surveys) used to assess the extent to which the turnover hypothesis holds. Chapter 7 discusses the magnitude of turnover in the surveyed projects and the impact it has had on deforestation. Finally, Chapter 8 transforms the theoretical framework developed in Chapter 5 into an empirical economic model that sets the conditions under which the turnover hypothesis can be assessed.

Chapter 9 presents empirical evidence that dispels the myth that poor regional agricultural performance is the main force that triggers turnover and deforestation in the Amazon. Here, the economic returns to farming are compared with its opportunity costs to assess whether colonists are faring well or poorly in frontier agriculture and, further, how performance in frontier agriculture is associated with turnover and deforestation.

Chapter 10 summarizes the findings of this study and, based on them, discusses policies that could be implemented to contain the causes of deforestation in the Brazilian Amazon.

1.4. DIMENSIONS AND LIMITATIONS OF THE STUDY

The objective of this study is to assess the appropriateness of the turnover hypothesis to explain the causes of deforestation in the Amazon, as far as colonization projects are concerned. For many years (actually decades), the government of Brazil and the international community have considered this hypothesis a 'mantra' upon which policies for the region are conceived and implemented with substantial foreign aid. This study challenges this hypothesis and finds that it is out-dated for dealing with the complexity of current Amazonian issues. This study also analyzes the extent to which economic policy can be used to reduce the share of deforestation caused by local farmers in colonization areas.

The empirical sections of the study analyze turnover and deforestation and assess how well, or how badly, small farmers are covering their opportunity costs of frontier farming. The conceptualization of these opportunity costs are rather limited, as they only represent rates of remuneration of factors of production in the economy as a whole. Broader alternatives, such as gold prospecting, drug trafficking, and extractivism are not dealt with explicitly.

Some terms are used interchangeably in this study, glossing over important differences that are relevant for other disciplines of the social sciences. Farming households are interchangeably called 'frontier farmers' (who represent the universe of the rural population in the Amazon), 'settlers' (farmers who may or may not have title to the land), 'colonists' (farmers who are owners of a colonization plot) and 'pioneers' (farmers who first arrived on colonization plots, either sponsored by the government or by private colonization companies). The terms 'family farming' (farmers whose only source of labor is family labor), 'small farming' (whose farming plots are small) and 'subsistence farming' (farmers who do not generate surplus output or savings) are often substituted for one another, as are the terms 'the Amazon' (the basin itself, which transcends the borders of Brazil), 'Legal Amazonia' (the nine states in Brazil that contain the rain forest; an administrative definition for the implementation of regional policy) and 'the North region' (one of the five geographic regions of Brazil, a region that includes six out of the nine states of Legal Amazonia). In the context of this study, the interchangeable use of these terms should not sacrifice interpretation.

The terms 'new (recent) frontiers' and 'consolidated (old) frontiers' are used throughout the text and have important specific meanings. A *new frontier* can be thought of as marginal lands in the initial stages of occupation, with low population densities, and where markets are nonexistent or very incipient. New frontiers can also be considered places that select for individuals with low opportunity costs, relative to more developed areas, given the thankless reality they have before them. New frontiers can be understood as places where land is an abundant resource that is often unclaimed or, if claimed, is unoccupied. Further, the total area already deforested in these places is low relative to more developed regions.

The term *consolidated frontiers* can be defined as places with increasing population pressure, where disputes over land are common and often violent. In consolidated frontiers, input, output and factor markets are still incipient and thin relative to developed areas, but are certainly more evolved than they are in new frontiers. Consolidated frontiers can count on basic infrastructure and on the provision of government services, although both can be very rudimentary and inadequate given the size of the population. Land resources that were abundant in new frontiers become scarce as frontiers consolidate. Deforestation is higher in consolidated frontiers than in new frontiers. Consolidated frontiers generally select for individuals with relatively higher opportunity costs.

The difference between these two types of frontier is crucial for understanding some of the points that are discussed in this study. For example, while the rate at which a small farmer deforests in *new frontiers* may be very high (because he expects the government to grant him a title over a multiple of the area that he has cleared), the rate of deforestation by the same farmer in *consolidated frontiers* may fall drastically (his marginal rate of deforestation is only that necessary to support family consumption rather than also to secure title). Therefore, the factors that influence farmers' decisions with regard to deforestation are different in new and consolidated frontiers. A clear space-time divide separates the two types of frontiers: new frontiers are located in *distant* places relative to the established economy and can be found in a very *early* stage of occupation; consolidated frontiers are places *near* the established economy at *later* stages of occupation.

There are several issues that this study does not attempt to treat. It does not analyze data on Amazonian deforestation beyond that caused by colonists. It does not discuss some of the broader consequences of Amazonian deforestation, such as its global environmental impact (e.g., climate change, carbon emissions) or the anthropological dimensions of deforestation (e.g., the deforestation by indigenous and native groups).

The issue of illegal logging is also ignored in this study. Small farmers may obtain additional income from illegally extracted wood, as they are thought to commercialize it in the informal market. Depending on the volume of the additional income, farmers may alter their choices with regard to deforestation and conservation. Studies on this issue are incipient, reliable data are scarce and the only source of evidence available is anecdotal.

Although this book does not attempt to offer an in-depth analysis of human capital, the data set used in this study does contain information that pertains to this issue. Ozório de Almeida (1992) and Ozório de Almeida and Campari (1996), using the same data set, offer more extensive research on human capital. Likewise, health conditions are not explicitly examined in the text even though they are known to correlate to economic performance. Finally, it was not possible to undertake an empirical qualitative analysis of the soils of sampled locations. There is no evidence, however, that government considered soil quality prior to settling farmers on the projects. The sample, therefore, is not biased in regard to soil type. All of these issues are beyond the scope of this study.

The new information and novel interpretations offered here are based on an analysis of the largest and most complete data set ever produced on the economic variables that influence small farmers in the Amazon. The empirical observation of the economic behavior of a panel of small farmers over a span of 20 years is unprecedented, from the major thrust toward Amazonian colonization in the early 1970s until the chaotic aftermath of the early 1990s.

One of the main lessons learned from this study is that Amazonian development and deforestation are an intra-Amazonian matter; interregional migrations no longer pose the threat to the forest they once did. If frontier farmers are not induced to settle where they are now, they will continue to move to areas meant to be reserved. Conservation of these areas, therefore, will not be possible unless intraregional migrations are contained.

By revealing the economic mechanisms at work in deforesting the Amazon today, this study hopes to contribute to the design of appropriate policies for use by the federal and state governments, multilateral institutions, lending agencies, international organizations, and to inform the academic debate on the causes of Amazonian deforestation.

2. Occupation, changing migration dynamics, and deforestation in the Brazilian Amazon

2.1. INTRODUCTION

Despite the front-page publicity given to deforestation, the Amazon embraces still the world's largest area of intact tropical rain forest. It has a relatively unexplored resource potential and is regarded as one of the last agricultural frontiers. Figure 2.1 shows that the Brazilian Amazon comprises the states of Acre, Amapá, Amazonas, Mato Grosso, Maranhão, Pará, Rondônia, Roraima and Tocantins, totaling an area of over 5 million square kilometers, equivalent to 60 percent of Brazil, and sufficiently large to accommodate the entire Western Europe. Of this, approximately 4 million square kilometers is covered by forest formations.

In the 1970s, the Brazilian government and people were blithely optimistic regarding the future of the Amazon region. The military regime (which had taken power in the previous decade) set out to colonize the region and tap its natural resources through a series of high-profile development projects. The federal government launched credit and tax incentive schemes to attract private capital to the region, and it financed the construction of the Transamazon Highway – an unpaved road extending some 5000 kilometers from the state of Maranhão in the east through Pará and Amazonas to the unpopulated Amazon basin to the westernmost state of Acre on the border of Bolivia.

The modernization of Amazonia was to be achieved through the National Integration Program, which envisioned colonization by smallholders on 100 hectare plots along both sides of the Transamazon Highway. Similar to the Homestead Act in the United States 100 years earlier, the government's attempts to colonize the Amazon were to create a prosperous small-farmer class by freely distributing agricultural land in sparsely populated territories. Colonists came from amongst poor farmers and rural landless in the overpopulated and poverty-stricken Northeast region of Brazil.

Figure 2.1. *The Brazilian Amazon*

Initial enthusiasm, however, soon gave way to the somber reality of the difficulties linked to agriculture in lowland tropical areas. The colonists settled by the federal government's Institute of Colonization and Agrarian Reform (INCRA) in Marabá, Altamira and Itaituba (the first projects in Pará) faced a myriad of difficulties, particularly in transporting produce to market. Nonetheless, the large flows of spontaneous migrants quickly swamped INCRA's capacity to provide services and to absorb them in the planned communities. As alternatives became scarcer, small farmers staked out land wherever accessible, falsely believing that any and all government lands not being cultivated could be claimed as a homestead.

One of the main initiatives of the federal government was the additional construction of roads off the Transamazon Highway, the main one being the Belém-Brasília Highway, which provided a corridor through which settlers occupied – either directed by the government in official colonization projects, or spontaneously – small plots of land in Pará (Figure 2.2). Furthermore, the 1970s were marked by highly profitable tax treatments and credit programs made available through SUDAM (the Superintendence for the Development of the Amazon, which was closed down in 2001 because of widespread corruption) to well-financed investors from southern Brazil. Some of these investors converted huge tracts of forest land to pasture, but most bought land to hold in investment portfolios as a hedge against inflation. In occupied areas, land conflicts became quite common when cattle ranchers, land grabbers, and peasant farmers competed for control of the newly accessible territories. The violence that ensued claimed the lives of thousands of people and bestowed on Pará its unfortunate notoriety as the 'Wild West' of Amazonia (Schmink 1982; Schmink and Wood 1992; Alston et al. 1999).

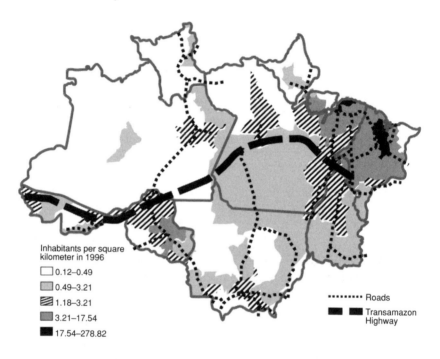

Inhabitants per square
kilometer in 1996
☐ 0.12–0.49
▨ 0.49–3.21
▨ 1.18–3.21
▨ 3.21–17.54
■ 17.54–278.82

········· Roads

■■ Transamazon
Highway

Figure 2.2.   Dispersion of the population along the highway system

By the middle of the 1970s, many of the small farmers who informally claimed untitled land had been driven off the plots they had cleared. The dispossessed faced a difficult and uncertain future. Many moved down the road. Others ventured further into the forest, only to fall victim again to eviction. A large number of families drifted from one site to another, temporarily employed by labor recruiters who had been contracted by ranchers to clear land for pasture during the dry season. Those with enough resources to do so returned to their states of origin. Many more lost their land but were too poor to return, seeking refuge in the new villages that sprang up along the roads or in the shantytowns on the outskirts of established cities. A few places that once had held a modest number of people exploded into makeshift towns of 15,000 to 20,000 (Schmink and Wood 1992). Most urban centers lacked sanitation, medical facilities, and educational services and offered displaced peasants and new migrants neither regular employment nor the means to support themselves. Most colonists whose stories are not generally told, however, stayed on their plots and were relatively successful in agriculture. These were the very fortunate, and their plots displayed increasing productivity, growth and deforestation.

The heavy influx of emigrants and the publicity given to the violent confrontations between ranchers and peasants, as well as the international outcry over deforestation and the threat to indigenous communities, served to undermine support for INCRA's colonization program at the time when frontier settlement came under growing criticism for being expensive and failing to live up to its original objectives. In the tradition of blaming the victim, the colonists themselves were faulted for their presumed lack of managerial skills, even though many of the problems they confronted were hardly of their own making (Wood and Schmink 1979). Business interests took the opportunity to wage a campaign arguing that a more 'rational' and less 'predatory' occupation of the region could be achieved by the private sector. By the late 1970s, pressure from the business lobby had succeeded, mainly in Mato Grosso, and public colonization, the only safe haven for the small farmer, was virtually abandoned in favor of privately owned and operated colonization schemes (Ozório de Almeida 1992; Ozório de Almeida and Campari 1996). Private colonization gained impetus in the early 1980s, as federal budgets for public colonization dwindled due to Brazil's economic crisis. When easy credit ceased to flow by the late 1980s, private companies lost interest in this type of colonization. Furthermore, issues concerning land occupation for agricultural development in the Amazon became increasingly complex as environmental concerns heightened.

The criticism of Amazonian development that began in Brazil in the late 1970s soon connected with the international concern about deforestation.[1] Conservation and environmental awareness lent both publicity and legitimacy to new priorities in the development of the region. By the early 1990s, the terms of the Amazonian debate had completely shifted. The environmental consequences of the development policy became the target of headline stories in Brazil and across the world. The expansion of cattle ranching in the Amazon, once the mainstay of the modernization program, was condemned in favor of environmentally and socially responsible development. The small farmers who had migrated to the frontier in the 1970s and 1980s shared a similar fate, and were either despised or labeled 'villains' in the deforestation process, when in fact they were lured to the Amazon as a new 'Eldorado' by federal programs and private colonization companies. The demise of colonization programs, without the appropriate social safety nets to reduce the short-term impact of the structural changes brought about by the economic crisis of the 1980s on small farmers, impelled prospective colonists to settle and farm whatever land they could possibly find. Given the lack of support, many of those already settled also gave up their plots and moved: some did not have another choice but to sell out, as land was bad and agricultural production could not be sustained without external financial assistance; others whose land exhibited high productivity chose to sell out to earn capital gains and also moved on to other plots further inland. A process of intense in- and out-migrations among the rural population was under way.

The purpose of this chapter is to explore the differences in the past and the current migration dynamics that are likely to have determined the outcomes that this study sets out to analyze: turnover on farming plots and its relationship to deforestation and land re-concentration in the Amazon. The environmental significance of turnover depends on whether an itinerant population of small rural households open new frontiers, grow crops and stay on the land for a few years before they sell out to newcomers, only to start the process again further into the forest. Those who come in later are thought to arrive with a different agenda, demanding larger land holdings and larger deforested areas than did initial settlers. The turnover hypothesis is based on the premise that a critical mass of farmers does make a difference in deforestation and land re-concentration. A good way to begin to examine this issue is by analyzing migration dynamics.

Section 2.2 discusses the differences in the patterns of migration in two periods, from the mid-1960s to the mid-1980s, when farmers responded to government incentives to migrate, and from then until 2000, when migrations became a response to local stimuli. Since the population dynamics of the agricultural frontier is assumed to be strongly associated with land use and forest clearing, Section 2.3 discusses the dynamics of deforestation from the early 1970s until the late 1990s. Section 2.4 discusses the effects that occupation and changing population dynamics had on the forest resource base.

2.2. THE CHANGING PATTERN OF MIGRATION DYNAMICS

Although the efforts on the part of the federal government to induce occupation of the Amazon began in 1964, it was not until 1970 that a significant number of migrants started to make a difference in the demographic landscape of the region (Alston et al. 1999). Table 2.1 shows the percentage of land in each region of Brazil that was in private farms from 1920 to 1985. In 1920, when the first census was taken, much of the land in the South and Southeast had already been transferred to private hands. The rate of growth of the values in the table indicates the extent and pace of settlement. The Amazon (the North) experienced virtually no increase in settlement from 1920 to 1970. Alston et al. (1999) argue that this is why the Amazon began to be perceived in the 1960s as the last frontier in Brazil. In contrast, in other areas of the country, especially in the South and Southeast, over 50 percent of the land had been placed in private farms by 1940.

Table 2.1.   Ratios of occupied land to total land (in percentages)

			Total Area in Farms				
	1920	1940	1950	1960	1970	1980	1985
Brazil	20.6	23.2	27.2	29.3	34.6	42.9	44.1
North (Amazon)	6.0	7.1	6.5	6.6	6.5	11.6	12.6
Northeast	23.2	27.6	37.6	40.6	47.9	57.0	59.3
Southeast	49.4	62.1	66.4	68.8	75.2	79.5	79.2
South	47.7	54.9	61.6	67.8	79.0	83.3	83.3
Center-West*	23.6	21.4	28.5	31.9	43.4	60.3	61.9

Notes: *Geographically, the state of Mato Grosso belongs to the Center West region, but administratively it belongs to the Legal Amazon. It was not until the late 1970s that it began to be colonized, which explains the big jump in the values for the Center West between 1960 and 1970.

Sources: Alston et al. (1999); IBGE, 1920–85 *Agricultural Census.*

The Amazon population today numbers over 21 million people, more than one-third of whom live in rural areas and show no intention of leaving the region (Table 2.2). Any realistic Amazon conservation scheme, therefore, must deal with the fact that, for the foreseeable future, over 6 million people are farming the Amazon (Ozório de Almeida and Campari 1996; Sawyer 2001).

The purpose of this section is to show that a significant number of small migrant farmers are still within the Amazon, and their movement creates demographic instability which is believed to have quite important consequences for deforestation. Contrary to the interregional migrations triggered by countrywide pressures in the course of the 1970s, during the 1980s, migrations largely responded to local-level dynamics. The section will show that fertility rates for Brazil are declining and that overall and regional rates of population growth are falling. As a result Amazonian settlement in the near future is not expected to experience significant population pressure from the outside. Turnover on farming plots is accelerating within the Amazon, however, and a large population of rural households is being displaced from time to time. Both these factors have spurred intra-Amazonian migrations and deforestation further inland to the very borders of Brazil, where farmers and ranchers are adding to the flow of prospectors and other migrants now spilling over into neighboring countries. Thus, reduction of population pressure on the forest requires taking into consideration *intraregional* rather than *interregional* migrations.

Table 2.2.   Population and land in the Amazon

State	Number of inhabitants	Population Urban	Rural	Area of State (Km²)	Population Density (people per Km²)
Acre	557,526	66%	34%	153,150	5.78
Amapá	477,032	89%	11%	143,454	3.64
Amazonas	2,812,557	75%	25%	1,577,820	1.78
Maranhão	5,651,475	60%	40%	333,366	1.44
Mato Grosso	2,504,353	79%	21%	906,807	4.94
Pará	6,192,307	67%	33%	1,253,165	3.33
Rondônia	1,379,787	64%	36%	238,513	4.16
Roraima	324,397	76%	24%	225,116	16.95
Tocantins	1,157,098	74%	26%	278,421	2.76
TOTAL	21,056,532	68%	32%	5,109,810	4.12

Source: Population Census (2000)

2.2.1.   Fertility Decline

High fertility is often believed to contribute to pressure on fragile environments by creating a large stock of potential migrants. Rising fertility rates would suggest a possible increase in the propensity to migrate, other factors held constant, whereas declining fertility rates would suggest a decrease. However, these hypothesized relationships have not held in Brazil during the past thirty years.

The weighted averages of total fertility rates for Brazil were 5.6 live births per woman for 1965, 3.2 for 1991, and 2.09 in 2001 (IBGE 2001). These figures indicate that the overall fertility rate has been falling and will probably continue to decline. Yet the drop in fertility rates has not resulted in a reduction in the rates of migration and urban growth. On the contrary, during the 1960s and 1970s throughout much of the country, migration remained high despite declines in fertility rates. Thus in general, migrations in Brazil and to the Amazon in particular seem to have been spurred more by economic and social factors than by population increase.

2.2.2. Lower Interregional Migration

The Brazilian agricultural frontier has historically been short-lived (Monbeig 1952; Roche 1959; Margolis 1973; Katzman 1977; Martins 1975; Foweraker 1981; Sawyer 1984, 1990; Ozório de Almeida 1992; Ozório de Almeida and Campari 1996; Alston et al. 1999). The main sending areas, once frontier themselves, soon began expelling emigrants at rates greater than those at which they were receiving immigrants. Table 2.3 shows that, during the 1960s, the growth in the rural population of the *cerrado* (a type of savanna vegetation) region of the Center-West – then considered Brazil's agricultural frontier – was 777,478 but that ten years later (1970s) the growth dropped to 233,668. In contrast to the reduction in the number of rural migrants to the *cerrados* during the 1970s (which had by then become an old frontier), the neighboring Amazon region – which had turned into Brazil's most recent agricultural frontier – absorbed 1,097,912 rural migrants, approximately twice the numbers seen during the 1960s (see Table 2.3).

Table 2.3.   Change in rural population in frontier areas, 1960–80

Frontier Area	1960–70	1970–80
Amazon	547,745	1,097,912
Cerrado	777,478	233,668
Total change	1,325,223	1,281,565

Source: Population Census 1960, 1970, 1980, and Ozório de Almeida (1992)

During the 1960s and 1970s, the geographical spread of occupied frontier areas was considerable. As the frontier 'shifted', it left behind low-density population pockets where small farming activities had once been carried out. Small tenants and squatters were evicted in large numbers. Many small landowners sold their plots, either moving further inland to re-establish their family farming, or going to nearby towns, seeking non-farm employment. The land was acquired by newcomers or successful neighbors. In either case, prosperous farmers consolidated small neighboring plots into large ones, converting most of the farmland into pastures.

Table 2.4 shows broad trends during two successive decades. During the 1960–70 period, the Southeast region of Brazil experienced the only loss in rural population, declining by 1,224,574 persons. During the 1970–80 period, the negative value in the Southeast increased, but it was exceeded by the South, where the rural population declined by 2,023,200 persons. This massive number of rural displacements in the South-Southeast during the 1960s and 1970s was caused by a number of factors, including the penetration of soybean and sugar cane plantations in these regions, changes in land laws and rural labor legislation, the effect of business cycle variations on real estate appreciation, and fiscal and credit policies favoring large farmers (Ozório de Almeida and Campari 1996; Mesquita and Silva 1987a, 1987b).

Table 2.4.   Change in rural population by region, 1960–80

Region	1960–70	1970–80
North (Amazon)	383,076	924,532
Northeast	1,945,981	957,853
Center-West	720,432	–178,430
Southeast	–1,224,574	–1,963,936
South	1,826,351	–2,023,200
Total change	3,651,266	–2,283,181

Source: Population Census 1960, 1970, 1980, and Ozório de Almeida (1992)

Tables 2.3 and 2.4 show that, during the 1970s, migrations from other regions to the Amazon were quite intense. ABEP (1998) reports, however, that in the 1986–91 period net migration to the region was only 131,218, falling to 60,844 in the 1991–96 period. The drastic reduction in net migration to the Amazon during the 1980s was the result of the suspension of large-scale government colonization programs, significant decline in infrastructure development, land conflicts, health concerns (such as endemic malaria in many areas), and the lack of government resources to stimulate migrations directly any longer (Sawyer 1990; Moreira and Moura 1997). The balance of the changes in Amazonian population during the 1980s (the period considered in the empirical chapters of this study) is depicted in Figure 2.3.

2.2.3.   Increasing Intraregional Mobility

The fall in interregional migration did not stop population instability within the Amazon (see Figure 2.4). Since the mid-1980s the region has exhibited

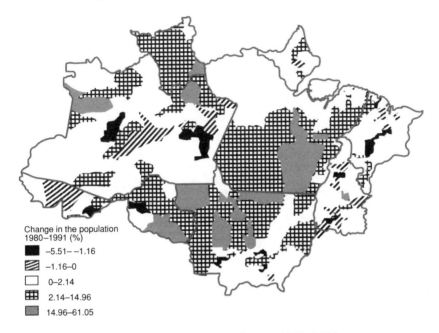

Change in the population
1980–1991 (%)

- ■ −5.51–−1.16
- ▨ −1.16–0
- ☐ 0–2.14
- ⊞ 2.14–14.96
- ■ 14.96–61.05

Figure 2.3.   Change in the Amazon population, 1980–1991

high numbers of migrants, most of whom, however, come from within the region rather than from outside. Net intraregional migration was 708,274 during the 1986–91 period, and 619,991 in the 1991–96 period (ABEP 1998).

In fact, Ozório de Almeida and Campari (1996) show that the decline in the number of small farmers in already settled areas assumed impressive proportions during the 1980s. The authors argue that the migrations of small farmers within the region creates a demographic hollow in previously occupied areas at the core of the frontier (see Figure 2.2). These migrations led small farmers away from the Transamazon Highway, which had drawn them in one decade before (Figure 2.4). Displaced migrants concentrated in northern Mato Grosso and along national boundaries, often going beyond them into eight neighboring countries (Marques 1993). In this study, a 'hollow' frontier means that a large number of small farmers have moved out and, consequently, that the person per hectare ratio has decreased. The existence of a demographic hollow in consolidated areas (old frontiers) does not mean that no economic activity is taking place. In fact, Chomitz and Thomas (2001) provide evidence that many of these areas are undergoing intensification of economic activity. This implies that land is becoming re-concentrated, which is one of the pillars of the turnover hypothesis.

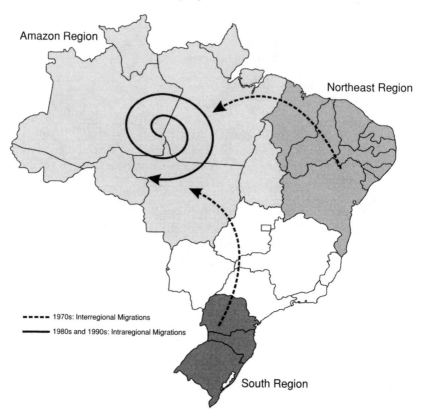

Figure 2.4.   Changing migration dynamics: 1970s–1990s

The destinations of intraregional migrants are mainly frontier cities, gold mines (especially in the state of Roraima), new settlements (especially in Pará and northern Mato Grosso), and previously unopened areas without any kind of physical or social infrastructure available. Migration analysts and sociologists who have studied intraregional migrations in the region have claimed that such instability is associated, in great part, with the instability of colonization projects, which forces settlers out, searching for improved livelihoods (Sawyer 2001; Martine 1982, 1992).

To end this section, a final remark must be made with regard to seasonal migration. While conducting the field research for this study, it was common to observe temporary out-migration among male farmers, heads of their families, who supplied unskilled labor to contractors, such as for deforestation and civil construction. This was most noticeable when the head of the household was not present to respond to the questionnaires at the survey sites. In this case, migration is seasonal and depends on the specificity of the agricultural activity undertaken by the migrant.

2.3.   DEFORESTATION

The process of occupation and the shift in the pattern of migrations (from inter- to intraregional) has triggered a process of forest conversion into agricultural land, which has been a source of considerable controversy. Biologists have voiced concern about species extinction (Pires and Prance 1977; Myers 1980), changes in hydrologic regimes (Gentry and López-Parody 1980), local and global climate change (Moliton 1975; Salati et al. 1979), and soil and resources degradation (Goodland and Irwin 1975; Goodland 1980; Sombroek 2000). Social scientists have pointed to the intense land conflicts (Schmink 1982; Schmink and Wood 1992), increasing peasant marginalization (Santos 1979; Sawyer 1979; Wood and Schmink 1979), extinction of indigenous groups (Davis 1977), and increased rural to urban migration (Aragón 1978; Martine 1982) all of which have accompanied the process of development through agricultural expansion into the Amazon region.

Notwithstanding the concerns of biologists and social scientists, Amazonian regional occupation and development has been described by others as necessary to ensure that millions of Brazilians are not condemned to lives of abject poverty (Alvin 1978, Ozório de Almeida and Campari 1996). In the end, the process of forest conversion into agricultural lands in the Amazon is nothing more than the legacy of public policy fostering occupation, as well as the consequences that different policy approaches have had on the patterns of demographic and economic dynamics. Since this study analyzes Amazon deforestation as a consequence of the economic occupation of the region, it would be unnatural to separate the two issues.

The objective of this section is to discuss facts and figures about deforestation using secondary data. Other chapters will discuss the driving forces behind forest conversion using other sources, including primary data.

2.3.1.   The Magnitude of Deforestation in Legal Amazonia

In this study, deforestation refers to the conversion of primary forest physiognomy by anthropogenic activities for the development of agriculture and cattle ranching. Relative to agriculture and ranching, the logging activity contributes little to the overall deforestation in the region, this work will not therefore give logging the emphasis it has received elsewhere (Schneider et al. 2000).

The best method available to observe the evolution of deforestation at the regional level is remote sensing. Figure 2.5 displays processed satellite images covering the entire Amazon region during the 1970s and 1980s. Taken together, they show the intensification of deforestation in old frontiers (those opened in the 1970s) and the spread of deforestation into new frontiers during the 1980s.

Only in 1988 did the Brazilian government's National Institute of Space Research (INPE) begin using remote sensing techniques to monitor the state of Amazon's forests. Given the unavailability of satellite images, Table 2.5 is used instead. The table shows that the average rates of gross deforestation[2] fluctuated widely between 1978 and 1999. During the 1977–88 period, the registered average rate of deforestation per year was 0.54 percent, and it reached its highest peak in 1994–95, at 0.81 percent. In the 1997–98 period, though, that rate dropped to 0.48 and remained the same for the following period.

Table 2.6 translates these rates into absolute numbers. The table indicates that in the 1978–88 period, the sum of the yearly average rates of gross deforestation was 21,130 square kilometers; gross deforestation peaked at 29,059 square kilometers in 1994–95, and went down to 17,259 square kilometers in 1998–99.

Table 2.7 shows that 570,000 square kilometers had been deforested by 1999, which correspond to 11.4 percent of the regional territory and to 14 percent of the original forest cover. Moreover, the table shows that 60 percent of the total deforestation occurred in only two states, Mato Grosso (25 percent) and Pará (35 percent), the two states surveyed for this study.

2.4.   SUMMARY AND CONCLUSION

This chapter sets forth the basic arguments of this study, i.e., that deforestation is a direct consequence of occupation dynamics. The causes of geographic mobility of the rural population during the 1960s and 1970s can be summarized as follows:

1. A combination of legal, political, economic, and agricultural factors that pushed small farmers and entrepreneurs out of established farming areas of the South and the Northeast. These included (a) legal and political changes in labor relations (Mesquita and Silva 1987a, 1987b, 1987c); (b) long peak in the business cycle which helped the 'Brazilian miracle',

Evolution of Amazon deforestation

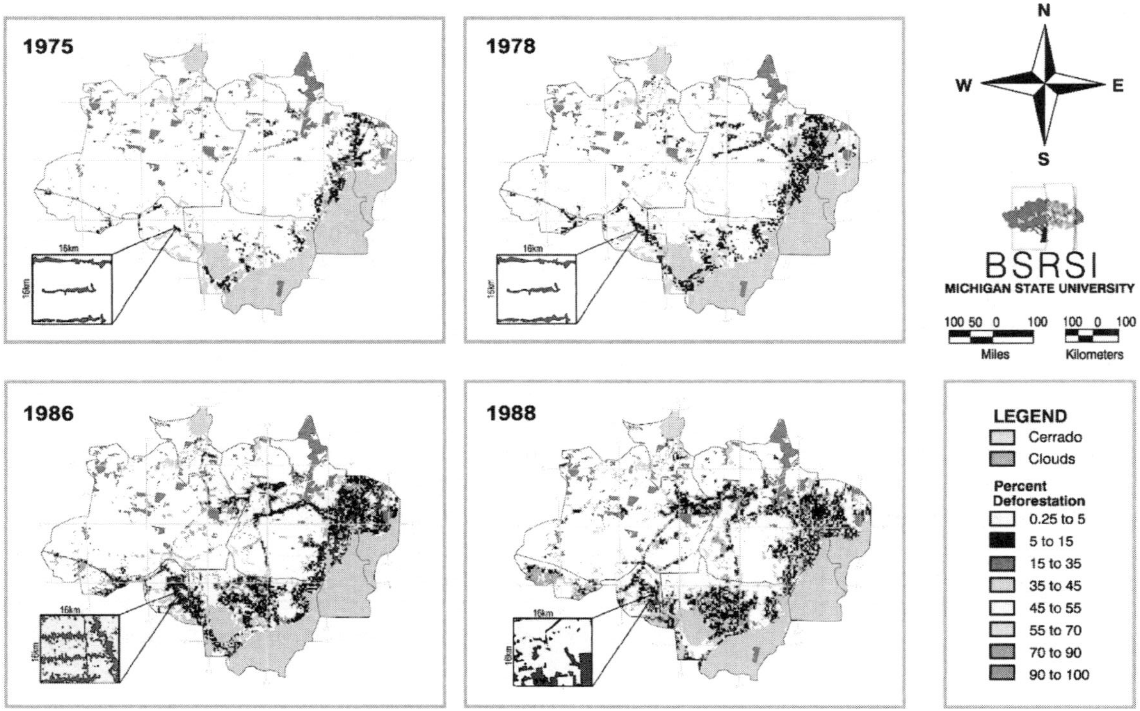

Figure 2.5.   Deforestation, 1970s and 1980s

Table 2.5. Mean rate of gross deforestation (%/yr)*, 1978–1999

Amazonian States	77/88**	88/89	89/90	90/91	91/92	92/94***	94/95	95/96	96/97	97/98	98/99
Acre	0.42	0.39	0.39	0.28	0.29	0.35	0.86	0.31	0.26	0.40	0.33
Amapá	0.06	0.12	0.23	0.37	0.03	–	0.01	–	0.02	0.03	–
Amazonas	0.10	0.08	0.04	0.07	0.06	0.03	0.14	0.07	0.04	0.05	0.05
Maranhão	1.79	1.30	1.03	0.63	1.07	0.35	3.21	2.01	0.40	0.99	1.21
Mato Grosso	1.01	1.31	0.90	0.64	1.05	1.40	2.43	1.56	1.25	1.56	1.71
Pará	0.62	0.55	0.47	0.37	0.37	0.42	0.78	0.62	0.41	0.58	0.51
Rondônia	1.11	0.78	0.91	0.62	1.27	1.46	2.75	1.45	1.18	1.23	1.44
Roraima	0.18	0.39	0.10	0.27	0.18	0.15	0.14	0.14	0.11	0.14	0.14
Tocantins	2.97	2.00	1.61	1.61	1.17	0.95	2.29	0.94	0.81	1.73	0.65
Total	0.54	0.48	0.37	0.30	0.37	0.40	0.81	0.51	0.37	0.48	0.48

Notes:
* Relative to the area of remaining forest formations
** Decade mean
*** Biannual mean

Source: Ministry of Science and Technology/National Institute of Space Research (INPE). *Monitoring the Brazilian Amazon by Satellite: 1999–2000 Report*

Table 2.6. *Mean rate of gross deforestation (sq. km/yr), 1978–1999*

Amazonian States	77/88**	88/89	89/90	90/91	91/92	92/94***	94/95	95/96	96/97	97/98	98/99
Acre	620	540	550	380	400	482	1,208	433	358	536	441
Amapá	60	130	250	410	36	–	9	–	18	30	–
Amazonas	1,510	1,180	520	980	799	370	2,114	1,023	589	670	720
Maranhão	2,450	1,420	1,100	670	1,135	372	1,745	1,061	409	1,012	1,230
Mato Grosso	5,140	5,960	4,020	2,840	4,674	6,220	10,391	6,543	5,271	6,466	6,963
Pará	6,990	5,750	4,890	3,780	3,787	4,284	7,845	6,135	4,139	5,829	5,111
Rondônia	2,340	1,430	1,670	1,110	2,265	2,595	4,730	2,432	1,986	2,041	2,358
Roraima	290	630	150	420	281	240	220	214	184	223	220
Tocantins	1,650	730	580	440	409	333	797	320	273	576	216
Total	21,130	17,860	13,810	11,130	13,786	14,896	29,059	18,161	13,227	17,383	17,259

Notes:
* Decade mean
** Biannual mean

Source: Ministry of Science and Technology/National Institute of Space Research (INPE). *Monitoring the Brazilian Amazon by Satellite: 1999–2000 Report*

Table 2.7. Accumulated gross deforestation (sq. km), January 1978 to August 1999

Amazonian States	Jan. 78	Apr. 88	Aug. 89	Aug. 90	Aug. 91	Aug. 92	Aug. 94	Aug. 95	Aug. 96	Aug. 97	Aug. 98	Aug. 99
Acre	2,500	8,900	9,800	10,300	10,700	11,100	12,064	13,306	13,742	14,203	14,714	15,136
Amapá	200	800	1,000	1,300	1,700	1,736	1,736	1,782	1,782	1,846	1,962	1,963
Amazonas	1,700	19,700	21,700	22,200	23,200	23,999	24,739	26,629	27,434	28,140	28,866	29,616
Maranhão	63,900	90,800	92,300	93,400	94,100	95,235	95,979	97,761	99,338	99,789	100,590	102,326
Mato Grosso	20,000	71,500	79,600	83,600	86,500	91,174	103,614	112,150	119,141	125,023	131,808	137,610
Pará	56,400	131,500	139,300	144,200	148,000	151,787	160,355	169,007	176,138	181,225	188,372	194,619
Rondônia	4,200	30,000	31,800	33,500	34,600	36,865	42,055	46,152	48,648	50,529	53,275	55,274
Roraima	100	2,700	3,600	3,800	4,200	4,481	4,961	5,124	5,361	5,563	5,791	6,112
Tocantins	3,200	21,600	22,300	22,900	23,400	23,809	24,475	25,142	25,483	25,768	26,404	26,613
Total	152,200	377,500	401,400	415,200	426,400	440,186	469,978	497,053	517,067	532,086	551,782	569,269

Notes:
* Decade mean
** Biannual mean

Source: Ministry of Science and Technology/National Institute of Space Research (INPE). *Monitoring the Brazilian Amazon by Satellite: 1999–2000 Report*

driving up real estate prices, mainly in the South, which in turn financed the spontaneous out-migration of southern family farmers (Rezende 1981; Brito 1987); (c) the penetration of the soybean crop in the South and Center-West, consolidating small holdings into large ones (Mesquita and Silva 1987b, 1987c); and (d) a severe drought in the Northeast in the early 1970s, expelling the rural population from a vast area;

2. A military dictatorship that promoted a policy of Amazonian occupation during a period of easy access to international finance for large-scale projects. This regime, motivated by national security interests, geopolitics, and development aspirations, catalyzed the forces that promoted occupation. Characterized by the concentrated decision-making of the executive power, the military government created vast resource-using projects in mining, smelting, hydroelectric power, and other industries, attracting to the Amazon hordes of workers and farmers from distant regions. Improvements in transport and telecommunications systems were made, facilitating long-distance, interregional migration; and the establishment of agricultural credit and fiscal incentives expanded agroindustrial and commercial agriculture in frontier areas. All of the above, together with official land titling and directed colonization programs, increased the accessibility of the Amazon to large and small farmers and to an increasing variety of agents (Ozório de Almeida 1991, 1992; Ozório de Almeida and Campari 1996).

This chapter further argues that patterns of migrations have changed from the early days of occupation until today. Table 2.8 displays a timeline showing dates down the middle with a summary of the main political and economic events on the left-hand side and the main population changes on the right-hand side.

From the 1960s until the mid-1980s, migrants arrived in the Amazon from other regions of Brazil. From 1986 to 2000, there was a clear halt in interregional migrations. However, population movements in the frontier have continued, with migrants now coming from within rather than outside the region. As the stock of migrants is mostly rural, the activities of these farmers are linked to deforestation, i.e., given the type of economic activity they practice, farmers must convert forest land into agricultural land.

Since deforestation is a direct consequence of the economic occupation of the region, this chapter also presented the figures regarding Amazon forest clearing during the past 30 years. Incremental rates at which forest is being converted, as well the accumulated area deforested during the same period show that deforestation has peaked in 1994–95 and reduced somewhat by the end of the 1990s. The data that are presented in this chapter do not paint an optimistic picture with regard to forest conservation, as 1998–99

Table 2.8. Timeline: summary of political and economic events and population changes

Political and Economic Events	Dates	Population Changes
Military coup and initial government support for regional development	1964	Initial stages of occupation, with emphasis on large farmers and ranchers
Mechanization of agriculture in Southern Brazil due to encroachment of soybeans Severe drought in the Northeast Beginning of colonization programs by the federal government (mainly the National Integration Program) Construction of the Transamazon Highway and road system in the Amazon	1970s	Displacement of small Southern and Northeastern farmers Migrations of small farmers from the South and Northeast regions of Brazil to the Amazon
Generalized economic crisis High inflation stimulated land sales offering capital gains for those who sold and a hedge against inflation for those who purchased End of support to public colonization programs Beginning of private colonization projects, although it was short-lived Growth in Amazonian economy	1980s	End of interregional migrations Beginning of intense intraregional migrations
Beginning of international pressures for conservation of the Amazon region Further reduction in federal budget to support small-scale agriculture	1990s	Acceleration of intraregional migrations

rates are the same as they were in 1989. The problem gains emphasis and can hardly be dismissed so long as a fluctuating population of small farmers move around the forest, clearing land as they go.

Small farmers' movement from old to new frontiers constitutes the core of the turnover hypothesis. At the heart of the hypothesis also is the question of what happens to land after they leave the frontier in a somewhat hollow condition (low population density). Since the out-migration of small farmers can be considered a response to government policies, then we must understand the policies that generated demographic instability during the 1960s, 1970s, 1980s and 1990s. They are quite different, at times contradictory, and are discussed in the next chapter.

NOTES

1. Deacon (1990), for example, explicitly links government policies and government instability to deforestation rates. Bunker (1985), Repetto (1989), Gillis and Repetto (1988), Binswanger (1994) and Mahar (1989) are critical of government development subsidies and land-tenuring policies that have distorted incentives and encouraged rapid deforestation of the Amazon.
2. Gross deforestation indicates that areas in process of secondary succession or forest recovery are not subtracted in the calculation of the rate.

3. The political economy of frontier expansion and deforestation in the Amazon

3.1 INTRODUCTION

This chapter discusses the background against which Amazonian development took place. The chapter analyzes occupation and the underlying causes of deforestation in light of the large development programs implemented by the federal government during the 1960s and 1970s, and its subsequent halt in support of Amazonian development during the 1980s. The chapter is organized in six sections. Sections 3.2, 3.3 and 3.4 discuss, respectively, the political and socio-economic contexts of the 1960s (marked by the military coup of 1964), the 1970s (marked by the shift in policy orientation from economic to social occupation of the region) and the 1980s (marked by the transition to democracy and by the withdrawal of federal government incentives for regional development). Section 3.5 discusses the role that specific tax provisions have had on regional occupation and deforestation. Section 3.6 summarizes and concludes the chapter.

3.2. THE 1960s: REGIONAL DEVELOPMENT STRATEGIES ADOPTED BY THE MILITARY REGIME

Brazil's military coup of 1964 was of the type that Barrington Moore (1968) would call 'revolution from above'. Although diverse political factions supported the coup (Stepan 1968), its outcome favored particularly the agroindustrial and industrial entrepreneurial elite from the Center-South of Brazil. The coup introduced a myriad of changes, both in kind and in emphasis, in the Brazilian economic scene. The outcomes of this transformation were reflected in increasing international investment, the strengthening of entrepreneurial capital, and significant modifications in the role of the Brazilian State in national and Amazonian development planning.

When the military seized power, it first had to address its legitimate right to govern. Second, it had to resolve many of the urgent economic constraints that had hampered the accumulation of capital by national elites (including wage demands, high inflation, import substitution industrialization policies, and lack of investment outlets). Third, it was bound to solve, or at least foster the façade contending with, the social and political problems of rural areas as reflected in stagnant agricultural production, low investment rates, and rural-to-urban migration (Knight 1971; Schmink and Wood 1992; Ozório de Almeida and Campari 1996).

The economic growth policies chosen by the new government relied heavily on international borrowing, increased participation of transnational capital in the economy, and expansionist monetary and fiscal policies (Fishlow 1973; Belassa 1979). Although the contribution of these policies to the 'Brazilian miracle' remains open to question (Fishlow 1973; Malan and Bonelli 1977; Belassa 1979), the regime certainly can take credit for the rapid growth of the economy during the late 1960s and early 1970s. Brazil's economy grew faster than any other economy in the world during this period (Encarta 99, 1999). The country's real GDP increased by more than four times, from 55,055 million *reais* in 1969 to 270,945 million *reais* in 1974, which resulted in double-digit annual real growth rates (World Bank 1999). It was this exceptional economic performance that supported the institutionalization of the various military governments that followed the 1964 coup.

Agricultural and agrarian problems demanded a profound reassessment of policy priorities as well. In the first half of the 1960s, the Brazilian agricultural sector suffered from a lack of credit and investment capital, high import tariffs that elevated the cost of agricultural inputs, high export taxes, and marked regional disparities in investment. Furthermore, an overvalued currency (*cruzeiros*) made Brazilian agricultural products relatively expensive in the international market, while national policies emphasized exports only as an outlet for surplus production (Knight 1971). The structural changes and mechanization of agriculture in Southern Brazil began seriously to diminish the access to land for tenant farmers and sharecroppers and to reduce agricultural options for the rural poor in this region (Foweraker 1981).

Government's efforts to counter these problems took the form of increased availability of funds for agriculture through subsidized interest rates for rural modernization and mechanization, export incentives, and devaluation of the *cruzeiro*. These policy initiatives intended to modify the production process at the farm level and in specific regions. Subsidized rural elites, agroindustrialists, as well as urban entrepreneurs were attracted to agriculture in order to diversify their investment portfolios and to take advantage of tax credits. The government argued that these initiatives would promote efficiency and rational economic behavior that would transform agricultural production in Brazil.

The agrarian problem's outward symptoms were rural-to-urban migration (Ozório de Almeida and Campari 1996) and peasant activism, problems addressed under the post-coup regime by repression and the opening up of a new agricultural frontier, the Amazon. Amazonian development forestalled the need for land reform and provided the appearance of a national will to include the rural poor in the government's development strategy.

The idea of occupying the Amazon was in line with other themes in the government programs. Perhaps the most important one was the military ideology of national security. The distress about the region was due to its large size, scanty population and unpatrolled borders shared with eight other countries, and with a history of annexation and conflict between them. The geopolitical importance of the Amazon region, reflected in the slogan *integrar para não entregar* (integrate in order not to surrender (the region to other nations)), is emphasized in the planning documents and propaganda pamphlets of that period.

The military rhetoric introduced the idea of regional occupation as the moral equivalent of war. The focus of the military was to unify national factions around a common national goal, justifying current sacrifices in welfare for a larger (future) good. In 1964, General Castello Branco stated that 'Amazonian occupation would proceed as though it were a strategically conducted war' (Hecht 1984). The first body of legislation concerning the Amazon during the new regime goes by the title of 'Operation Amazonia'. The efforts of the military government to occupy the Amazon stimulated the regional economy through investment in heavy industries and infrastructure development.

Another policy theme closely associated with national security was national integration, promoting linkage of the distant Amazon region to urban centers. Integration can be regarded as a version of Manifest Destiny, an idea consistent with the orthodox economic approach to the region. The purpose of national integration was facilitated by the development of infrastructure and the creation of investment credits. Regional disparities came under sharp attack and the image of the developed Center-South was conceived as the achievable future of Brazil's hinterlands.

International forces played an important role in emphasizing that ranching would be the main development alternative for the Amazon in the mid-1960s (Hecht 1984). In 1964, the United Nations Food and Agricultural Organization (FAO) and the Economic Commission for Latin America (ECLA) published an influential report summarizing the international perspective on the expansion of the Brazilian herd (FAO/ECLA 1964). The FAO report indicated that while Brazil's existing productive capacity was rather low, it had great potential for expansion through the incorporation of new land and the rationalization of production. The report argued that overcoming certain bottlenecks, primarily related to credit, would be essential for Brazil to capture a sizable market share of world beef production. This document concluded that beef markets were buoyant and would continue to expand as national and international demand increased, a tendency that was particularly strong in the mid-1960s.

Furthermore, Brazil was conceived as an appropriate area for the use of Australian pasture technologies. This technology involved the identification and introduction of adaptable grass varieties into specific soils (with appropriate drainage) as well as the recognition of the importance of the stocking rate, rather than grazing systems, as the major determinant of animal productivity per hectare (Australian Academy of Technological Sciences and Engineering 1988). If the conditions of long-term credit and better grass varieties were met, the report pointed out that Brazil could become one of the premier beef exporters. This influential document frequently underlay the great push toward ranching throughout Latin America in the 1960s, the precise period when the policy for the Amazon was being developed. Various international agencies such as the World Bank were able to argue that with the proper technology and better credit lines, livestock represented an excellent investment for development. As a consequence, during the mid- to late 1960s, financial resources (national and international) poured into livestock projects, mostly developed in the Amazon (Hecht 1984; IADB 1971–76). Feder (1979) suggests that public and private investment in cattle ranching development in the 1960–75 period was minimally US$15 billion, not including operational capital.

Developing the Amazon not only guaranteed Brazilian sovereignty over the region, but also made it possible to extract its potential wealth, thereby contributing to the rapid economic growth and modernization goals envisioned by the military regime. Reaching these goals meant encouraging new flows of migrants and capital into the region. Through various policy initiatives, the new agricultural frontier in the Amazon was expected to resolve critical economic and ideological questions and thus serve important political and legitimizing functions for the new military regime. The forces operating at the international level, particularly with regard to availability of investment funds, fit well with the development ambitions of Brazil's military regime, particularly with regard to geopolitical and balance-of-payments concerns. It was against this scenario that, after several trips to the Amazon, General Castello Branco laid the groundwork for Operation Amazonia.

3.2.1. Operation Amazonia

In 1966, the Superintendence for the Amazon Economic Valorization Plan (SPVEA) was replaced by Superintendence for the Development of the Amazon (SUDAM). This administrative change represented the start of Operation Amazonia. President General Castello Branco began a new era in planning that would set the tone of regional development in the Amazon. The emphasis was that planning would give precedence to technical considerations and avoid corruption that had dominated the previous planning agency (SPVEA). The expansion of the Amazon frontier through large-scale agriculture and cattle ranching in the 1960s was also conditioned by high inflation periods that increased the importance of land in corporate as well as private portfolios. The fiscal incentives associated with the land allocation system provided by the government in the Amazon facilitated land acquisition and contributed to the increase in the real value of land in the region. These incentives were largely made available through SUDAM, which administered a series of credit benefits and fiscal incentives to large entrepreneurs, mainly ranchers. Those who benefited from SUDAM's incentives made enormous capital gains simply by buying and holding on to land, not necessarily using it productively (Margulis 2001). It is important to emphasize that smallholders did not qualify for the incentives offered by SUDAM (Alston et al. 1999; Schneider 1995); their only source of support was the federal government's National Institute of Colonization and Agrarian Reform (INCRA).

Operation Amazonia was based on Law No. 5.1744 (October 1966), which provided fiscal incentives by stipulating that 50 percent of a corporation's tax liability could be invested in Amazonian development projects, essentially permitting taxes to become venture capital. The projects could be either new ones or expansion of existing enterprises. Since several large landowners in Southern Brazil already had substantial land investments in the Amazon, this was an attractive means for increasing the value of existing holdings.

To those enterprises that had already been established by 1966, the law provided exemptions of 50 percent of the tax liabilities for 12 years; for projects implemented prior to 1972, it provided for exemptions of up to 100 percent. Qualifying firms were permitted to import duty-free capital (machinery and equipment) and were exempted from export duties for regional products (e.g. timber). The states of the Legal Amazon provided their own additional incentives (usually land concessions), while international lending institutions such as the World Bank and the IADB also made special agricultural development credit available for the region (Pompermeyer 1979; Hecht 1984; Binswanger 1994).

Furthermore, the new incentive provisions made grace periods on loan repayments more generous. Foreign corporations were also eligible for loans and tax concessions, although it is worth noting that foreign investments in the Amazon were relatively low compared to the amount invested by the Brazilian government. Further, foreign investment in Brazil was characterized during the 1964–78 period by its involvement in the industrial sector rather than agriculture.

Fiscal incentives combined with other credit lines resulted in an explosion of ranching in the Amazon; livestock production was the most promising investment to be made in the region. The extraordinary fiscal incentives and the seemingly relatively low risk associated with ranching created an unparalleled stimulus for the conversion of forests to ranch land. As Mahar (1979) shows, investment in crop production in the Northeast (where incentives were also available) was comparatively risky, as was most crop production in the North. But if land values increase, then land becomes an attractive investment, especially because it tends to hold value in inflationary economies (Ozório de Almeida and Campari 1996). This was certainly the case in Brazil throughout the 1960s and 1970s. Although it is argued that infrastructure development in a region like the Amazon also increased the value of land (Schneider 1995), the field data used in this study do not corroborate this statement (see Chapter 9). The government granted generous incentives for land acquisitions during the 1960s as a form of compensation to those who were helping it incur the costs of regional development. These incentives led to a situation in which the real value of Amazonian land increased at 100 percent per year (Mahar 1979). Speculation was driven in part by the hope of future returns to agricultural production, the future value of natural resources (wood, gold, diamonds), or simply because Amazonian land was so artificially cheap because of the credit and tax incentives that it was worth keeping as a store of value. Two points are worth emphasizing: first, land and its modification by ranching became the primary vehicles for capturing enormous subsidies, and second, in the late-1970s, the nature of land in the Amazonian economy began to change in a fundamental way: land itself, not its product, became a commodity. Land values rose sharply, regardless of resource productivity, due to speculative behavior (Ozório de Almeida 1992; Ozório de Almeida and Campari 1996; Margulis 2001).

In the late 1960s, criticism of the expansion of corporate livestock operations was mounting, both for ecological and social reasons. Partly because the laws were so obviously biased in favor of large holders, and partly because of the pronounced drought in the Northeast, President Médici in 1970 adopted a new direction for Amazon policy.

3.3. THE 1970s: RURAL DISPLACEMENT AND THE NATIONAL INTEGRATION PROGRAM

The National Integration Program (PIN) was launched in 1971 to bring colonists to the Amazon. The PIN shifted the focus of policy from the purely economic approach of the 1960s to a social perspective. The previous slogan 'Amazon is your best business', was replaced by *O Homem é a Meta* ('Man is the goal'). From the misery of the drought-wrecked Northeast, 'people without land' would be linked via the Transamazon Highway and other infrastructure programs to the 'lands without people' in the Amazon. A more cynical version of the new programs saw the Transamazon Highway linking poverty and misery (the highway was named the 'Transbitterness' by those who settled there early on). The new policies expressed in the first National Development Plan (PND) reiterated the themes of the agricultural frontiers as escape valves for surplus population, the importance of national security, and the necessity of national integration.

It is against this scenario that directed colonization began under the auspices of the federal government's Institute for Colonization and Agrarian Reform (INCRA). The goals of the entrepreneurs and of advocates of Amazon colonization by small farmers came into sharp conflict. Inter-ministerial rivalry became quite severe between SUDAM (which had not retreated from its position that corporate development was the best means of Amazonian occupation), INCRA, and the Ministry of the Interior. During the 1970–74 period, INCRA suffered pressures from a variety of interest groups. Interagency rivalry and INCRA's advocacy of 'social occupation' of the Amazon came under sharp attack (Bunker 1979; Pompermeyer 1979).

Brazil's worsening economic situation in the late 1970s made social concerns a luxury. Tensions became so extreme between INCRA and the private sector that it was necessary for the government to sell areas of public land (under INCRA control) so that SUDAM could designate a new group of entrepreneurs for ranching development. A deliberate policy decision was made by Reis Velloso, the Minister of Planning from 1974–79, who traveled along the Transamazon Highway with 20 entrepreneurs to whom he offered land that had been reserved for colonization projects and agrarian reform (Pompermeyer 1979).

3.3.1. Subsidies, Credit, and Corruption

Despite the will to colonize and populate the Amazon, it became clear in the second half of the 1970s that the government's colonization program fell short of its objectives. In part, failure resulted from an uncontrolled migratory flow, mainly from the impoverished Northeast region. INCRA was unable to cope with the demand for demarcation of individual plots, recording claims, formal surveying, titling, and provision of other promised services and inputs such as infrastructure, education and health care, seeds and fertilizers (Moran 1975, 1981; Ianni 1979; Fearnside 1986).

In 1975, the government re-evaluated its policy toward the Amazon and announced the Polamazonia program together with the Second Development Plan for the region. The new plan represented another policy reversal, i.e., a shift from occupation through colonization programs to an emphasis on large-scale agriculture and cattle enterprises. This program expanded the earlier fiscal incentives managed by SUDAM.

The legacy of subsidized rural credit is reflected in the prevalence of very large properties with unproductive land. An extreme example is the abuse of the SUDAM Program by firms and large farmers who set up 'ghost ranches', i.e., enterprises owned by fictitious people who exist only in paper, as a means to receive the subsidies. On the one hand, while the Program gave incentives for firms and individuals to propose agricultural and ranching projects in order to receive subsidies, on the other hand, it provided little or no incentive to establish a bona fide operation, particularly in remote frontier areas where transportation and production costs were high. Gasques and Yakomizo (1986) report on a sample of 29 SUDAM-subsidized cattle ranches with an average size of 16,334 hectares, finding that 14 sold no cattle at all, and only two reached more than 50 percent of their operational target between 1974 and 1985.

The recent media attention given to 'ghost projects' led to the closing down of SUDAM in 2001 on account of corruption. Public prosecutors have found that SUDAM's rural credit has, in most cases, been totally diverted to non-farm uses that were more profitable than agriculture – thus the prevalence of so much privately owned idle land in the Amazon.

Another important factor in the propensity to hold unproductive land in the Amazon is the Brazilian land tax, known as ITR (rural territorial tax), which has been systematically evaded by most landowners. The government conceived the land tax as a major instrument for land reform in the Land Statute of 1964, complementary to the use of expropriations. Despite several changes in its rules, the ITR never managed to achieve its purpose. During some periods the tax rates were set too low, and during others the value of the land used to calculate the tax was notoriously underestimated because the owner himself reported the value. Curbing evasion was difficult politically and logistically. Alston et al. (1999) report that while only 32 percent of the landowners with properties of up to 100 hectares in size evaded the ITR in 1995, 74 percent of those with properties from 1,000 to 50,000 hectares evaded the tax, with the number going up to 94 percent for properties from 50,000 to 500,000 hectares. The authors report further that the total amount collected through the ITR in Brazil in 1995 was slightly less than US$100 million, an amount that represented only 0.03 percent of the federal government's budget revenue and only 0.21 percent of the total amount collected in net taxes. (Land taxes and other types of taxes will receive special attention later in the chapter.)

These large tracts of land, held largely uncultivated and unused, together with the large contingent of landless peasants left stranded on the frontier, due to the reversal in the government policy focus from small to large-scale agriculture, provided sufficient elements for land invasions and conflicts to occur. In order to settle these conflicts, INCRA was forced in many cases to step in and expropriate the disputed farms. During the last half of the 1970s and early 1980s, INCRA increasingly was put into the reactive policy position of responding to land conflicts through expropriation, indemnization (compensation), and the creation of settlement projects on the disputed land. Government-sponsored colonization projects faded into the background and since then INCRA's position has been the same. It is still very common for large landowners themselves to induce the invasion of their own farms by the landless poor, so that they can receive compensations from the government that are a large multiple of the true value of the land.

While SUDAM's agricultural subsidies and credit policies were exceptionally favorable for large farmers, small farmers did not have access to the same benefits. Since credit was not equally available to farmers at different wealth levels, the subsidies increased the difficulty faced by poor people when trying to buy land. Gaining access to subsidized credit required some form of land title or certificate of land occupancy. Thus land with acceptable papers as collateral had a higher value than land without such collateral. The increase in the credit subsidy increased the demand for titled land and provided its owners with a capital gain. Conversely, it reduced the demand for untitled land and led to capital losses for those farmers who did not yet have a title to the land. Untitled farmers, however, sold their land despite non-existent property rights at prices below the market value. Furthermore, the increase in the credit subsidy also increased the flow of investments from the nonagricultural sector into farms with titled land and thereby provided an additional force toward increased ownership holdings.

While the amount of credit disbursed in the Amazon was small and declining over time, compared to the total agricultural credit volume, it was a significant factor in accelerating deforestation until the early 1990s. As with the income tax preference for agriculture, subsidized rural credit tended to increase the demand for land, leading to a more rapid expansion of crop and pastureland. Moreover, subsidies were partly capitalized into land values, reinforcing the regressive impact of the income tax system. Furthermore, subsidized credit encouraged mechanization, reduced employment and tenancy opportunities in agriculture. The system thus increased the migrations of small farmers from old to new frontiers.

3.4. THE 1980s: THE TRANSITION TO DEMOCRACY AND ECONOMIC CRISIS

The first half of the 1980s brought the start of a decade-long period of macroeconomic crisis in Brazil with profound consequences for Amazonian settlement policy. The occupation of the region as a means of resolving the problem of landlessness was abandoned, at least temporarily. Interest in the occupation of the Amazon waned, although tension over land distribution increased. One might think that the crisis of the 1980s would have reduced migrations, since neither the political elements of the military regime nor the financial resources were available to sustain the policies of the previous decade. However, Chapter 2 showed that migrations accelerated within the region, and so did deforestation. This section discusses the political and socio-economic contexts associated with this issue.

3.4.1.   National Economic Context of the 1980s: Shifts in Fiscal Revenues

The 1980s were marked by a return to democracy. Federal authority for macroeconomic management in Brazil experienced a profound transformation as a result of democratic elections in 1984 and institutional changes that culminated in the new federal constitution of October 1988. This constitution provided for greater decentralization of responsibilities, a considerable redistribution of revenues, and an increase in the power of state and municipal governments. The growth of frontier economic activity and the constitutional reform inserted the Amazon into the broader national economic context.

The fact that most strikingly distinguishes the Amazon of the 1980s from that of the 1970s is its capability to generate tax revenues locally. The tax code, which until the late-1980s essentially exempted agriculture and converted it into a tax shelter, changed in a fundamental way. Up until 1988, it was relatively easy to claim any frontier activity as agricultural in nature, contributing to the demand for land by urban investors and corporations attempting to diversify their asset portfolios (Mahar 1989; Serôa da Motta 1991; Binswanger 1994). With the constitutional reform, however, the tax code was revised and most of these exemptions disappeared. The tax revenues that began to be generated locally somewhat counterbalanced the loss of fiscal and credit incentives from the federal government that occurred during the crisis of the 1980s (Ozório de Almeida and Campari 1996). Table 3.1 shows that these incentives began to decline during the early 1980s, and subsidized rural credit was practically nonexistent by the end of the decade (Mahar 1989).

Table 3.1.   Official rural credit for the legal Amazon, 1970–85

Year	Amount (US$)	Year	Amount (US$)
1970	61,692	1978	775,219
1971	89,220	1979	1,062,085
1972	153,763	1980	1,095,666
1973	178,498	1981	748,273
1974	118,669	1982	506,628
1975	288,321	1983	275,168
1976	523,506	1984	115,352
1977	573,674	1985	172,795

Source: Ozório de Almeida and Campari (1996)

The evidence presented in Chapter 2 showed that deforestation and migrations continued to occur throughout the 1980s, in spite of the absence of the forces that stimulated them during the 1970s. Thus migrations and deforestation were responding to new forces. The main difference is that, since the early 1980s, the forces that have impelled people to migrate and deforest are generated locally rather than outside the region.

3.4.1.1.   Reduction in federal activities
Escalating external debt and deteriorating commodity prices made the Brazilian government more vulnerable to those who opposed expanding the agricultural frontier. As pressures from international agencies and NGOs grew, the general public became more interested in, and informed about, Amazonian issues.

Dwindling federal budgets killed many federal infrastructure investments, while local urban centers, swelled by newly urbanized voters with political clout, increasingly defined local priorities. The process of urbanization at the frontier was accompanied by the creation of a critical mass of politicians and civil society organizations that determined local priorities. Political and economic opposition to large-scale federal projects such as hydroelectric dams grew, while state and municipal projects multiplied.

Federal investments in infrastructure and development programs that had cost billions of dollars during the 1970s fell drastically, further discouraging potential interregional migrants during the 1980s (Sawyer 1990). Although vast tracts of land continued to be auctioned off to private colonization firms or to forestry-agroindustrial businesses from the South and from abroad, they could no longer benefit from the same incentives as they once did during the heyday of land purchasing credit and other fiscal incentives (Ozório de Almeida 1991). Some large-scale projects were initiated and/or continued during the 1980s in mining and smelting, hydro-electricity, and other industries, although these tended to have only a local impact. The broadest one was the Great Carajás Project. This project was established in 1980, and it is one of the largest development schemes ever undertaken in the Amazon. It covers an area of 880,000 square kilometers, almost 11 percent of the Brazilian territory. The project was established to exploit the extensive reserves of iron, copper, manganese, cassiterite, nickel, bauxite, and gold. The area where the Great Carajás was developed hosts the world's largest iron ore deposit (18 billion tons). Major investments were undertaken in iron-ore mines, smelters, two aluminum plants, a hydroelectric power plant, and the construction of roads and railways.

Thus, as the national economic crisis dragged on throughout the 1980s, the forces that had promoted interregional mobility during the 1970s weakened, while new ones emerged that might have reduced interregional mobility even further. Despite the strong reduction in credit and fiscal incentives to agriculture, and reductions in other federal initiatives in the region, Chapter 2 showed that intraregional migrations and forest clearing did not correspondingly decline during the 1980s. This suggests that Amazonian migrations and deforestation during the late-1980s responded to intra-frontier forces different from those of the 1970s. Similarly, Ozório de Almeida and Campari (1996) argue that although the speculative motive for deforestation might have begun with incentives from the federal government in the 1970s, by the late-1980s it was already being fed by local stimuli.

3.5.   TAXES, LAND USE AND DEFORESTATION

This section discusses the role of preferential tax treatments that have influenced farmers' decisions with regard to conservation and deforestation. Specific provisions of the tax code, associated with the rules of land allocation discussed in the following chapter, have determined most of the deforestation in the Amazon.

3.5.1. Taxes on Agricultural Income

From Brazilian colonial times until the late-1980s, Brazilian income tax laws virtually exempted agriculture and converted it into a tax shelter. This exemption added to the demand for land and made urban investors and corporations compete aggressively for land in consolidated areas of the frontier. This competition resulted in unequal land ownership holdings, as large farmers bought out small ones, and it increased the rate of conversion of forest to cropland and especially pasture.

Binswanger (1994) argues that by using a variety of special provisions of the income tax code, corporations could exclude up to 80 percent of agricultural profits from their taxable income and individuals could exclude up to 90 percent. The tax code contained very favorable treatments for agricultural expenditures and investments. Landholders could choose between two tax policies. They could elect to be taxed at 10 percent of their gross agricultural revenues, or they could choose to pay higher income taxes and deduct the cost of modern inputs or investments from gross agricultural income.

Fixed investments, animals, buildings, machines and vehicles could be depreciated completely in the first year, and also depreciated several times over by using a multiplication factor that ranged from two to six. Up to 80 percent of farm profits could be sheltered in this way. If the resulting multiples of expenditures and investments exceeded current income, the deductions could be carried forward to reduce the tax liabilities of the next four years. The net effect was that almost all agricultural income escaped taxation.

Neither corporations nor individuals could offset agricultural losses against nonagricultural taxable incomes. However, some consumer expenditures could be disguised as agricultural costs, and it was thereby possible to shelter some nonagricultural income as well.

Corporate agricultural profits were taxed at a rate of only 6 percent. Combined with the depreciation provisions, the tax on corporate agricultural profits could be as low as 1.2 percent. Corporate profits from other sources were subject to a tax rate between 35 and 45 percent.

The implication of this tax treatment is that private and corporate investors would undertake projects in agriculture, even though the projects had a lower economic rate of return than nonagricultural projects. Therefore the demand for land by corporations and individuals in high-income tax brackets increased, resulting in potentially faster expansion of agriculture in frontier areas.

During one of the interviews carried out to finalize this study, a senior environmental economist from the World Bank reported that, despite the decline in land values after that period, farmers and ranchers continued to make considerable profits from land sales due to the large magnitude of the subsidies they received at the time when land was acquired. Another interview[1] revealed that some of the holdings that were purchased in the north of Mato Grosso during the 1970s, and left unproductive since that period, are so large that their owners face severe difficulties in selling the entire property, even at values slightly below the market value. The interviewee reported that these huge holdings are being dismembered and sold to different owners. Further, he pondered that in some regions of Mato Grosso land is likely soon to become less concentrated as this process continues. This suggests that Amazonian agriculture may not have economies of scale.

The income tax treatment not only provided no benefits to the poor, but it also affected the poor negatively. If agricultural income is taxed at lower rates than nonagricultural income and agriculture is a tax shelter, the market price of land contains a component capitalizing these tax preferences. In consolidated frontiers, the market price for land becomes too high for the small and poor to buy, even if given credit. Legally, poor farmers could only gain access to Amazonian lands through colonization projects sponsored by the government or by private companies.

In a perfect market, the value of land reflects the present value of agricultural profits, capitalized at the opportunity cost of capital. If poor farmers outside of colonization projects – where they used to get land for free from the government – have to use credit to buy land at its market value, the only income stream they have available for consumption is the imputed value of family labor. They must use the remaining profits to pay for the loan. If these farmers could get the same wage in the labor market, then they would be no better off as landowners than they would be as workers. This example is, moreover, an ideal situation where the interest rate paid by the poor farmer is equal to the interest rate that the most creditworthy borrowers can get. Therefore, if the value of the land exceeds the capitalized agricultural income, then poor farmers must cut consumption below the imputed value of family labor to pay for the land. This situation is aggravated when small farmers obtain loans in the informal economy. Although this situation cannot be generalized, this case is typical of farmers settled along the Transamazon Highway, where poverty associated with subsistence agriculture prevents settlers from saving.

The income tax shelter was not the only distortion capitalized into the land value. With the size of populations growing and the demand for land increasing in consolidated frontiers, some of the expected future appreciation of the land price was capitalized into the current land price. The only way a poor farmer could have access to that income stream was by selling a small parcel of land every year to pay for his interest cost. (Although this would, at first glance, seem infeasible for small landowners, selling or leasing parts of their plots was a common practice observed during the field work; this tendency persists to this day.) For those who obtained land for free from the government, as in the early days of public colonization, this presented a unique opportunity to reap gains, as the asset the government gave them would be worth more. In fact, this is the origin of the itinerant strategy of capital accumulation: small farmers move from place to place in order to obtain land for free from the government, only to sell it after a few years. This point is further discussed in the following chapters, particularly in Chapter 9.

In addition, Brandão and Rezende (1988) show that high and unstable inflation rates in Brazil clearly increased the land price, and that credit subsidies also were partly capitalized into the land price. These factors made it increasingly difficult for small farmers to buy land. This encouraged them to move to the frontier in search of unclaimed land, with the rational expectation that INCRA would later regularize the situation.

3.5.2. Property Taxes

In principle, a progressive property tax on the size of ownership holdings could offset the effects of the favorable income tax treatment on the land market by making it less profitable to have land in large holdings. Brazil's land tax code, though progressive in principle, contains many exceptions so that effective tax rates are not progressive in practice.

Up until 1996, legislation provided for a progressive property tax. Farms smaller than two modules paid no land taxes, while farms larger than 100 modules paid 3.5 percent of the unimproved value of their land each year. Binswanger (1994) argues that apart from direct evasion, the land tax could be reduced by a factor of up to 90 percent, increasing with the intensity of land use and the productivity of the farm. Both tax formulas used reduction factors directly and positively related to the use of the land.

The key point is that, until the mid-1990s, forestland was considered unused. A farm containing forests was therefore taxed at higher rates than one containing pastures or cropland. Converting forests to pasture on larger farms would therefore reduce the land tax, providing incentives for deforestation. The major impact of this legislation was likely to be felt in settled areas where the enforcement of the land tax was fairly strict.

In December 1996, the Brazilian Congress approved a new land tax law that sharply raised the tax for unproductive properties. The tax rate for unproductive properties above 5,000 hectares was set at 20 percent of its value. That law provided owners of large holdings with an incentive to either use or sell the land to someone willing to make it productive. One of the purposes of the law is to reduce the price of land and thereby reduce the cost to INCRA of obtaining land for settlement projects. Other articles in the law sought to ensure that owners declared the true value of the land for tax purposes. In addition, the law made evasion more difficult (Alston et al. 1999). It is still too early to tell if this law will achieve its goal, or if it will simply be a dead letter, as so many of its predecessors have been.

3.5.3. Stumpage or User Taxes

No stumpage or user taxes were ever charged per hectare for deforesters, large or small, colonists or not.

3.5.4. Other Federal Taxes

No other federal tax regulations, such as capital gains or commodity taxes, appear to contain provisions that affect deforestation. There are, however, a number of regional and sectoral tax breaks that encourage investment in enterprises using cleared forestland.

3.6. CONCLUSION

The existing literature on Amazon development provides a mixed scorecard for the Brazilian government in the management and planning of the frontier. Ozório de Almeida (1992), Ozório de Almeida and Campari (1996), and Schneider (1995) are reasonably positive in their evaluation of the impact of frontier occupation on the welfare of smallholders. These authors emphasize the opportunities that remain for the development of effective government policies to facilitate environmental management in the region. Gillis and Repetto (1988), Spears (1988), Mahar (1989) and Binswanger (1994), however, are critical of government subsidies for particular settlement and land use activities, such as road construction and ranching. As we have seen in this chapter, however, most of these subsidies have long been dropped. Additionally, concerns about the extent of deforestation and the benefits of Amazonian settlement in face of feared high environmental costs are raised by Goodland (1985), Serrão et al. (1996), and Smith et al. (1996). Bunker (1985), Bakx (1990), and Walker and Homma (1996) find that, in general, the policies of the Brazilian government to occupy the Amazon failed, as frontier settlement led to increased itinerancy of the rural population, rural to urban migrations, and unequal land distribution in the region.

Table 3.2. Timeline: summary of political and economic changes, actions and impacts on regional development and deforestation

Political and Economic Problems and Events	Dates	Government Actions and Their Impact on Regional Development and Deforestation
Military coup marked the beginning of government support for Amazonian development Stagnant agricultural production Reassessment of agricultural and agrarian questions because of lack of credit and investment capital, high import tariffs, high export taxes, and marked regional disparities Overvalued currency made agricultural products expensive in international markets Agricultural mechanization began to displace labor in the South Increased poverty among the rural population Rural to urban migrations caused violence in urban areas Creation of SUDAM to oversee regional development and finance large agricultural operations in the region Launching of Operation Amazonia to institutionalize through legal means tax exemptions and credit incentives Beginning of the 'Brazilian miracle', an unprecedented growth of the Brazilian economy	1960s	Increased availability of funds for agriculture through subsidized interest rates for modernization and mechanization Export incentives for agricultural products Subsidies to agroindustrialists and urban entrepreneurs to diversify their investment portfolios in frontier agriculture High international borrowing from multilateral institutions to finance structural changes in agriculture Opening up of the Amazon agricultural frontier to relieve social tensions Adoption of new pasture technologies in the Amazon Expansion of cattle ranching
Mechanization of agriculture in Southern Brazil and encroachment of soybeans in areas previously occupied by small farmers Severe drought in the Northeast Shift in government policy focus from large businesses to small farming, then another policy reversal favoring large farmers again	1970s	Large investments in Amazonian development continued throughout the decade Subsidies and agricultural credit increased, expanding agroindustrial interests in frontier areas Induced migrations from other regions to the Amazon through the National Integration Program (mainly from the South and Northeast regions of Brazil)

	Beginning of colonization programs by the federal government (mainly through the National Integration Program) Construction of the Transamazon Highway and a road system into the Amazon Institutional conflicts between INCRA (which supported colonization by small farmers) and SUDAM (which continued to give emphasis to corporate interests in the region) Increasing availability of funds to large-scale agriculture.	Settlement of small farmers along the Transamazon Highway The creation of vast resource-using projects in mining, smelting, hydroelectric power, and other industries attracting to the Amazon hordes of workers and farmers from distant regions Improvements in transport and communications systems facilitated interregional migrations
1980s	End of military regime Generalized economic crisis End of subsidies and credits End of infrastructure development Escalating external debt New Constitution of October 1988 High inflation stimulated land acquisitions as a hedge against inflation End of support to public colonization programs Beginning of private colonization projects By the end of the decade, international pressures for conservation of the Amazon region began	Decentralization of responsibilities, redistribution of revenues, and increasing power of state and municipal governments End of interregional migrations The growth of frontier economic activity replaced, to an extent, the loss of fiscal and credit incentives Beginning of intense intraregional migrations, which began to respond to local stimuli as opposed to forces outside the region Increase in regional tax revenues Rapid urbanization Increase in the rates of deforestation

This chapter has argued that federal government intervention in Amazonian regional development had three distinct phases during the 1960s, 1970s and 1980s:

- *The 1960s*: This phase was characterized by a military regime, motivated by national security interests, which promoted regional development mainly by introducing a growth-oriented approach based on subsidized credit for large-scale agriculture, mainly cattle ranching, as well as generous tax relief for investments in the Amazon;
- *The 1970s*: During this decade, agricultural mechanization in the South and a severe drought in the Northeast prompted the government to relieve population pressures in these regions by promoting a social-oriented approach to Amazon development, creating large colonization programs, the first ones along the Transamazon Highway. These programs, however, were short-lived. In the second half of the decade, subsidies and credit incentives gained impetus, mainly for large entrepreneurs;
- *The 1980s*: This phase was marked by the transition from a military to a democratic government, in a context of generalized economic crisis, which shifted the focus of the government's attention away from the Amazon, as most investments in infrastructure were cut off, as well as credit subsidies and tax reliefs.

Table 3.2 displays a timeline summarizing the main issues associated with the political economy of Brazil from the mid-1960s until the late 1980s. The dates are placed down the middle, the political and economic problems and events are placed on the left-hand side, and government actions associated and the impact that they had on regional development and deforestation are placed on the right-hand side.

NOTE

1. Interview carried out with the President of the largest soybean business in Brazil.

4. Deforestation and the rules of land allocation

4.1. INTRODUCTION

The Amazon frontier has always been a source of optimism, and it has traditionally elicited strong emotional connotations of economic opportunity, liberty, and hope for a better future. With low population densities and rich endowments of land and other valuable resources, the region has spawned the country's principal migrations, and it continues to do so today.

To understand why land is cleared and, further, why it is probably being cleared excessively, then one must understand the rules of land allocation in the region. These rules are important because they strengthen the market distortions discussed in Chapter 3, leading to a situation of excess deforestation.

This chapter is organized in five sections. Section 4.2 discusses how the rules of land allocation have encouraged deforestation. Section 4.3 argues that these rules render inadequate the standard models that attempt to explain deforestation based on the premise of rent maximization. Section 4.4 discusses the economic behavior of farmers in the Amazon, particularly with regard to the practice of extensive agriculture. Section 4.5 summarizes and concludes the chapter.

4.2. THE RULES OF LAND ALLOCATION

The majority of the land in Brazil's 5-million-square-kilometer Legal Amazon has, until recently, been in the public domain either under the federal or state governments. Land is incorporated into private property in many ways. Legally, public land can pass to large private owners through occasional offers of land for sale through sealed tenders, while small plots are sold to colonists in government-sponsored settlement areas. In the early 1970s, the heyday of colonization, these plots used to be granted for free to settlers in public projects. The plot areas distributed to settlers decreased from 100 hectares in the 1970s to 50 hectares in the 1980s. The land was sold on favorable terms with five-year grace periods and 6 percent annual interest – far below the rate of inflation at the time. In practice, opportunities have usually been rare and are now nonexistent for obtaining public land through these legally correct avenues: while large areas of public land were distributed in this way in the 1970s, such distributions have not occurred since 1987. Instead, a long tradition from colonial times has carried out most transfers to private ownership through illegal invasions, mainly by small actors, the role of INCRA being a later regularization or legalization of the land holdings that exist on the ground (Fearnside 2001).

How do small farmers show that they have a solid claim on land? During the 1980s, they began doing this most effectively by squatting. The right known as *direito de posse* has been formally recognized since 1850, but goes back to the method of settling land disputes in colonial times. This right states that a squatter, or *posseiro*, who lives in unclaimed public land (*terra devoluta*) and has used it 'effectively', i.e., to produce crops or rear cattle, for at least one year and one day, has a usufruct to over 100 hectares. If the *posseiro* fulfills the condition of living on and effectively using the land for more than five years, he has the right to a title. Land can also be obtained by squatting on private land for a time without being challenged by the owner.

These rights may appear to favor the establishment of relatively small farms. Up to 3,000 hectares of lands under federal control may be claimed by using the *direito de posse* and the attendant administrative and regulative procedures. In some areas of the Amazon, INCRA used the following rule: a claimant who lived on the land would get preference to obtain a title for up to three times the area of forest he cleared. Therefore, any squatter had an incentive to deforest large areas rapidly, even if his agricultural operation did not justify it.

In Mato Grosso and Pará, the two states surveyed for this study, these or similar rules have resulted in the allocation of most public land to individually owned ranches or to large corporations. The reason is that, after a frontier consolidates, corporations and large ranches have a major advantage over poor individuals in the rush for land: they have the capital to build their own access roads into the forest. This advantage enables them to lay claim to land much farther from major highways than can poor settlers. Small farmers have difficulties in finding land for squatting. They can typically claim land only a few kilometers from public roads, as they can neither market products nor have access to health or education facilities if they venture further. Often, their alternative is to invade land that already is clearly privately claimed, leading to land disputes, or to wait until new colonization projects are established.

4.2.1. Deforestation and Land Allocation in Colonization Projects: An Example

In order to understand the relationships between colonists, newcomers and squatters and the process of deforestation in a typical colonization project, a series of diagrams are displayed in Figure 4.1. A colonization project begins when a forested area is demarcated by INCRA and all land is divided into small plots of generally 100 hectares each. In the diagrams, each square represents a plot. A letter in each square indicates the type of agent occupying the plot, and the patterning of the square indicates the extent of deforestation. The thick line circumscribing the plots along the road indicates the area demarcated for the project. Diagram A exhibits a situation

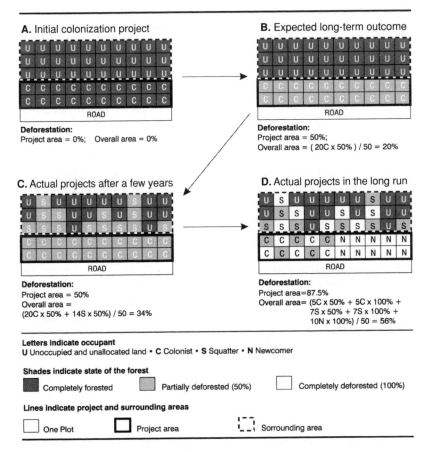

Figure 4.1. Deforestation in colonization projects

in which land has been allocated, but no one has moved in yet. In this case, the area where the project will be established is completely forested.

Diagram B shows the outcome expected by the government in the long run. This diagram depicts an ideal situation in which all colonists would deforest only the amount of land they are legally entitled to clear according the 1965 Forest Code, i.e., half of their property. Colonists (C) were expected to use the deforested area to plant crops, while they could use the remainder of their land to extract forest products. In this situation, deforestation would be 50 percent of the project area and 20 percent of the overall area where the project is established. The important point here is that deforestation was an expected outcome of colonization, but it would be restricted to the planned project area.

Diagram C shows the squatters (S) moving into the neighborhood of established projects. This diagram depicts a very common situation during the early 1970s when squatters moved into forested lands at an early stage of human settlement, motivated by the factors that triggered migrations discussed in Chapter 2. Because of the squatters, total deforestation (project area plus surrounding area) rises to 34 percent, already higher than the long-term projection in diagram B.

Diagram D shows what the actual project and the surrounding area look like in the long run, after colonists and squatters have had the chance to complete any deforestation intended, and after colonists have had a chance to sell their land to newcomers. Deforestation in the project area is now 87.5 percent, which is 37.5 percent higher than the government had expected. Deforestation in the overall area is 56 percent, which is 36 percent higher than the long-term government projection. This diagram assumes that the probability that a C or an S will deforest completely is 50 percent, but new owners (N) deforest completely since they are generally large farmers, mainly ranchers, who are unconstrained by labor supply and can count on government incentives to do so.

Comparing the outcome of diagram D with the intended outcome in B, deforestation in the overall area exceeds the intended target by 36 percent (56 percent minus 20 percent). From this example, we can attribute this excess deforestation to different sources:

N raise deforestation on 5 plots from 50% to 100%: $(5 \times 50\%)/50 = 5\%$
S raise deforestation on 14 plots from 50% to 100%: $(7 \times 50\% + 7 \times 100\%)/50 = 21\%$
C raise deforestation on 5 plots from 50% to 100%: $(5 \times 100\%)/50 = 10\%$
TOTAL   36%

Within the planned colonization project, excess deforestation (37.5%) can be distributed as follows:

N raises deforestation on 10 plots from 50% to 100%:   (10 x 50%)/20 = 25.0%

C raise deforestation on 5 plots from 50% to 100%:   (5 x 50%)/20 = 12.5%

TOTAL   37.5%

This is only an example to illustrate that since the beginning of a project, the government expects some degree of deforestation, because farmers are legally entitled to deforest 50 percent of their holding. It also shows that deforestation can easily be in excess of the government target because of the squatters who arrive in the early stages of settlement and because of the newcomers who arrive later, when the frontier consolidates.

Although this study focuses on small farmers, large private and corporate ranches account for most of the land of the Legal Amazon: of the total area of private lands (including forests) in the Amazon, 62 percent was in holdings of 1,000 hectares or larger, as of the last full agricultural census in 1986 (IBGE 1989). Often, these large holdings are consolidated in areas that have once been destined for colonization. Furthermore, the fact that more than 80 percent of the deforestation occurs in properties that are larger than 200 hectares[1] implies a clear relationship between plot size and deforestation. In Figure 4.1, this situation could be depicted as if Diagram D had only one N owner for the ten plots. This is precisely the situation that establishes the linkage between land re-concentration and deforestation in consolidated frontiers, which is an important part of the underlying hypothesis of this study.

The rules for land allocation encourage rapid deforestation on individually owned farms because the final amount of land that receives title under regularization is a multiple of the area covered by crops or pasture. Some colonists allege that it may be enough to clear land of the original forest – only to let secondary forest grow back – as irrevocable user certificates are issued after one year of occupation. The importance of this phenomenon, however, is not easy to assess. The process of forest conversion into private property in new frontiers would not be possible without the generous future granting of property rights and generalized corruption. These irregularities have always been facilitated by Brazil's byzantine system of land-title registration, with a multitude of different registry offices (*cartórios*) where a variety of types of documents dating from different historical periods may be filed and legally recognized. Land claims frequently overlap, which lead to disputes (often violent) over land tenure at the frontier. During an interview, public attorneys in Mato Grosso admitted this to be not only one of the most critical points in the whole land occupation process in the Amazon, but also one of the most difficult to reverse. The Public Attorney General himself feels incapable of launching operations that could even minimally threaten the established practices. The reason is that several areas that are currently titled could be legally contested, since the conversion of government land into private land with recognized title depends on the prior review of the tenure history of the land, something that is simply not done in the vast majority of cases.

Squatters are often accused of contributing greatly to deforestation. While they may be responsible for deforestation in new frontiers, they are less of a problem than ranchers in consolidated areas. Yet within their allocated plots, the system will reduce forest area rapidly. Primary forest formations are destroyed in the process of extensive crop production, as previously productive areas are quickly abandoned and replaced by secondary forest formations or by pasture. Soil degradation is initially perceived to be minimal because the land is covered by vegetation for all but short periods during the first few growing seasons, and because initially the highest quality soils are chosen. But, as under all extensive cultivation systems, large areas are abandoned as soon as soil fertility declines and weed infestations become a serious problem (after the first few seasons). Future chapters will provide field evidence showing many cases in which such fertility decline did not occur and, therefore, cannot be generalized.

4.3.   THE INADEQUACY OF STANDARD MODELS

Most economic analyses of the use and management of forestland are undertaken in countries where, unlike the Brazilian case, agricultural frontiers are fairly stationary. Few studies take into account how the management of existing farmland is influenced by the ready availability of land that can be cleared for crop or livestock production (Burt 1981; McConnell 1983). The option to bring idle land into production is incorporated in some models of natural resource development. For example, control theory has been used to characterize a socially optimal sequence of stages of growth in an agricultural economy. That sequence generally involves geographical expansion before major investments to increase yields are made, which can include the application of conservation measures (Hochman and Zilberman 1986). Regardless of how well such models describe how land should be used and managed, however, they do not fully explain the resource development decisions made by small farmers living on or near the developing world's agricultural frontiers, because they are based on the premise that the rental value of natural resources is maximized.

The premise of rental maximization is invalid for a causal analysis of deforestation in the Amazon for many reasons, most of which are associated with the rules of land allocation and government policies. First, because farmers must deforest land to acquire formal tenure or informal usufruct, they are obliged to disregard non-agricultural rents. Second, farmers clear unclaimed land in new frontiers beyond the point that justifies their agricultural operations. They act on the expectation of capturing profit through later sale, since deforested lands become more valuable than forested areas as the frontier consolidates. Such expectation is based on the experience that, as time passes, technological progress and new roads quickly promote the integration of previously unclaimed land into the emerging formal economy, which will make deforestation profitable as frontiers mature and land markets emerge. Third, the uncertainty introduced by this tenure regime restricts farmers' decisions regarding the timing of resource development activities, timing that is the primary focus of most dynamic models used to describe how the present value of a stream of rents can be maximized. Any farmer realizes that he would risk losing land that is not 'demarcated' by deforestation (a process that commonly determines the perimeter of a plot) if he ever acted on the basis of a judgement that forest conservation, or even delayed deforestation, is more profitable than present land clearing. Fourth, missing credit markets, combined with poverty, induce small farm households to discount future income heavily, which may lead them to ignore the long-term effects of their land management decisions. Therefore, settlers do not forego the opportunity to clear any parcel immediately if agricultural rents can be captured by doing so. Finally, the market distortions introduced by government policies (discussed in Chapter 3) tend to strengthen the behavior outlined above.

In the early stages of settlement, the lack of land tenure forces farmers to make short-run decisions regarding deforestation. Since pioneer farmers are family farmers, their only source of labor is family labor. This means that they are constrained by their labor supply rather than by the land they have available on the frontier. The result is that squatters will deforest as much land as their labor supply allows, so that they can be granted the future right to the property. The payoff is that when regularization takes place, these farmers will be entitled to a multiple of the area they have deforested. This rapid deforestation to secure title, however, happens only once, generally upon arrival. Subsequent land clearing is much slower, as continued rapid clearing would divert the scarce labor from planting crops for consumption.

Chayanov (1966) developed the first farm household model to analyze typical farm household behavior in the Russia of the early twentieth century, which had practically no land markets or labor markets, and so households varied the amount of land they farmed in response to changes in the age and numbers of their members. Ozório de Almeida and Campari (1996) confirm that certain aspects of this model can still be applied to the process of Amazonian settlement today.

4.4.   THE BEHAVIOR OF AMAZONIAN FARMERS

Farmers' choices with regard to the way land is managed and deforested are not irrational decisions. These decisions are based on: government's development policies; the frontier's tenure regime; imperfect information and markets; farmers' opportunity costs, and the different opportunity costs of the various agents with whom farmers interact at different stages of occupation (Schneider 1995; Ozório de Almeida and Campari 1996; Kaimowitz and Angelsen 1998; Alston et al. 1999). Chapter 7 further discusses the issues associated with opportunity costs of frontier farmers.

Farmers in the Amazon – large and small, titled or not – typically employ extensive practices and, for that reason, they are regarded as the primary source of deforestation. These households can simultaneously be considered producers and consumers. Low population densities and poor infrastructure contribute to weak communications systems and high transaction costs. This leads to pervasive market imperfections (Binswanger and McIntire, 1987). Since land is abundant in new frontiers, often no land market exists when the pioneer front arrives. Markets develop only as time passes and infrastructure improves. Interestingly, land in the Amazon frontier is traded regardless of whether it is titled or not. Similarly, credit, labor, input and output markets may be absent or very imperfect in the initial stages of occupation. For example, pioneer colonists may be able to find off-farm employment only during certain seasons or may experience difficulty in obtaining credit. This affects household behavior, including their choice about technologies and their decisions about whether to clear forest. Under such circumstances, household decisions about production and consumption depend on one another and on specific technology. Market and household characteristics determine many of the outcomes.

The literature on the economics of rural organization shows that imperfect information leads farmers to consider hired labor a poor substitute for family labor (Feder 1985). This partially explains the frequently found inverse relationship between farm size and efficiency (Berry and Cline 1979; Feder 1985; Heltberg 1998). Moral-hazard situations due to imperfect information cause rationing in credit markets (Stiglitz and Weiss 1981). Cash and credit constraints also contribute to labor market imperfections, which explains why land-abundant agricultural economies such as in new frontiers in the Amazon region have many Chayanovian features.

As frontiers consolidate and markets emerge, the situation changes. Boserup's (1965) theory of the evolution of agricultural development describes a general tendency for production to become more intensive as labor productivity falls in response to greater population pressures. In the Amazon, this can be observed only in consolidated frontiers where agriculture can be considered successful. In such places, as population density rises, successful farmers substitute labor for land and turn from shifting cultivation to long fallow, short fallow, permanent and multiple cropping systems. In the case of new frontiers, farmers do not even reach the stage where they would practice shifting cultivation. Land is abundant, which encourages them to deforest and, after a few years when productivity declines, either sell or abandon the deforested part of the plot and move on to deforest another area. Further, they do not generally experience labor shortages for crop production, nor do they work as hard as they can, because they have no need or incentive to do so. They are small subsistence farmers who are not integrated into the market economy. However, when farmers adopt fallow systems or permanent cultivation in consolidated frontiers, labor becomes a limiting factor for production. The demand for labor in these systems has more pronounced seasonal peaks, particularly for land preparation and weeding, and the physical yields of cropped areas (excluding fallow) are lower than in shifting-cultivation systems. This implies that extensive agriculture offers many desirable features for farm households in sparsely populated areas, such as in new frontiers in the Brazilian Amazon.

In new Amazonian frontiers, colonists continue their extensive practices, often associated with slash-and-burn (a technique in which farmers deforest part of the plot and burn the logs, so that the ashes will replenish the land with its nutrients). They do so even after they have exceeded the plot's carrying capacity, i.e., the point at which the farming system starts to collapse due to nutrient mining (slash-and-burn can be sustained for only a few seasons, as the process displays clear diminishing returns). As a result, fallow periods become shorter, and the system becomes unsustainable. With regard to deforestation, the situation becomes really bleak when empirical evidence indicates that poor colonists' discount rates are much higher than the rate of forest regrowth (Schneider 1995). Under such conditions, Alston et al. (1999) have shown that poor colonists will have a short-term view and disregard the future benefits of forest regeneration.

4.4.1. The Impact of Extensive Agriculture on Regional Deforestation

In the Amazon, extensive agriculture applies to small and large farmers. This scale varies according to the labor supply and technology available. In the case of family-based agriculture, settlers in consolidated frontiers clear three to four hectares in order to plant annual crops for two or three years, taking advantage of the fertility of recently cleared land (see Chapter 9). Following a period of high yields, the deforested lands begin to exhibit diminishing returns due to nutrient mining caused by slash-and-burn (the most common production technique used by Amazonian farmers). Farmers abandon that part of the plot and deforestation continues in another piece of land. When small farmers own their plots, they may or may not plant pasture on the lands they no longer cultivate. When they do plant pasture, they typically raise cattle, although on a very modest scale. Surrounding large landowners may lease these pastures to grow their own cattle, but at very low productivity levels (Chomitz and Thomas 2001; Margulis 2001). When small farmers are squatters or tenants, they usually plant pasture expressly for landowners. Thus they incorporate into their behavior the expectation of future eviction from current plots and subsequent occupation by ranchers (Ozório de Almeida 1992). This is the classic sequence of the moving frontier. Its consequences are extensive agriculture and ranching and low-level technology for both large and small producers.

Given the abundance of land in new frontiers and the practice of extensive agriculture, land is surely not seen as a fixed factor of production to be preserved and recovered for permanent reuse. Rather, most of the deforestation literature argues that frontier agents view land as a variable factor, an input, that one uses up and throws away, or leaves behind. Chapter 9 will contest this assumption. The implications of land-extensive technology for deforestation are obvious. The deforested area is a large and growing multiple of the area in use.

4.5.　CONCLUSION

This chapter has shown that the economic decisions of farmers about whether to conserve or deforest is not irrational, given their preferences, resource constraints, limited access to information, imperfect markets and opportunity costs (theirs as well as those of other agents). Such behavior is influenced by specific government policies that promote deforestation and penalize conservation. An extensive production strategy that accelerates deforestation in the Amazon is aggravated by uncertain property rights, rules of land allocation, special tax incentives, and the subsidized credit for agriculture.

Land-tenure issues affect virtually every decision in the Brazilian Amazon, from the investments of labor and capital by small farmers to the migration of populations. Deforestation is a direct outcome of these decisions. The current pattern of land occupation unfolds as an environmental symptom of the absence of enforcement of the rule of law, including woefully inadequate property law and a system of financing that is characterized by routine fraud.

Rules of public land allocation provide incentives for deforestation because the rules solidifying claims and ensuring maximum land areas encourage land clearing. A claimant used to be allocated two to three times the amount of land cleared of forest. In addition, land clearing provides protection against competing claims and against invasions. Gillis and Repetto (1988), Spears (1988), Mahar (1989), and Binswanger (1994) and have been particularly critical of government policies, both for a failure to provide well-defined property rights and for encouraging migrations and deforestation as a means of staking claims to land and relieving ingrained social pressures in other parts of the country. To reform these rules would require changing the rules of land allocation to remove incentives for clearing land simply for purposes of solidifying land claims and increasing the size of allocations. Although the 1988 constitution attempted to reverse these trends, deforestation continues.

For many years ranchers have considered themselves to be 'obliged' to deforest to guarantee their tenure because, despite legal restrictions, any landowner who did not deforest would, in practice, risk losing the land either through expropriation (since forested land was considered unproductive and, therefore, likely to be expropriated for agrarian reform); or to land invasion. Land tenure problems have always led to both direct and indirect effects, speeding deforestation by both large and small landowners. The practice of extensive agriculture among small and large farmers is associated with the fragile tenure regime in the frontier. Extensive agriculture and consequently deforestation give the farmer an informal property right in the short run. This informal right is the quickest way to obtain a formal title later. The farmer is granted the right to a multiple of the area deforested, since deforestation is considered by the government as an indicator of 'productive' land use. Extensive agriculture is also attractive because it is much cheaper for farmers to produce crops on free forested lands rather than to upgrade already deforested areas.

This study comes at an opportune moment in the Amazonian debate. Although this chapter is largely about the economic behavior of colonists in the Amazon, one cannot dismiss the recent policy developments that might, in the long run, alter such behavior. Very little, however, has been done in practice to correct the distortions outlined in this chapter that culminated in concentrated land structures and more deforestation throughout the region. The linkage between concentrated landed property and deforestation is the topic of the following chapter.

NOTE

1. Interview with the Director of the Forest Resources Department of the State Foundation Environment for the Environment in Mato Grosso.

5. The turnover hypothesis of Amazon deforestation: conceptual framework

5.1. INTRODUCTION

Although the underlying economic and political forces that stimulated migrations during the 1970s had disappeared by the mid-1980s, the Amazon continued to experience demographic instability, deforestation and concentration of land. Although in the 1970s migrants arrived in the Amazon from other regions, the difference in the 1980s was the end of *interregional* migrations and the beginning of *intraregional* migrations. Moreover, during the 1980s, the Amazon developed a critical mass of politicians and a local élite that began to define local priorities. During that period, the region acquired its own socio-economic dynamics that began to influence migration patterns with direct consequences for deforestation and land re-concentration. Therefore, in the 1980s, locally generated stimuli replaced external forces.

Throughout the 1980s and 1990s, the source of demographic instability in the Amazon continued to be the migrations of the rural population, mainly that of small farmers. These farmers have always been the first ones to arrive and, therefore, are considered the initial source of deforestation in new frontiers. It is conjectured that, after arrival, they engage in a sequence of predictable uses of land, which ultimately culminates in the sale of their plots to new owners, who, for different reasons and purposes, deforest even more. The hypothesized process of pioneer settlers arriving in a directed colonization project, settling in for a few years, deforesting part of the plot for agricultural production, and then selling out the land to a newcomer is called *turnover*.

For many years, several authors in many disciplines have provided quite different analyses of the causes of turnover. What is widely agreed is that the current process of in- and out-migrations generates demographic instability in the region, with an adverse impact on the forest resource base as new areas are constantly being opened and occupied. It is also understood that the migration of small farmers in the region compromises the equitable distribution of land among the rural poor, as newcomers arrive and re-concentrate land, undermining the primary goal of colonization. It is believed that newcomers not only increase the deforested area measured in numbers of hectares (*an absolute amount*), but they are also thought to deforest a larger fraction (*percentage*) of their lands than do small colonists. The difference in the relative rates of deforestation (percentages) is the distinguishing characteristic in the two types of agents.

The purpose of this chapter is to develop the conceptual framework of the turnover hypothesis of deforestation in the Amazon. Section 5.2 introduces the logic of the hypothesis. Section 5.3 discusses a set of necessary conditions for the hypothesis to hold. Section 5.4 formalizes a model of the turnover hypothesis. Section 5.5 summarizes the discussion and concludes the chapter.

5.2. THE TURNOVER HYPOTHESIS: A CIRCULAR APPROACH TO THE CAUSES OF DEFORESTATION

Small farmers who migrated from other regions to the Amazon in the 1970s and early 1980s became agricultural colonists for many reasons. They were frequently obliged to leave land that they and their forebears had long cultivated. Socially disruptive rural development strategies were pursued, often with the support of government, such as mechanized agriculture and the encroachment of soybean plantations in the south of Brazil. Or they were forced to migrate as land became exhausted of its nutrients, as is the case among the groups of migrants who went to the Amazon to escape from the chronic drought in the Northeast region of Brazil.

Since the mid-1980s, however, the rural population in the Amazon has been a source of regional demographic instability, as family farmers move from place to place, opening new areas to farm only to sell out again a few years later. It is argued that the main cause of demographic instability in the countryside is the failure of Amazonian soils to sustain agricultural production.

The turnover hypothesis links plot size with deforestation. It holds that pioneer colonists are bound to deforest less than newcomers, as initial land endowments are small, generally less than 100 hectares per family. Pioneer colonists are also constrained by labor, which reduces even further their capacity to deforest. The growth in farm sizes increases deforestation in two ways. First, newcomers increase the deforested area because they need more land to carry out large-scale agriculture, cattle ranching, or both. Second, the arrival of newcomers influences the decision of pioneer farmers to move further into the woods, where they will deforest in order to reproduce their family farming system. This becomes a vicious cycle that is repeated over again, and it is unconstrained by land resources since these are readily available in new frontiers. This is a typical characteristic of the Brazilian agricultural frontier where land, in the initial stages of occupation, is an open access resource available for free. In the absence of government, all the conditions are present for the indiscriminate use of land and the degradation of the rain forest.

Figure 5.1 presents a diagram showing the hypothesized relationships between turnover, land re-concentration and deforestation. While the top part of the diagram (shaded area) is related to the production/deforestation dynamics of small farmers in new frontiers, the bottom part of the diagram (not shaded) is associated with production and land clearing carried out by newcomers as frontiers become mature (consolidated). Dotted lines represent turnover itself, i.e. the arrival and departure of farmers in colonization plots. Solid lines represent the interaction between production and deforestation. In terms of the turnover hypothesis, the relevance of deforestation is depicted as follows: (i) the arrival of small farmers into new frontiers (dotted lines in the top part of the diagram); (ii) the replacement of pioneers by newcomers as frontiers mature (dotted lines in the bottom part of the diagram); and (iii) the production-deforestation cycle by newcomers in old frontiers (solid lines in bottom part of the diagram). Figure 5.1 makes it clear that the behavior of the pioneers who choose to stay (solid lines) is secondary in terms of deforestation. This happens because they are thought to deforest little because they produce little due to labor constraints.

The turnover hypothesis is intuitive, its dynamics are simple to understand, and it seems to tackle well the relationships between farming and deforestation, as well as the interdependence between the scales of both. The most common arguments used to explain turnover are undefined property rights, declining yields, or inappropriate government policies to contain migrations. This study challenges these arguments by showing evidence that even without those conditions (i.e. with relatively well-defined property rights, increasing yields, and no government policies stimulating migrations), turnover in colonization projects continues to occur. The following chapters show that arguments of the turnover hypothesis provide only partial insights into the problem of deforestation.

5.3.   NECESSARY CONDITIONS

This section develops a set of three conditions for the turnover hypothesis to hold. In this conceptual framework, plots in colonization projects are

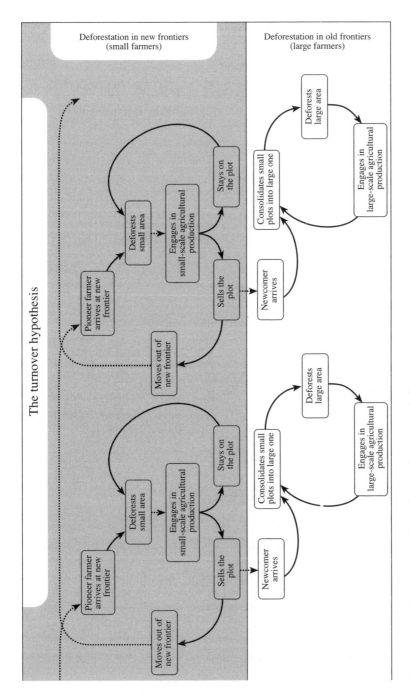

Figure 5.1. The turnover hypothesis of Amazon deforestation

classified into two categories, depending on whether or not they are sold to new farmers in a given period. Plots where ownership remains the same during this period are labeled *survivors'* plots. Plots where ownership changes are labeled *newcomers'* plots. Turnover happens every time a plot is sold.

Three conditions are necessary for the turnover hypothesis to hold:

Condition	Why is it necessary?
(1) *Survival rates* among original settlers in Amazon colonization projects must be low relative to similar projects elsewhere in Brazil	*Implies that displacement of Amazonian small farmers is high.*
(2) Over time, *plot sizes* where turnover occurs (newcomers' plots) tend to become larger relative to those plots where ownership remained the same (survivors' plots)	*Implies that newcomers are re-concentrating land to some extent.*
(3) Over time, *deforested areas* in plots that turned over (newcomers' plots) tend to become relatively larger than those where ownership remains the same (survivors' plots)	*Implies that newcomers' deforestation must be larger (in absolute and relative terms). Further, this condition suggests that different categories of farms have been subject to different farmers' behaviors with regard to forest consumption over time.*

These conditions are discussed below.

5.3.1. Condition 1: Low Survival Rates

The hypothesis is constructed upon the assumption that a large number of initial settlers who receive land from the government in public colonization or who buy property in private projects must abandon or sell their plots to another farmer after settling for only a few years. If this is the case, then survival rates among colonists must be low, as they receive (or acquire) land and sell it afterward, only to begin the process over again in another place in the frontier. One of the major strengths of this study is that this assumption is testable. This condition has been conjectured in other studies, but it has never been tested using plot-level surveys over a long period as is done here.

5.3.2. Condition 2: Relatively Larger Farms among Newcomers

Newcomers who buy plots from initial settlers are assumed to be commercial farmers whose activities would require more land than is available in the plots they have just acquired. For this reason, newcomers are assumed to increase the size of their land holdings by consolidating small neighboring plots either by acquisition or leasing. In either case, a typical newcomer is able to expand the size of the plot. Therefore, over time, plots where turnover occurs must become a multiple of their initial size.

This condition can be formalized by two inequalities, where L is the size of the plot (land) in hectares, the first subscript is the time period (T or $T+1$), and the second subscript is the owner that period (S refers to settler survivor, and N refers to newcomer):

$$L_{T+1, N} > L_{T, N} \tag{5.1}$$

$$L_{T+1, N} > L_{T+1, S} \tag{5.2}$$

The first condition says that the size of plots that experienced a change in ownership is larger after turnover (in period $T+1$) than beforehand (in period T). The second condition requires that plots that were passed onto newcomers in period $T+1$ are larger than survivors' plots in that period; this situation characterizes land re-concentration in the hands of newcomers. While condition (5.1) is a comparison *over time* of plots that changes hands, condition (5.2) is a comparison *across farm groups* in the period that follows turnover.

5.3.3. Condition 3: Relatively Higher Deforestation among Newcomers

Deforestation is a positive function of plot size. Therefore, initial settlers deforest little because they are generally constrained by the small size of their plots and by their labor supply (family labor). In the case of newcomers, the situation is quite different. Since they have more land and easier access to capital market than do small farmers, it is reasonable to assume that they also deforest larger areas. They carry out commercial agriculture and grazing, based on extensive practices. Thus, in the Amazon, the scale of deforestation is associated with the size of the plot. Further, because newcomers are less labor-constrained than pioneer settlers, the hypothesis also assumes that they are likely to deforest a larger fraction of their plots than survivors. In this case, compared to survivors, newcomers would display higher rates of deforestation. Let D represent the fraction of the plot deforested. Then we have two other conditions emerge:

$$D_{T+1,\,N} > D_{T,\,N} \qquad\qquad (5.3)$$
$$D_{T+1,\,N} > D_{T+1,\,S} \qquad\qquad (5.4)$$

Condition (5.3) requires that the fraction of the plot deforested is lower before turnover (period T), and higher after it occurs (period $T+1$). This condition compares deforestation in plots that turned over at two points in time, i.e., before and after turnover. Condition (5.4) requires that ultimate deforestation in newcomers' plots is greater than in survivors' plots. Again, while condition (5.3) is a comparison *over time* in plots that changed ownership, condition (5.4) is a comparison *across groups* in period $T + 1$.

5.4.   A MODEL OF THE TURNOVER HYPOTHESIS

The above conditions require that newcomers have larger plots *and* deforest larger fractions of their plots than survivors. These conditions force newcomers to deforest larger areas than survivors. Therefore, deforestation is greater with these conditions than without any of them. Letting L represent the size of a farmer's plot and D represent the fraction of the plot that has been deforested, then $H = L.D$ represents the number of hectares deforested per plot. If the turnover hypothesis holds, then the total excess deforestation due to the behavior of newcomers (H^{TOT}) can be expressed as follows:

$$H^{TOT} = \sum_{i \in N} (H_{T+1,N}^{i} - \hat{H}_{T+1,S}^{i}) \qquad\qquad (5.5)$$

where: $\hat{H}$ = hypothetical number of hectares deforested in a plot that turned over, had this plot been owned by a survivor instead of a newcomer; N = set of newcomers; S = set of survivors; i = plot.

Rewriting (5.5) yields:

$$H^{TOT} = \sum_{i \in N} H_{T+1,N}^{i} - \sum_{i \in N} \hat{H}_{T+1,S}^{i} \qquad\qquad (5.6)$$

which leads to:

$$H^{TOT} = N\,(\bar{H}_{T+1,N}^{i} - \bar{\hat{H}}_{T+1,S}^{i}) \qquad\qquad (5.7)$$

where: N = number of plots that turned over (i.e., where there is a newcomer). $\bar{H}$ and $\bar{\hat{H}}$ represent averages.

Alternatively,

$$H^{TOT} = N_{TOT} \cdot \pi \cdot (\bar{H}^i_{T+1,N} - \bar{\hat{H}}^i_{T+1,S})$$

(5.8)

where N_{TOT} = total number of plots in the colonization project; π = fraction of plots that turned over.

If the turnover hypothesis provides a good theoretical framework of Amazon deforestation, then excess deforestation in a new project can be predicted as follows:

$$\hat{H}^{TOT} = N_{TOT} \cdot \hat{\pi} \cdot (\bar{H}^i_{T+1,N} - \bar{\hat{H}}^i_{T+1,S})$$

(5.9)

where $\hat{\pi}$ estimated probability that turnover happens.

5.5.   SUMMARY AND CONCLUSION

Turnover in colonization plots is characterized by the out-migration of small farmers and the arrival of newcomers who replace them. The literature on Amazonian development argues that the effects of turnover are disastrous in terms of equity of land distribution and environmental losses. First, turnover generates the demographic instability of the rural population discussed in Chapter 2. Second, it is assumed to lead to land re-concentration in the hands of newcomers who are considered large farmers, undermining the main goal of colonization (i.e., to distribute land among the rural poor). Third, and most important for the topic of this study, it is argued that turnover promotes deforestation in two ways: first, small farmers move into new frontiers and deforest once again, and second, newcomers arrive and consolidate areas that once belonged to small farmers, deforesting them to a larger extent than did previous owners in order to carry out commercial agriculture or grazing.

The turnover hypothesis differs from two simpler alternatives: (a) small farmers deforest a small amount of land, farm it for a few years and then migrate; newcomers then take over the land but do not really deforest more than pioneer colonists would have done, or (b) small farmers do not deforest much because they are constrained by labor supply, but they sell out to newcomers who then undertake most of the deforestation. The turnover hypothesis actually hinges on the interaction of the two groups: it claims, implicitly, that deforestation is higher than it would have been with just small farmers alone (even if they do move around a lot), or with just newcomers alone (i.e., if newcomers had to do all their own clearing).

In order to analyze turnover and its impacts on deforestation and land re-concentration, this chapter formalized a conceptual framework by outlining three conditions for the hypothesis to hold. To test this hypothesis, a large data set that covers 20 years of colonization experience has been assembled. Chapter 6 will describe how this data set was conceived and organized as well as the main questions that were asked in the surveys. The chapter will also display the field locations surveyed for this study. Chapter 7 will later assess whether the conceptual framework put forth in this chapter holds.

6. Colonization projects: field work

6.1. INTRODUCTION

The data for this study were collected from surveys of colonization projects in the Brazilian Amazon that were carried out in 1981 and 1991, under the auspices of the federal government's Institute of Applied Economic Research (IPEA) in Brazil and the National Institute for Colonization and Agrarian Reform (INCRA). The partnership established in 1980 between IPEA and INCRA turned into a project called 'Internal Migrations and Small Agricultural Production in Amazonia: An Analysis of INCRA's Colonization Policy'. The project lasted for four years, from 1980 until 1984, and is summarized in six volumes that are currently held by IPEA in its Rio de Janeiro branch. The 1991 data set was an undertaking by IPEA alone.

From 1992 until 1995, the data set was maintained by the World Bank's Poverty and Social Policy Department (PSP), where research and analysis continued with updating (which included further field visits). At IPEA, the data were mostly used for cost-benefit analysis of public versus private colonization. At the World Bank, the purpose of the work was to study the frontier's rural poor with respect to their dependence and impact on the natural resource base.

Figure 6.1 shows the locations surveyed. Surveys were carried out in the states of Pará and Mato Grosso, in the eastern and western Amazon, respectively. Frontier farmers, merchants and institutions were interviewed to establish a broad picture of economic, social, political and institutional conditions of directed colonization in the Amazon. In this study, only the agricultural surveys on farmers are used, because the primary data sources on merchants and institutions were very poorly maintained by IPEA and, therefore, do not provide additional reliable information on the issues that this study wishes to address.

Thus far, two pieces of work have been published using these data. Ozório de Almeida (1992) focuses on the 1981 data set; Ozório de Almeida and Campari (1996) focus on the 1991 data set. Since 1995, the data have been exclusively used for this book, and it is the first attempt to bring the two data sets together as a single panel sample.

The 1981 sample covered 363 farms; the 1991 survey revisited 336 farms from the original sample. The years 1981 and 1991 were chosen for several reasons. They were near census years that provide general information on the universe being sampled (1980 and 1990). They were normal agricultural years for the Amazon in general, and in the sampled locations in particular, with no extraordinary positive or negative trends that would bias the analysis. Therefore, the ten-year comparison can be assumed to be unbiased. Finally, these years bracket the 1980s, a period when the economic and political landscapes in Brazil changed drastically.

Furthermore, a new round of interviews was conducted in October and November 2001. The purpose of these latest interviews was to register the perceptions of relevant sources about whether the findings of this study are still robust, given that the data set used here was ten years old. These interviews were conducted mainly in the state of Mato Grosso with: (i)

Figure 6.1.   Field work locations

Mayors and Secretaries of Rural Development and Environmental Policy of the municipalities of the northwest region of the state; (ii) local small producers in the municipality of Juina, a municipality that faces strong turnover problems; (iii) the State Secretary for Environmental Policy; (iv) the local representative of the Ministry of the Environment's Secretariat for Amazonian Affairs; (v) State Public Attorney Officers; (vi) technical staff from INCRA's local office; and (vii) the CEO for the largest soybean business in Brazil. The following were also interviewed: (viii) consultants and environmental advisors from the Ministry of the Environment; (ix) technical consultants from the Pilot Program to Conserve the Brazilian Rain Forests, known as PPG7 (the largest multi-donor environmental program in the world, financed by the G7); (x) economists and task managers of the World Bank's Rain Forest Unit; and, finally, (xi) one manager and several senior-level environmental, social and livelihoods advisors from the Department for International Development (DFID) in Brazil. These interviews, often conducted informally, are used here to illustrate many points of this study.

6.2. SURVEY DESIGN

The same farming plots were surveyed in 1981 and 1991, and the same survey methods were used in both years in order to assess the performance of farmers in directed colonization over time at the farm level. Although a complete record of settlers' characteristics is available from the survey questionnaires, it is important to note at the outset that the unit of observation in this study is the farming plot and not the farmer who occupies the land. In many cases, colonists interviewed in 1981 were no longer on the same plots in 1991. The respondents were always the heads of the households, i.e., those responsible for making decisions with regards to land use and agricultural production within each plot, regardless whether they were owners, tenants, or sharecroppers.

This section presents the data, the main questions that were asked, the underlying hypotheses, and the variables of interest for the IPEA/INCRA research team. Then, it discusses the parts of the data that are used in this book.

6.2.3. Stratification of the Sample

It must be noted that, although the data collected by IPEA/INCRA were used in this book to address the issue of frontier deforestation, the main goal of the survey project was to collect information to test hypotheses associated with the performance of Amazonian colonization. The choice of the types of households surveyed as well as the underlying hypotheses associated with that choice are outlined below:

(a) *young and old households:* to test life-cycle hypotheses;
(b) *colonists who had recently arrived on the land as well as those who had been on the plot for a long time:* in order to test hypotheses associated with the fixation and itinerancy of frontier colonists;
(c) *'southern' and 'other' migrants:* to test hypotheses regarding the impact of previous experience in agriculture in Southern Brazil on the performance of frontier colonists (e.g., regarding technology, community development, access to credit through cooperatives, and banks);
(d) *colonists who owned small and large properties:* to test hypotheses about the appropriate size of plots for family farming;
(e) *farmers in public and private colonization projects:* to test hypotheses about the effect of type of colonization on colonists' performance.

6.2.2. Criteria for Household Selection

Specific criteria were used to determine the characteristics of the households in the sample. These are:

(a)   Age   Households were considered 'young' when the wife of the head of the household was at most 35 years of age, and 'old' otherwise. This criteria was used because, according to IPEA's health advisors, female fertility in Amazonia tended to decline after that age. This is a fundamental factor in determining the size of the colonists' families and, therefore, the supply of household labor (the only source of labor available to colonists).

(b)   Time on plot   In 1981, households were considered 'recent' when they had arrived on the plot up to three agricultural seasons (years) before the survey was carried out and 'old-timers' otherwise. This criterion was based on the literature reviewed, which argued that itinerant migrants are unable to use the same farmland after three harvesting seasons, after which land loses its nutrients and yields decline. Therefore, fixation or itinerancy on plots could only be observed after three years. Fixation of the farmer on the land was assessed by the introduction of permanent crops as well as the improvements made by the farmer on his land that led to a more intensive use of deforested areas.

(c)   Origin   Colonists were considered 'southerners' when they had a previous farming experience in the South of Brazil (in the states of Paraná,

Santa Catarina and Rio Grande do Sul; see Figure 2.4 in Chapter 2) and 'others' otherwise. This criterion is not related to farmers' place of birth, or to their previous migratory origin before reaching the Amazon. The important point for the survey is whether farmers retained the knowledge and techniques previously acquired in southern agriculture – considered the most efficient in Brazil – and brought this knowledge to the Amazon. Even a short tenure in the South could have had an important and decisive impact on farmers' performance on the Amazon frontier.

(d)   Plot size   The goal of the survey was to study the performance of small farmers in the Amazon. However, if the sample had been truncated by plot size and large plots discarded, then an important part of the story would have been missed, namely, 'successful' farmers who started out small and grew over time. The survey would also have missed the differences in the scale of operations that could determine certain advantages of large and medium farmers over small ones. A household with techniques that could be considered primitive, without mechanization, and constrained by labor supply, was assumed to be unlikely to deforest and farm more than five hectares per year. Since the oldest farmers (those settled along the Transamazon Highway) had been in the Amazon frontier for at most ten years, the typical deforested area among small producers in these locations should reach, at most, 50 hectares. Given that in 1981 the typical size of a colonization plot was 100 hectares, plots were considered 'small' when no more than 50 hectares had been deforested – which represents 50 percent of the plot area – and 'large' otherwise.

(e)   Type of colonization   Public and private colonization projects were considered. Among the public ones, only those established by INCRA (federal government) were surveyed (state-funded projects were not considered). State-funded projects were not considered because the goal of the study was to assess INCRA's settlement policy against the performance of private ones. Although state-funded colonization projects also deserved attention because of their impact on farming and regional deforestation, these were excluded for reasons of time and resource constraints. Private colonization projects were established by different companies, Indeco and Mutum.

6.2.3.   Variables

6.2.3.1.   Measurement of performance
The goal of colonization is to provide the conditions for successful agriculture to individuals who arrived in the Amazon from other regions.

The *performance indicator of a colonization project* is, therefore, the average of the sum of the performance indicators of individual colonists. If some colonists are successful while a large number fail, then a project can be implicitly considered unsuccessful. The choice of analytical variables, therefore, was guided by the hypothetical relationships that the study wished to address regarding the performance of Amazonian colonists.

The *performance indicator of a colonist*, however, is not associated only with the conditions of the project where he is currently settled. His performance is also related to other factors from his background, individual characteristics, and previous farming experiences in other places. The analysis of a colonist's performance, therefore, requires the survey of three types of information: (a) that associated with the colonist's background; (b) that in regard to the current site; and (c) that associated with individual characteristics.

A farmer's performance is very difficult to assess. Would it be the colonist's own perception of success or failure, his current income, or accumulated wealth since arrival on the frontier, the agricultural productivity of his plot, or the surplus that the farmer produces? The choice is difficult and depends on the issue that the researcher sets out to analyze. In the surveys carried out by IPEA, three standard microeconomic variables were chosen to assess individual performance: (1) income; (2) investment; and (3) asset accumulation.

These variables were measured for each household in the survey. In cases where a single plot hosted multiple households (related by family ties or not), but with a single economic decision-maker, then all households were surveyed, but all the information was added and entered into a single questionnaire. In cases with multiple and independent households (decision-makers) within a single plot, then the information for each household was recorded in a different questionnaire.

Income, assets and investments of each household were measured as follows:

1. Income Income is defined as the value of all goods and services generated in the household, or received from outside sources, in payments or transfers, monetary or in kind, during the agricultural year between 1 July 1980 and 30 June 1981 (in the case of the first survey); the same dates were considered tens years later, i.e. 1990–91 (in the case of the second survey). For incomes received 'in kind', local market values were imputed to the quantities received of the goods and services in question:

1a. Agricultural income: all incomes generated by agricultural production, grazing, and extractivist activities on the plot;

1b. Non-agricultural income: all incomes generated that are not associated with agricultural production, grazing or extractivist activities on the plot or outside of it (excludes family income, see 1c);

1c. Family income: all incomes generated from wage work and transfers received by the household;

1d. Total income: the sum of 1a + 1b + 1c.

2. Investment Investment is the value of all expenditures, monetary or in kind, incurred during the year comprehended between 1 July 1980 and 30 June 1981 (in the case of the first survey); the same dates were considered ten years later, i.e. 1990–91 (in the case of the second survey), aimed at generating all income after the periods in question. Agricultural investment, non-agricultural investment, family investment, and total investment are measured the same way as in 1a–1d, above (except that instead of 'income', the term 'investment' should be used).

3. Assets Assets were measured as the value of all goods, stocks and net balances, monetary or in kind, owned by the household on 30 June 1981 in the case of the first survey and 30 June 1991 in the case of the second survey. Agricultural assets, non-agricultural assets, family assets, and total assets are measured the same way as in 1a–1d and 2a–2d above.

The main difficulty faced by interviewers during field work was how to measure variables 1–3 above. The measurement of income required quantifying all agricultural production, grazing and non-agricultural production. All present remuneration and transfers were registered. Household own-consumption was assessed in great detail (e.g., even fuelwood for cooking). To measure investments, all of the following were assessed: deforestation, construction, expenditure on permanent crops, the value of improvements to the plot, stock variations, the acquisition of equipment and durable goods for production. Assets were measured by stock, all animals, construction, improvements, total land (regardless of its use), all production and consumption goods, as well as all financial balances. To test the 'consistency' of all three variables, all expenditures were computed and only the questionnaires that presented robust accounting balances were considered satisfactory for the purposes of the IPEA study.

6.2.3.2. The precision of measurement

In spite of the difficulties reported by the research team in collecting data on income, investments and assets, during the field work as well as in the later correction of data, the efforts paid off. A high measurement precision was reached through the application of consistency tests and a return to the field to correct the questionnaires that were considered unsatisfactory.

The following features of this study are not common in field research: the interviews lasted, on average, three to four hours; the farming households were surveyed on all economic activity; consistency tests were applied on the spot contesting the information provided by the farmer; the same household was revisited one or more times (sometimes days, sometimes months apart between one visit and another). All of the above tasks maximized the number of questionnaires that are considered satisfactory.

It is usually assumed that farmers, particularly the illiterate ones who are unfamiliar with accounting methods, would not remember the details of their own economic life. It is also assumed that measurement precision is compromised as time passes and as the level of detail of information requested grows. The field experience, however, shows that the contrary happens. Whoever takes great economic risks – such as the one to move to an inhospitable frontier of settlement – is fully aware of the elements available to him which, in a way, can determine his performance. The households interviewed generally knew in great detail what they had planted, harvested, transacted, manufactured, and how much they worked during the agricultural year. Furthermore, they remembered with great precision what they had brought with them to their current plots: equipment, stocks, furniture, cash; generally, farmers provided accurate information without hesitation.

The type of research design carried out by the IPEA team was innovative in terms of field surveys. It did not intend to have the non-intruding behavior most commonly found in anthropological surveys that seek the 'truth' in the spontaneity of information and behavioral observations of the household. In the case of the IPEA research, only a few pre-established microeconomic variables were quantified. The 'truth' in this case was sought in the accuracy of information, demanding from the household coherence of information with accounting identities unknown to him and which, often, are not applicable to the logic of a frontier economy where markets are nonexistent or are very thin. These identities, however, controlled the entire survey process and determined the extent to which a questionnaire was satisfactory or not. For example, before assets and liabilities were balanced (i.e., balanced accounting), the questionnaire could not be considered satisfactory. As strange as it may sound, it did not matter to the research team how irritated or uneasy the household became after hours of exhaustive interviews and re-visits (Ozório de Almeida 1985).

Many advantages were associated with the exhausting field work. Quite a few variance tests were performed on different subsamples in all the variables that compose income, investments and asset accumulation by colonists to try to identify biases that were not detected by the consistency tests, or that would have been generated by data entry. Only a few cases had large variances due to data entry error, which means that the efforts of the research team in the field paid off.

The methodological option adopted by the research team, which consisted of long pre-coded questionnaires, with direct consistency tests and many returns to the sampled plots, were also often frustrating to the team. The microeconomic analysis is dry and not very interesting in itself. It was only worthwhile carrying out this task because the underlying theory predicted precise results on the linkages between income, investment and asset accumulation. Once these variables were appropriately measured, then it was possible to assess the extent to which their interactions are influenced by frontier conditions in colonization projects – the most interesting part of the research. Most of this information is discussed in Chapter 9.

6.3. LONGITUDINAL DATA ON FARMING PLOTS

The panel constructed for this book used the data described above to offer detailed information on the changes that occurred during the 1980s in colonization projects in the Amazon at the plot level, mainly with regard to turnover, land accumulation and deforestation (Chapters 7 and 8) and performance indicators that affect these variables (Chapter 9). Table 6.1 shows how the panel used in this study was constructed. All the observations in one survey year that did not have the equivalent information in the other year were excluded. One location in Mato Grosso (São José do Rio Claro) was deleted from the original sample because it was located in the *cerrado* zone of the state, an area which is not forested; furthermore, there were

Table 6.1.   The panel of plots

1981 sample:	363 observations Less 48 observations not sampled in 1991
1991 sample:	336 observations Less 21 observations not sampled in 1981
Matched data:	315 observations Less one location in MT: no forest (17 observations) Less observations with missing values for the variables of interest and internal inconsistencies (26 observations)
Final panel:	272 observations

only 17 observations in that location. The number of questionnaires in 1991 was 336, so that sets the maximum size of the panel. After the data were retrieved and cleaned for the variables of interest, the size of the panel was reduced to 272 observations:

The 1981 sample covered 7 percent of the total population in the corresponding census districts. It is difficult to estimate the representativeness of the sample in 1991 for several reasons. First, the size of the sample was smaller due to a reduction in the 1991 research budget, which prevented the team from revisiting all farms. Second, aggregation and disaggregation of the original plots reduced the number of properties that qualified for the panel. Third, several municipalities were dismembered during the inter-survey period, making it difficult to estimate the variation in the population size of each location. Fourth, in other instances, there was no one around to answer the questionnaires, or plots had been abandoned. It was not possible, however, from the data available, to differentiate among the four factors. Finally, the areas of the projects grew, as did the population. Given the above factors, the 1991 sample was certainly not as representative as the 1981 sample.

The following sections display the most important variables considered to assess the turnover hypothesis. The descriptive tables that contain the other variables discussed in previous sections are located at the end of the chapter.

6.3.1.   Directed Colonization: Public and Private

The type of colonization considered here is *directed colonization*. Directed colonization can be divided into two types, public and private. While INCRA had an executive role in all official projects, it had regulatory authority over all private colonization projects. Directed colonization was mostly carried out during the 1970s and 1980s and refers to the settlement of farmers by government agencies on public lands, and by private colonization companies in their own lands. Since the early 1990s, the role of the government with regard to directed colonization declined substantially, and colonization has been limited to regularizing the tenure situation of squatters. It is worth noting that squatters do not account for much of the deforestation problem, since they settle mostly in areas already deforested. Farmers in directed colonization benefit from a more stable property rights system than do their counterparts in spontaneous fronts. A farmer in directed colonization needs effectively to occupy the land, i.e., engage in agricultural production, and stay on the plot for a few years before he can claim permanent title to his plot.

Ozório de Almeida and Campari (1996) observe strong differences between the two types of colonization with regard to: farmers' origins (mostly northeasterners in public colonization, and southerners in private projects); initial capital brought to the frontier (higher in private colonization); infrastructure (better in private); and extension services provided by the government (better in public). All of these can influence the way in which farmers manage and deforest land.

6.3.2. Different States

The states of Pará and Mato Grosso were chosen for data collection because they account for the largest deforested areas and the largest number of colonization projects. In addition, Pará was selected because it contains the highest number of public colonization projects and because it is the state where the pioneer front was settled in the early 1970s along the Transamazon Highway. Thus Pará has a longer colonization history than elsewhere in the country.

By the time the first survey was carried out in 1981, more than ten years had passed since the pioneer front arrived in all sampled projects in Pará. By 1991, Pará could be considered a consolidated frontier. Thus, at the time the second survey was carried out, Pará provided insights into the dynamics of colonization over a 20-year period.

Mato Grosso was selected because it is the state with the highest density of private colonization projects in the country. In contrast with Pará, Mato Grosso was a very young frontier when the first survey was carried out in 1981. Private colonization had barely started and southern settlers were still adapting to the place. This is evident from the fact that many households interviewed in 1981 consisted of male farmers, a typical characteristic of early frontiers in which the head of the household arrives before his family. The process of evolution in colonization projects in this case is observed ten years later, by the time the second survey was carried out in 1991. Pará and Mato Grosso were also selected on the basis of their geographical position within the Amazon, i.e., these two states represent the eastern and western flanks of the region, respectively. The idea is to observe whether frontier processes of deforestation respond to the exogenous characteristics of farmers in the two states, or whether these processes are frontierwide phenomena.

Finally, Pará and Mato Grosso were selected because of their representativeness in terms of regional deforestation. Today, these states account for 60 percent of the total deforestation in the Amazon and are widely known as the main states in the 'deforestation belt'.

6.3.3. Different Projects

The projects surveyed for this study are highly heterogeneous. Regarding the maturity of the projects, Figure 6.2 shows that a variety of situations emerged in 1991. The figure shows the frequency distribution of the number of years that survivors had been on the land in 1991. The horizontal axis represents the universe of the projects surveyed. The vertical axis displays the number of years that survivors had been on the plot. The first three boxes refer to public projects in Pará; the other three refer to projects in Mato Grosso. The distributions are displayed in box and whisker diagrams, which represent quartile ranges: the bottom whisker shows the lower quartile, i.e., the range of the 25 percent lowest values of the sample; the box represents the interquartile range (values between 25 percent and 75 percent) of the sample; the median, i.e., the fiftieth observation, is represented by an asterisk within the box; the top whisker represents the sample's top quartile.

Farmers in official colonization projects in Pará (Anapu, Pacajá and Monte Alegre) had a longer history on the site than did farmers in Mato Grosso's private colonization (Alta Floresta, Paranaíta and Mutum). Since colonization in Mato Grosso did not begin until the late 1970s, figures for this state must be considered relative to 10–14 years of colonization experience. In Pará, government-sponsored projects began much earlier. In Monte Alegre, for instance, some colonists' families had been on the land for a very long time; many of them migrated to the Amazon in the first quarter of the century and were officially settled by INCRA during the 1970s.

6.3.3.1. Sites in Pará (public colonization)
Four colonization projects were surveyed in Pará. Three of them (Anapu, Pacajá and Pacal) are part of the Altamira Colonization Program, which extended 400 kilometers along the Transamazon Highway. The Altamira Colonization Project is divided into various sub-projects, three of which have been surveyed: Pacal, Anapu and Pacajá. Since these three projects were approximately ten years old when the 1981 survey was conducted, a fourth project was included in the sample to represent an older colonization scheme. The project selected was Monte Alegre.

Pacal   The Pacal Project was created in 1972 as a Joint Colonization Project (*PAC – Projeto de Assentamento Conjunto Abraham Lincoln*) and was integrated into the municipality of Medicilândia in the late 1980s. Colonization plots were located on the stretch of the road that runs between kilometer 75 and kilometer 130 of the Transamazon Highway, between the municipalities of Altamira and Itaituba. Those colonists who

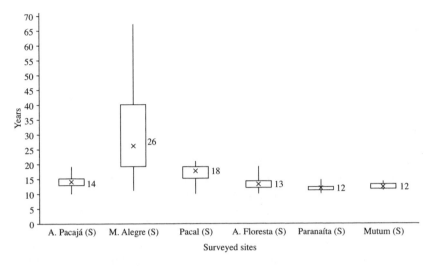

Figure 6.2.   Number of years on plot in 1991: survivors

occupied the first 200 plots benefited from a long stretch of *terra roxa* (a very fertile type of soil). Further, INCRA provided to colonists plots with deforested lands, assisted with soil preparation, and had established a sugar cane refinery (Usina Abraham Lincoln). In 1981, most colonists planted sugar cane since the refinery absorbed most of the production. In 1981, the project had secondary access roads, averaging 15 kilometers of extension in reasonably good conditions for transport during the dry season. Until today, all access roads, as well as long stretches of the Transamazon Highway, remain unpaved.

Colonists in Pacal also engaged in the extraction of Brazil nuts, and in the production of cocoa, black pepper, coffee and, to a lesser extent, rubber. Among the colonists surveyed in Pará, the ones in Pacal are indeed the most successful in agriculture.

In 1991, prosperity in Pacal was evident. The colonists had benefited from good urban infrastructure and extension services from the government. The project had more than doubled its size, with a total of 479 families settled.

Upon revisiting in 1991, it could be observed that the production of perennial crops faced severe difficulties. Among these difficulties were: (a) lack of rural extension, (b) financial resources at subsidized rates for the purchase of agricultural inputs and for maintenance of newly deforested land, and (c) low agricultural prices and expensive rural credit.

Anapu   Anapu is a project located between kilometers 130 and 175 of the Transamazon Highway, on the stretch of road between Altamira and Marabá. In 1981, it had 38 secondary access roads, of which 17 offered good transport conditions in the dry season, from July to November. The infrastructure in Anapu was the worst among all sampled locations. It included only a few roadside merchants (although this is endogenous), a cooperative trading post (frequently closed down), and an office of agricultural extension with no staff. Public services in the locality were scarce.

Upon revisiting in 1991, little had changed in Anapu. The rural extension office of EMATER had three staff members and a grammar school teacher. Malaria had remained endemic throughout the decade. Municipal government administration (executive and legislative) had no buildings.

Approximately 50 percent of the plots in Anapu produced coffee, cocoa, black pepper, rice, corn and beans. Almost all of them had some degree of cultivated pasture. In 1991, the project had 255 settled families. Mechanization in agriculture was very low, and generally only manual tools were available.

The houses of the colonists remained the same throughout the decade, i.e., wooden houses provided by INCRA in the early 1970s. The situation was no different in Pacal and in Pacajá. The main difficulties faced by colonists in Anapu were, according to colonists, the lack of subsidized rural credit, lack of public health services, lack of a community school, malaria, and diseases that affected black pepper cultivation.

Pacajá   The Pacajá Project started as a spontaneous settlement, and it later became a public colonization project. The area began to be occupied in 1972 when the Transamazon Highway was opened. In that year, INCRA started settling northeastern farmers. The project was established in a stretch of 65 kilometers along the Transamazon Highway, with 22 secondary access roads that in 1981 were still being opened. In 1981, urban infrastructure was reasonably well developed considering frontier conditions and in comparison to the neighboring Anapu project. Since access roads were still being built, however, access to most of the plots was only possible by foot or on horseback.

Pacajá gained emancipation as a municipality in 1988. By 1991, 603 families had been settled. The condition of the access roads remained precarious: 60 percent had absolutely no access, and the remaining 40 percent were accessible only during the dry season. Agriculture did not seem to have evolved much during the inter-survey period, mainly because of poor soils. Besides subsistence crops, colonists planted low quality coffee and black pepper and *guaraná*, all on a small scale.

Monte Alegre　　Monte Alegre, an older area of settlement, was included in the sample so that long-term trends could be depicted. Human settlement in Monte Alegre dates back to 1926, having begun as an initiative of the state government of Pará to settle a wave of Japanese migrants who arrived in Brazil during the first quarter of the century. Later, in the 1970s, these and a large number of spontaneous settlers received title from INCRA.

Generally, the age of the head of the household in this project was a lot higher than in other projects in the sample. The plots exhibit much technological diversity, ranging from those completely devastated and abandoned by early settlers (northeasterners) to those with notable productivity (generally belonging to Japanese migrants who have specialized in the production of vegetables to supply the Manaus and Belém markets).

6.3.3.2.　Sites in Mato Grosso (private colonization)

In Mato Grosso, three private colonization projects were surveyed. Two projects, Alta Floresta and Paranaíta, were located in the north of the state and one, Nova Mutum, in the center. With the exception of two families (squatters), all farmers in Mato Grosso's projects were southern. Capital endowments and net worth are quite different between settlers in Mato Grosso's private projects and in Pará's official projects.

Alta Floresta　　Situated in the north of Mato Grosso, Alta Floresta was founded in 1976 as part of the private colonization project carried out by Indeco, a private colonization company. In 1979, Alta Floresta gained independence and became a municipality.

Commerce, churches, education and several other institutions were brought in by Indeco, along with migrants actively recruited from the state of Paraná. This commercial and institutional infrastructure was sustained by gold prospecting until a violent conflict was waged by the colonization company to expel prospectors who had invaded the project in the early 1980s.

In 1991, 65 percent of the local population was engaged in agriculture, cattle ranching and gold mining. The municipal administration considered agriculture the third most important economic activity. Local commerce was sustained by gold mining, which had again become the main economic activity followed by cattle ranching. Coffee and cocoa were the main cash crops until 1991, but most crops had been replaced by grazing. Soils were not as good as expected by Indeco, and the coffee planted was unsuitable for the local soil type (arabica instead of robusta).

Paranaíta   Paranaíta is located north of Alta Floresta and, as such, was an Indeco colonization project. Paranaíta and Alta Floresta are similar in terms of migrants, crops, soils and problems. Paranaíta is switching to grazing at an even greater pace than Alta Floresta.

The project was founded in 1979 and by 1986 had gained independence and become a municipality. Although 55 percent of the total population lived in rural areas when the second survey was carried out, gold mining and grazing rather than agriculture was the main activity.

Mutum   The Mutum project is located in the municipality of Nova Mutum, situated in the center of Mato Grosso along the Cuiabá-Santarém Highway. Colonization in Nova Mutum began in 1978 with the Mutum Colonization Company. The interesting feature of this project is that it is located in a transition zone between the Amazonian *cerrado* (a type of savanna) and the rain forest. Nova Mutum gained independence as a municipality in 1989.

This locality is, in many ways, very different from the others, as it is a solid example of successful agriculture. It was founded by an entrepreneurial cooperative that brought its own members from the state of Rio Grande do Sul. Originally small farmers, these migrants exchanged highly appreciated plots during the 1970s – the heyday of real estate appreciation in the south of Brazil – for larger plots (400 to 1,000 hectares) on the frontier. In 1981, rice was the main cash crop. In 1991, Mutum had become a monoculture of soybeans. Located near a market road and retaining commercial, institutional and cultural ties to the prosperous south of Brazil, the project boomed. Until today, the urban center has been too small to provide the infrastructure demanded by its wealthy colonists, who demand services directly from the state's capital, Cuiabá. This is the most successful project in the sample.

7. Turnover on farming plots

7.1. INTRODUCTION

Law No. 8629 of 1993, which complements the 1988 constitution, states that beneficiaries of settlement projects can only sell the land they receive after ten years of continued occupation. In practice, this law and all other legal restrictions that preceded it have never been observed by colonists in the Amazon. Even without official documents attesting property rights, settlers have always bought, sold and leased land. Alston et al. (1999) have an interesting explanation for land transactions that occur in the absence of official property rights. They argue that squatters on public land sell their right to be granted the land in the future, and squatters on private land sell their rights to be compensated for any improvements they made on the land in case they are evicted by the owner. Among squatters on public land, deforestation is deemed necessary because during the regularization process they are entitled to a multiple of the land they have cleared. For squatters in private lands, a major component of the so-called 'improvements' is deforestation; so that they are likely to be compensated for this improvement at the time of eviction.

Ozório de Almeida and Campari (1996) observe that even in the presence of legitimate property rights – e.g., in directed colonization projects where titles are granted to settlers (freely, in public colonization, or purchased by the settler, in private colonization) – turnover is by no means low. Therefore, colonization plots in the Amazon experience changes in ownership regardless of whether land is titled or not, and despite the legal obligations imposed on colonists. This gives rise to the hypothesis that turnover is unlikely to be associated with the formal ownership of land. Alston et al. (1999) and Schneider (1995) further elaborate on this discussion.

The association of deforestation with frequent in- and out-migrations of farmers has been studied by many authors. Most studies, however, fail to provide supporting evidence for the conjectures they raise and even fewer are undertaken in the field of economics. A few exceptions are Schneider (1995), Ozório de Almeida and Campari (1996) and Alston et al. (1999).

Chapter 5 formalized a conceptual framework of the turnover hypothesis and outlined the necessary conditions for the hypothesis to hold. This chapter discusses the variables associated with high turnover and indicates whether turnover in the sampled projects is actually high compared to national indicators. Furthermore, the chapter examines how often farmers tend to move. This chapter also discusses the issues of how recently newcomers have arrived on the project (time on current plot) and previous migratory experiences farmers may have had prior to arrival in the current location.

The purpose of this chapter is to observe whether transience on Amazonian farming plots is indeed high relative to retention rates of similar projects in the rest of Brazil. The most comprehensive assessment of colonization projects in Brazil was carried out by FAO/UNDP in 1992 in a joint effort with the Ministry of Agriculture and Agrarian Reform (FAO/UNDP 1992). The results of the FAO/UNDP (1992) report point out that the overall retention (survival) rates in Brazil ranged between 97 and 100 percent (Schneider 1995, p. 50). The FAO/ UNDP (1992) report takes into account the date that each project was established and 1991, the year of the survey. The report provides the baseline indicator against which the performance of the projects sampled for this study is assessed.

Section 7.2 displays retention rates for the sampled projects and compares them with the baseline indicator set by FAO/UNDP (1992). Section 7.3 shows how recently newcomers had arrived in the surveyed locations when re-sampling was undertaken in 1991. Section 7.4 discusses whether newcomers are more prone to migrate than survivors. Section 7.5 summarizes the results and concludes the chapter by discussing possible economic forces that triggered turnover during the inter-survey period.

7.2. SURVIVAL RATES

Survival rates tell what percentage of the 1981 sampled farms remained under the same ownership in 1991. *Survivors* refer to farms in which the occupants remained the same during the 1981–91 period. *Newcomers* refer to plots where ownership changed during the period. Table 7.1 summarizes the results for each surveyed location.

Overall, 71 percent of those interviewed in 1991 had been on the same plots in 1981, but this percentage varied widely across projects. Retention rates were higher in Pará's official colonization projects (77 percent) than in Mato Grosso's private colonization projects (62 percent).

In Pará, the survival rate was higher in Pacal (87 percent) and lower in Anapu and Pacajá (59 percent), the poorest locations in the entire sample. In the Anapu/Pacajá grouped sample, it was not uncommon to find plots where the farmers being interviewed were the seventh or eighth owners of the same piece of land during the ten-year period between surveys. In Monte Alegre, which was in its third generation of farmers in 1991, the survival rate ranked second in the sample (75 per cent).

Table 7.1. Survival rates

	Number of Farms in the Panel	Number of Survivors	Number of Newcomers	Survival Rates
Para	167	129	38	77.2%
Anapu-Pacajá	47	28	19	59.5%
Monte Alegre	33	25	8	75.7%
Pacal	87	76	11	87.3%
Mato Grosso	105	65	40	61.9%
Alta Floresta	53	34	19	64.1%
Paranaíta	34	19	15	55.8%
Mutum	18	12	6	66.7%
Total	272	194	78	71.3%

In Mato Grosso, the highest survival rate is observed in Mutum (66 percent). The lowest rate is observed in Paranaíta (55 percent), a project where soils were not as suitable for agricultural production (so turnover was initially expected). In Paranaíta, pioneer settlers left in large numbers, and gold mining and grazing became the main activities. Alta Floresta shared a similar history, although turnover is less accentuated (64 percent).

By no means can the survival rates displayed in Table 7.1 be considered high, especially if compared to the 97–100 percent survival rates in other regions reported in FAO/UNDP (1992). The situation is especially worrisome in the recent frontier of Mato Grosso, where approximately four out of every ten families sold their land by 1991 (in 1991, projects were no more than 12–14 years old). Thus turnover on farming plots in colonization projects in the Amazon has been occurring, and by no means at low rates. Often itinerancy occurred within the same plot as successive areas were deforested and abandoned until the limit of the plot was reached and the plot was sold to a newcomer, even if land was exhausted of its nutrients. Plot abandonment was more frequently observed in Monte Alegre and along Transamazon Highway than in Mato Grosso, and not only on the locations surveyed for this study.

When a colonization project begins, be it public or private, the farmers who arrive tend to be very similar in their exogenous attributes (more so in private colonization), such as: place of origin (e.g., 100 percent of the households in private projects had southern origin); initial capital; agricultural know-how; and education. Chapter 9 presents descriptive tables that show the similarities of these exogenous attributes. Therefore, the data contain no evidence that colonists who sold land in any given location later in the decade were initially different from those who arrived with the pioneer front and who remained on their plots. In other words, in 1981 all farmers on any given site were pioneer colonists with similar exogenous attributes compared to each other and, initially, had a common motivation to migrate to the frontier.

7.3.   TIME ON PLOT

Considering the conceptual framework developed in Chapter 5, turnover becomes a chronic problem for deforestation if it is a common behavior among colonists. The time that colonists stay on the plot is an important piece of information to describe the temporal aspect of turnover: the faster the pace of turnover, the faster land will be cleared of the original forest cover. Although Jones et al. (1992) found no correlation between time on plot and deforestation, it would still be useful to know when turnover happened. This is done by observing how long, prior to the 1991 survey, newcomers had been on their plots.

Figure 7.1 shows wide variation across and within projects. The figure depicts the distribution of newcomers in terms of the number of years that they had been on the land when projects were surveyed for the second time in 1991. The first three boxes refer to the public colonization projects in the state of Pará: Anapu/Pacajá, Monte Alegre and Pacal. The other three boxes refer to private projects in Mato Grosso: Alta Floresta, Paranaíta and Mutum. The number inside each box represents the median. For each surveyed location, the bottom whisker displays the distribution range of the first quartile of the sample; the box represents the interquartile range; and the top whisker shows the range of the remaining 25 percent of each sample distribution.

This figure shows that the distributions are somewhat more skewed to the low tenure in projects where turnover was highest, i.e., Anapu/Pacajá and Paranaíta. Although Paranaíta and Alta Floresta display similar distribution ranges and medians, the Anapu/Pacajá sample is unequivocally different from the other two projects in Pará. Of all samples, the oldest

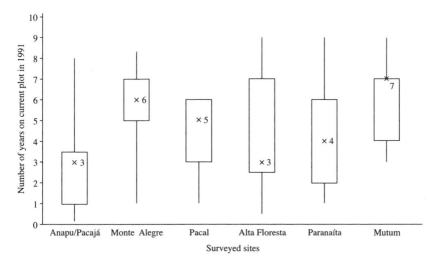

Figure 7.1. Time on plot: newcomers in 1991

newcomers were detected in Mutum, the project with the lowest turnover in private colonization.

Half of the latest newcomers in the Anapu/Pacajá samples – the poorest of all sampled locations and the one with the highest rate of turnover in public colonization – had been on the land for less than three years when the second round of interviews was carried out. These projects were characterized by intense in- and out-migrations, and the problem of land abandonment because of poor soil was evident during the field visits.

In Pará the location with the highest turnover was also the one hosting the most recent newcomers, but this did not occur in Mato Grosso. Paranaíta exhibits the lowest survival rate, but does not rank highest in terms of newcomers with a recent history on the land. Unlike the case of Anapu/Pacajá, in- and out-migration was intense in Mato Grosso, but for reasons other than land abandonment. These reasons are associated with real estate speculation during the 1980s, an issue that will be treated later.

It would be interesting to compare time on plot between newcomers and survivors. It would also be especially useful to check whether a difference in behavior is seen between the two groups of pioneer farmers, i.e., those who stayed (survivors) and those who decided to sell their plots (old-timers). However, the information regarding time on plot could not be retrieved from the 1981 data set (missing data); the information was therefore retrieved from the 1991 survey, which did not contain information on old-timers (since they had already left). Based on experience with Amazon colonization, an educated assumption can be made to circumvent the need for that missing piece of information. As soon as settlement opportunities appeared in the 1970s, the market for land in colonization projects is cleared almost immediately. Both in public and private projects, colonists are recruited to occupy the plots. In the case of private colonization, entire communities from Southern Brazil were taken to the Amazon to occupy a single region. There, they replicated the same lifestyle they had had before, with the same productive and socio-economic structures. INCRA operates in a similar way, as potential colonists wait for a long time before they are called to occupy the land. So, upon arrival, pioneer colonists did not present exogenous characteristics that would make them different from each other. Therefore, we have no reason to believe that, *ex ante*, those who left were any different from those who stayed. However, innate differences might have been unobserved and not revealed by the available data, and other differences might have been created subsequently. This does not mean that differences did not arise after arrival.

Time on the current plot is an important part of the turnover hypothesis. Although colonists may be small deforesters on any single site, they may cause quite a large impact on deforestation over their life cycle. The faster farmers move from place to place, the more they will open the frontier and deforest; this also implies that small farmers will rapidly sell out again to newcomers who end up re-concentrating land and deforesting even more.

7.4.   PROPENSITY TO MIGRATE

If Moran's (1989) argument that previous mobility is a strong predictor of future mobility is correct, the implications of the turnover hypothesis pose a real threat to the forest. The likelihood to move out once again can be observed by the farmers' propensity to migrate. Figure 7.2 shows the distribution of newcomers and survivors with respect to the number of times they established residence elsewhere before reaching the current (1991) plots. The figure depicts newcomers (Newc) and survivors (Surv) side by side in each project. The medians in the figure show this tendency. According to Figure 7.2, in most projects, newcomers were significantly more prone to migrate than survivors.

Once again, a variety of situations emerged. Overall, the farmers interviewed had a long history of migration, many having established residence elsewhere up to ten times before reaching the surveyed location (see Anapu/Pacajá). Some followed the typical itinerant cycle of ex-squatters and ex-sharecroppers who rarely stayed in one place for more

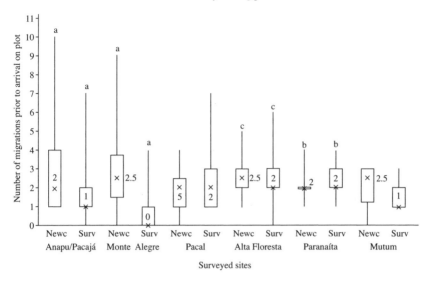

Notes: The presence of a common character indicates that differences between survivors and newcomers are statistically significant at the 1 percent level (a), 5 percent level (b) and 10 percent level (c).
The absence of a character indicates that no difference was found at the 10 percent level.

Figure 7.2.   Number of previous migrations (1991)

than five years (Ozório de Almeida 1992). Others were itinerant owners, for whom buying and selling land is part of a strategy to accumulate wealth (this point is discussed in Chapter 9). Both types have historically had a temporary relationship with land which is very hard to reverse. The problem of turnover for the forest does not reside in the fact that small farmers move a lot, but rather, in how they use land, and what large newcomers decide to do with it after they buy it from pioneer settlers.

Figure 7.2 and Table 7.2 show that the only two projects where the difference in the number of moves between newcomers and survivors did not reach statistical significance were Mutum and Pacal. These two projects are the ones with the highest survival rates in private and public colonization, respectively.

This simple exercise shows that newcomers who migrated to projects characterized by high turnover are likely to move once again, replacing pioneer colonists with each move. This result provides corroborating evidence to Moran's (1989) argument that newcomers have an inherent propensity to migrate. Ozório de Almeida and Campari (1996) show that this tendency indicates a clear strategy among newcomers to accumulate wealth with each move. Alston et al. (1999) develop this hypothesis further by introducing a life-cycle component; they argue that the number of moves will tend to decrease over time, as farmers display increasing wealth with each additional move, and will eventually stop as they become sufficiently capitalized, covering the opportunity costs associated with another move. These two contributions provide a corrective element to the literature on Amazonian development: for a small farmer, moving is an economic strategy, not fate.

It would be interesting to test statistically whether the number of migrations among pioneer settlers who left is significantly different from those who stayed. This information, however, does not exist for the 1981 data set. This might raise doubts on whether those who left (old-timers) behaved similarly to those who replaced them (newcomers). This important relationship, however, cannot be tested here.

7.5.   CONCLUSION

Figure 7.1 shows that colonists in high turnover locations in Mato Grosso (Paranaíta and Alta Floresta) chose to sell their plots at about the same time as farmers in Anapu/Pacajá, the sample with the highest turnover rate in Pará. Except for Mutum, the decision to sell was made in the second half of the 1980s (1991 minus median time on plot). Since projects in Mato Grosso were not more than 12–14 years old in 1991, the original colonists remained on the plot for, at most, seven to eight years before selling out to a new farmer.

The dynamics of land sales worked differently in different locations. In Mutum, where retention rates are the highest in private colonization, turnover occurred six years after the pioneer front had settled (1978). When the second survey was carried out in 1991, most of the land transactions had come to an end, and newcomers had been on the plot for approximately seven years. In Alta Floresta and Paranaíta, places where turnover is high, newcomers had been on the plot for three to four years.

In Pará, sales also peaked during the same period, i.e., 1986–87. In Anapu/Pacajá, the project with the highest turnover, newcomers had been on the plot for only three years when the research team revisited the project. These are high turnover locations where some plots had several different owners during the inter-survey period. The data however, lacks information on the different owners that each plot must have had between surveys. So the newcomers surveyed in this project are not likely to have been the second owners at all.

The peak in turnover in the second half of the 1980s is associated with strong underlying economic forces, the main one being a rise in land values all over the country, especially in 1986. Although land values for particular land uses in Pará and Mato Grosso are quite different, Figure 7.3 shows that in both states the sharp rise in land values coincided with the period in which turnover reached its peak. This is not due to coincidence. The rise in land values in the mid-1980s was provoked by a macroeconomic stabilization plan known as the Bresser Plan. This rise in land values triggered speculation and provoked a run on land at a time when inflation rates were very high, offering the opportunity for colonists to reap huge capital gains from selling their plots. At the same time, land has always served as a good hedge against inflation for those who wanted to invest.

Another important factor that drove land transactions (and turnover) to a peak in that period was a drop in international market prices for agricultural products and a rise in production costs. According to colonists and the institutions interviewed, international market prices for many permanent crops in the sampled projects suffered a drop during the mid- to the late-1980s. Cocoa, for example, was sold at US$2,000 per ton in 1987 and fell to US$980 per ton in 1989. The distance from main domestic product markets and export corridors further reduced the final prices paid to farmers. Moreover, high inflation caused an adverse impact on farmers with regard to financial payments on loans, as interest rates were indexed to inflation. For farmers who depended on outside labor, the rise in wages paid to workers, which were also indexed to inflation rates, had a detrimental impact on the economic stability of the farming system. Inflation provoked a substantial increase in agricultural input prices, which made the situation even worse. The exchange rate policies brought about by the three stabilization plans during the 1986–89 period (Cruzado Plan in 1986, Bresser Plan in 1987, and the Summer Plan in 1989) provoked stagnation in prices of nontraded goods despite the growth in the costs of production.

The adverse economic situation undermined the basis of the labor-intensive production technology in the Amazon. It was not uncommon, during this period, to observe colonists abandoning their permanent crops (mainly cocoa) because harvest costs exceeded the market value of these products. In this way, many farmers were led to subsistence agriculture.

In Pacal, for example, the agricultural department of the INCRA's local sugar cane processing plant (Usina Abraham Lincoln) reported that during the 1987–88 season, harvesting costs represented 53 percent of the gross value per ton. In 1988–89 the proportion reached 70 percent. This represents a 17 percent cost increase in this phase of production alone, i.e. harvesting.

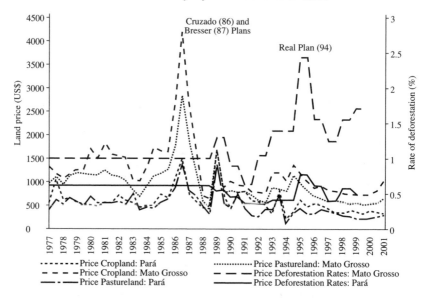

Figure 7.3.   Evolution of land prices and deforestation rates

Upon delivery of the product to the processing company, after deducting harvesting costs, other duties and legal taxes, farmers retained only 30 percent of what they had been paid in the previous season.

The underlying economic forces that affected sugar cane producers in Pacal were the same as affected other farmers in the sample. Revisiting in 1991 and following questionnaire updates undertaken in 1992, the research team observed that it was not rare to find originally well-off farmers facing a situation of insolvency ten years later. The land that had been put up as collateral for previous bank loans was in danger of being taken away. Many farmers did not have the means to harvest their crops in the past season, a labor-intensive activity that demands daily cash payments to workers. It should be pointed out that this process is a very expensive one, since it demands seasonal employment that, in the case of Pará, is generally supplied by another state, mainly Maranhão. Hiring labor from another state is necessary because in areas of colonization the only labor force available is that of the settlers' families and, consequently, there is no surplus labor supply in these areas. In Pacal, many poor families left their own permanent crops (cocoa and sugar cane, mainly) to supply labor and become wage workers of other farmers in the same project. These economic forces may have led to the peak in turnover and deforestation depicted in Figure 7.3.

Thus, although the conditions that led to a peak in turnover during this period varied, the underlying cause was strong domestic and international economic forces operating throughout Brazil in general, and the Amazon in particular, creating a detrimental impact on the livelihoods of some farmers, while it offered unprecedented opportunities for others. It is important to emphasize that in Pará the main reason for turnover was that high inflation elevated production costs and interest rates at a time when international agricultural prices were depressed, leading farmers to insolvency in places where agriculture could not be sustained due to the poor quality of soils. In Mato Grosso, however, insolvency and declining productivity were not so much the problem, but selling land was certainly advantageous to farmers as they reaped the capital gains in a period of high inflation. The farmers that gained most in the inflationary period of the 1980s were the very large ones, who had benefited from SUDAM's subsidized credit for purchasing frontier lands during the previous decade.

Since land transactions in rural areas necessarily imply the displacement of a part of the rural population, and since turnover may be linked to deforestation, the legacy of the peak in turnover on deforestation in the latter half of the 1980s cannot be underestimated. In the 1988–89 period, the mean rate of deforestation in the Amazon was 0.48 percent, the highest in the 1988–94 period (see tables in Chapter 2). In Mato Grosso, that rate was 1.31 percent, and in Pará 0.55 percent (Figure 7.3). The data to compute these rates were collected in 1989, during the Summer Plan, which also coincided with an increase in land values. However, the Summer Plan came three years after the first stabilization program, the Bresser Plan, was implemented in 1986 when land values peaked. The rates for the 1988–89 period are only lower than those in the 1994–96 period, the years of the Real Plan, another macroeconomic stabilization plan of the current administration. The rate of deforestation in the Amazon was 0.81 percent in the 1994–95 period (2.43 percent in Mato Grosso and 0.78 percent in Pará), and 0.51 percent in the 1995–96 period (1.56 percent in Mato Grosso and 0.62 percent in Pará).

Although this study does not intend to investigate the possible relationships between macroeconomic stabilization programs and Amazon deforestation, a clear trend relates the implementation of such programs to the rise in the rates of Amazon forest clearing. It would be interesting to analyze whether the impact of these programs on the forest resource base can be sensed through rising land values, which trigger land sales, turnover, migrations and, finally, deforestation. This study, however, will not undertake this task. A thorough discussion of this issue can be found in Reydon and Plata (2002).

HYPOTHESIS TESTING FOR DIFFERENCE IN NUMBER OF PREVIOUS MIGRATIONS BETWEEN SURVIVORS AND NEWCOMERS

Table 7.2 summarizes the results of testing the hypothesis that newcomers tend to migrate more than survivors. The method used is the robust Wilcoxon scores, because the samples are highly skewed. Two observations were lost due to missing values, one in Alta Floresta and one in Paranaíta. The variable used to test this hypothesis was the number of migratory steps taken by the settler prior to his arrival on the current (1991) plot. The probabilities displayed in Table 7.2 are associated with a one-tailed test, reflecting the hypothesized relationship that newcomers are more prone to migrate than survivors.

The first and second columns of the table show, respectively, the number of survivors and newcomers that entered the subsample (two observations were lost due to missing values: one in Alta Floresta and one in Paranaíta); the third column displays the probabilities associated with the normal approximation of the Wilcoxon test statistic; the fourth column shows t-approximation significance; and the final column shows the one-way ANOVA (Kruskall-Wallis Test) associated with the Wilcoxon scores.

Table 7.2.   Propensity to migrate (probabilities)

	Number of Survivors	Number of Newcomers	Wilcoxon normal approx. (Pr>|Z|)	t-approx. significance	Kruskall-Wallis Test (Pr>χ^2)
Para	129	38	0.08	0.08	0.08
Anapu-Pacajá	28	19	0.01	0.01	0.01
Monte Alegre	25	8	0.00	0.00	0.00
Pacal	76	11	0.17	0.17	0.17
Mato Grosso	65	38	0.18	0.18	0.18
Alta Floresta	34	18	0.08	0.08	0.08
Paranaíta	19	14	0.05	0.06	0.05
Mutum	12	6	0.12	0.13	0.11
Total	194	76	0.005	0.005	0.005

The probabilities displayed show a tendency for the number of previous migrations among newcomers to be larger than among survivors. It also shows that these differences were statistically at the 1 percent level in Anapu/Pacajá and Monte Alegre; at the 5 percent level in Paranaíta; and at the 10 percent level in Alta Floresta. In Pacal and Mutum, no statistical significance was found.

8. Deforestation and land re-concentration in the Amazon frontier

8.1. INTRODUCTION

One of the issues that most concern analysts of Amazonian development is land re-concentration. The turnover hypothesis, in its simplest form, considers land re-concentration a distributive problem, not necessarily an environmental issue. The theory developed in Chapter 5 refines the turnover hypothesis and associates land re-concentration with deforestation. In light of the theory developed in Chapter 5, the purpose of this chapter is first, to assess empirically the extent to which deforestation is associated with land re-concentration and, second, whether the behavior of newcomers is different from survivors in that regard (i.e., whether newcomers hold more land than survivors and, for that reason, deforest more land than survivors). The discussion draws from the information provided in the field surveys described in Chapter 6.

Section 8.2 shows recent satellite images of the dynamics of deforestation in selected colonization projects sampled for this study. Sections 8.3 through 8.5 discuss the background and linkages between deforestation and land re-concentration in the Amazon and the reasons why the two issues cannot be separated. Section 8.6 uses the theoretical framework developed in Chapter 5 to analyze deforestation empirically. Sections 8.7 to 8.11 assess the extent to which the most important aspects of the turnover hypothesis hold. Section 8.12 analyzes the turnover hypothesis in Anapu/Pacajá and Alta Floresta, the only two locations where it fails to be rejected. Section 8.13 examines the relationship between plot size and deforestation in the top 25 percent largest farms in the sample in order to quantify the relative shares of land re-concentration and deforestation of newcomers and survivors. Section 8.14 discusses whether deforestation is a convex function of plot size. Section 8.15 summarizes the main results and the lessons learned from the chapter. Finally, the statistical procedures and results are discussed at the end of the chapter.

8.2.   THE DYNAMICS OF DEFORESTATION IN SELECTED PROJECTS

When the first survey was carried out in 1981, projects in Mato Grosso were at most five years old: Paranaíta, two years old; Mutum, three years old; Alta Floresta, five years old. Before private colonization companies began clearing land for settlement, each of the sites was covered with pristine forest. Two of these projects were located in dense forest (Alta Floresta and Paranaíta) and one in a transition zone between the Amazonian *cerrado* (a type of savanna) and the rain forest (Mutum). Thus, most of the deforestation that occurred prior to 1981 is associated with the arrival of colonization companies and its migrants.

Using recent satellite images (LANDSAT 7) processed exclusively for this study, Figures 8.1 to 8.3 show the state of the forest in Mato Grosso's projects through December 2001.

Three pictures are used to monitor deforestation in each project on a bi-annual basis. Since the monitoring of the state's forest by satellite started in 1992, no processed satellite images are available prior to that date. Thus these pictures show deforestation prior to 1992 and periodic changes after that. (Unfortunately, a similar set of images could not be obtained for projcts in Pará.)

An important result can be seen from these figures: most of the deforestation in these sampled locations was undertaken prior to 1992. Since the area deforested prior to the arrival of colonization companies was nearly nonexistent, then the projects can be held accountable for all of the land cleared before 1992. Since then, deforestation has evolved, sometimes at accelerating rates (see periodic rates in the boxes displayed on each image).

The satellite images can be used to determine the fraction of total deforestation in the project area that is accounted for by plots sampled in the 1991 survey. The results are shown in Table 8.1.

The samples selected for this study account for a reasonable share of the total deforestation in the projects. In Paranaíta, the sample accounted for only 2.3 percent, but in Mutum 50 percent of the project's total deforestation was undertaken in the plots surveyed for this study.

This section showed that deforestation in colonization projects was substantial by 1991. However, whether deforestation is associated with turnover, plot growth, and land re-concentration is an issue that warrants further analysis.

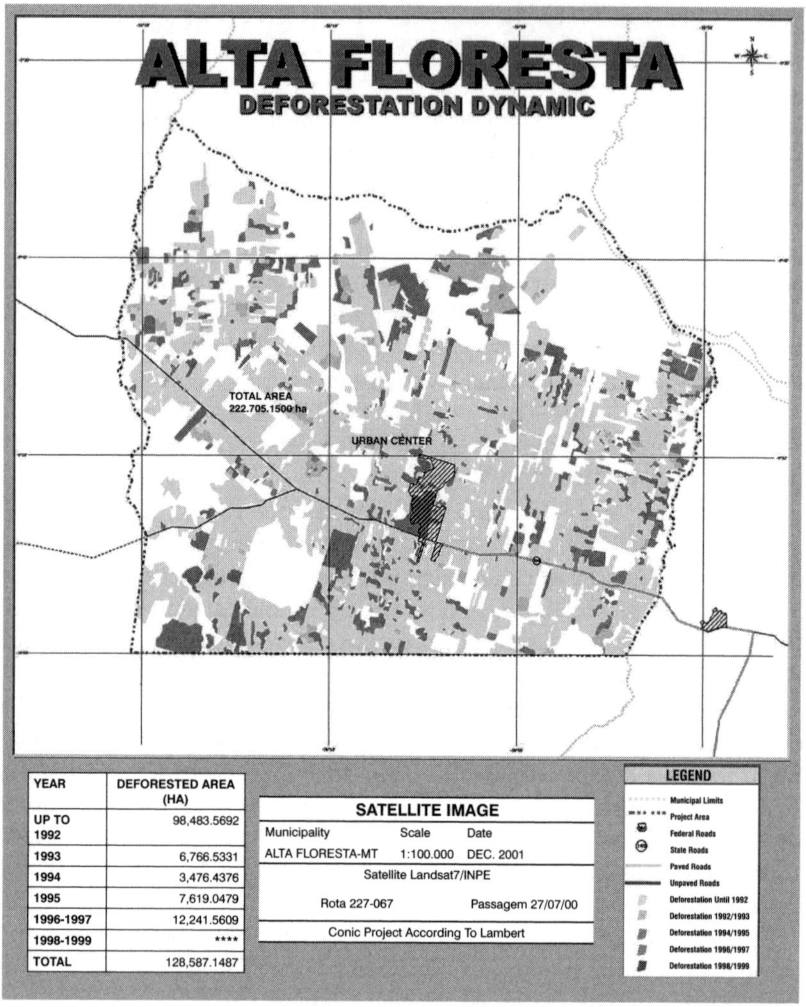
ALTA FLORESTA
DEFORESTATION DYNAMIC
TOTAL AREA
222.705.1500 ha
URBAN CENTER
SATELLITE IMAGE
Municipality Scale Date
ALTA FLORESTA-MT 1:100.000 DEC. 2001
Satellite Landsat7/INPE
Rota 227-067 Passagem 27/07/00
Conic Project According To Lambert
LEGEND
Municipal Limits
Project Area
Federal Roads
State Roads
Paved Roads
Unpaved Roads
Deforestation Until 1992
Deforestation 1992/1993
Deforestation 1994/1995
Deforestation 1996/1997
Deforestation 1998/1999

YEAR	DEFORESTED AREA (HA)
UP TO 1992	98,483.5692
1993	6,766.5331
1994	3,476.4376
1995	7,619.0479
1996-1997	12,241.5609
1998-1999	****
TOTAL	128,587.1487

Note: Full set of colored satellite images can be found in Campari (2002)

Figure 8.1. Incremental change in deforestation in Alta Floresta through 1999

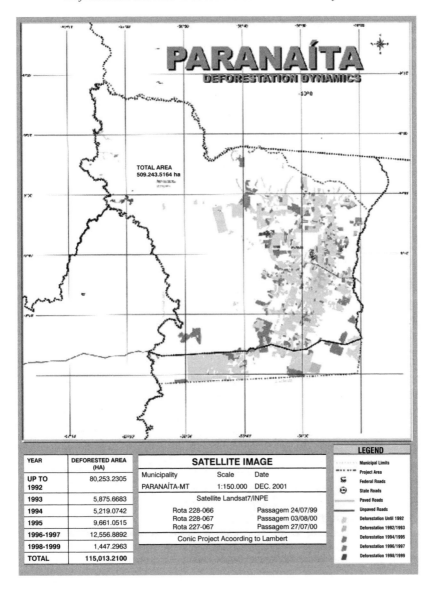

YEAR	DEFORESTED AREA (HA)
UP TO 1992	80,253.2305
1993	5,875.6683
1994	5,219.0742
1995	9,661.0515
1996-1997	12,556.8892
1998-1999	1,447.2963
TOTAL	115,013.2100

SATELLITE IMAGE

Municipality	Scale	Date
PARANAÍTA-MT	1:150.000	DEC. 2001

Satellite Landsat7/INPE

Rota 228-066	Passagem 24/07/99
Rota 228-067	Passagem 03/08/00
Rota 227-067	Passagem 27/07/00

Conic Project Acoording to Lambert

LEGEND

- Municipal Limits
- Project Area
- Federal Roads
- State Roads
- Paved Roads
- Unpaved Roads
- Deforestation Until 1992
- Deforestation 1992/1993
- Deforestation 1994/1995
- Deforestation 1996/1997
- Deforestation 1998/1999

Note: Full set of colored satellite images can be found in Campari (2002)

Figure 8.2.   Incremental change in deforestation in Paranaíta through 1999

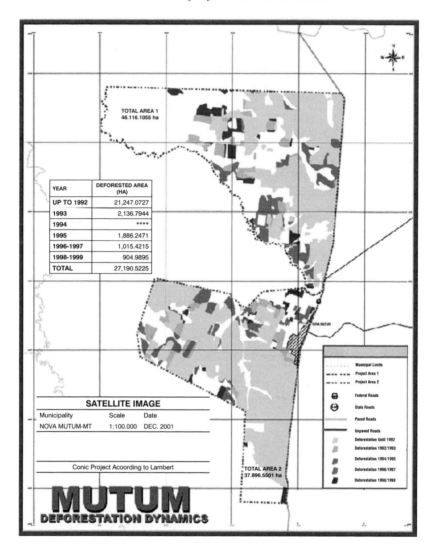

The table visible within the figure:

YEAR	DEFORESTED AREA (HA)
UP TO 1992	21,247.0727
1993	2,136.7944
1994	****
1995	1,886.2471
1996-1997	1,015.4215
1998-1999	904.9895
TOTAL	27,190.5225

Note: Full set of colored satellite images can be found in Campari (2002)

Figure 8.3.   Incremental change in deforestation in Mutum through 1999

Table 8.1.   Contribution of sampled plots to projects' overall deforestation

Project	Total deforestation in the project area in 1991 (ha)	Total deforestation in sample in 1991 (ha)	Percentage of the project's total deforestation attributed to the sample in 1991
Alta Floresta	98,483	6,781	4.5
Paranaíta	80,253	3,734	2.3
Mutum	16,404	8,192	50.0

8.3.   PLOT GROWTH AND LAND RE-CONCENTRATION: CONCEPTUAL DIFFERENCES

Conceptually, plot growth and land re-concentration are two distinct issues. It could be argued, however, that the former might lead to the latter if a fixed amount of land is available for human settlement. If such a condition held over time, and if land is originally equitably distributed among colonists, then the growth of any given plot (e.g., due to acquisition or invasion) would imply that at least one other plot became smaller, leading to a situation of unequal land ownership. To assume that colonization projects remain the same size over time, however, is not realistic in the case of the Brazilian Amazon.

Chapter 4 pointed out that when a project is established, it attracts spontaneous settlers (squatters) who are generally seeking a 'free ride' to a future title, or are willing to take advantage of the infrastructure available to colonists, or both. The result is that projects often become larger than initially planned in order to absorb and attend to the needs of an unexpected additional population. Given the added demographic pressure, the demand for land rises – initially in undisturbed lands in the periphery of projects, and later, as plot areas grow, within the projects themselves – and so do violent conflicts between colonists and squatters.

To avoid social unrest and to circumvent the need for unpopular political action, the unplanned and informal expansion of colonization projects is either endorsed or ignored by the government. Restrictive measures on the occupation of unclaimed lands by squatters are difficult for the government to enforce, as the political costs associated with such action would be too high. Squatters thus remain on the periphery of projects, burdening the inadequate infrastructure provided by INCRA or private companies. Eventually, these squatters too are regularized.

In view of the growth of the area available for *de facto* colonization, plot growth and land re-concentration may no longer have the same meaning, especially when colonists, following the example set by squatters, also start invading unclaimed land to expand the areas of their own farms. In this case, an increase in the area of some plots may not imply a reduction in the size of other plots, since land is abundant in new frontiers. This chapter was designed to take this issue into account when discussing land re-concentration.

8.4.   PLOT GROWTH AND DEFORESTATION

The turnover hypothesis assumes that deforestation in the Amazon is a positive function of plot size. The scatter diagrams in Figure 8.4 show that such a relationship held well between 1981 and 1991. The average plot size is shown on the horizontal axis and the area cleared is displayed on the vertical axis. Most samples show a clear positive relationship between the increase in average plot size and the area deforested. These diagrams, however, depict a relationship that is necessarily positive, since the scatter could not appear above the dotted lines (if graphs were drawn to scale, these lines would be 45-degree lines). While Figure 8.4 can be used to show growth of plots and deforestation in hectares, Figure 8.5 is more insightful.

Although it is quite obvious that larger plots would be expected to have larger cleared areas than small ones, it is less obvious whether they would display higher rates of deforestation – i.e., the fraction of the total plot area that is deforested. The diagrams in Figure 8.5 were drawn to show this relationship. For each project, the diagrams show the distribution of the sample in 1981 and in 1991. The horizontal axis represents average plot sizes in hectares. The vertical axis shows the fraction of each plot that has been cleared. The diagrams are divided into four quadrants. The vertical line that crosses the horizontal axis at 100 divides the sample into small and large plots. This value was the one used by INCRA and by private colonization companies to allocate land to colonists during the 1970s. Plots to the right of this line are considered large and, to the left, small. The horizontal line that crosses the vertical axis at the 50 percent mark represents the legal maximum that the government expected colonists to deforest at the time, according to the Forestry Code of 1965. Plots above this line are characterized by high deforestation; below the line, plots are characterized by low deforestation.

The figure shows clearly that while in 1981 most plots were small (darker dots), in 1991 these same plots had grown substantially (lighter dots). This can be observed in Anapu/Pacajá, Alta Floresta, Pacal and Mutum. Monte

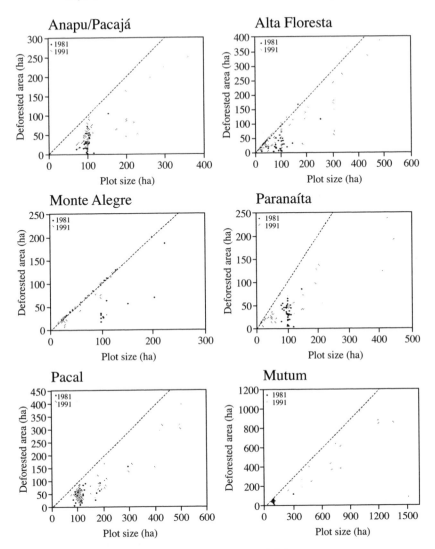

Note: Full set of colored figures can be found in Campari 2002

Figure 8.4.   Plot size by deforested area, 1981 and 1991

Alegre and Paranaíta are exceptions, since many plots were smaller in 1991
than they had been in 1981. In terms of deforestation, the fraction of each
plot deforested in 1991 (lighter dots) was unambiguously higher than it had
been in 1981 (darker dots) only in Mutum. In other projects, this trend is
not as clear.

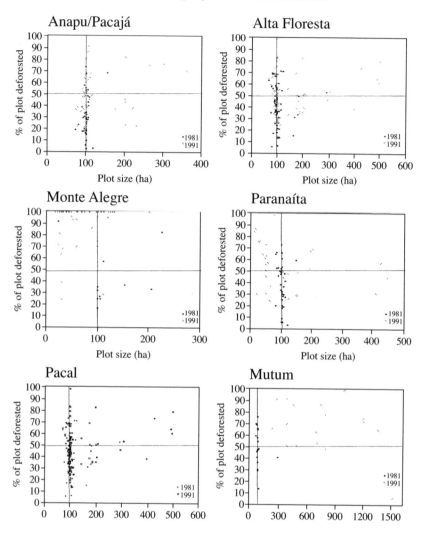

Figure 8.5.   Plot size (ha) by percentage of plot deforested

The turnover hypothesis holds that plots in 1991 should be in the northeast quadrant, depicting a situation in which they were both larger *and* with a higher fraction deforested compared to 1981. Although Mutum shows this situation quite clearly, turnover in this project is quite low. Pacal shows the expected tendency, but this particular project has the highest survival rate in the sample. Paranaíta and Monte Alegre are clear exceptions where the hypothesis is unlikely to hold. Anapu/Pacajá and Alta Floresta show a movement northeast between 1981 and 1991, and seem to support the turnover hypothesis since they exhibit high turnover rates.

Contrary to the turnover hypothesis, in Monte Alegre and Paranaíta many small plots in 1981 became even smaller by 1991 with accompanying high deforestation. In these two projects, a process of agricultural involution can be observed to this day. In Monte Alegre, this process is characterized by the abandonment of cleared lands which became unproductive between 1981 and 1991 (which reduced the reported size of the plot between 1981 and 1991) and the subsequent deforestation of new areas within the smaller plot (which increases the reported percentage deforested since the plot became smaller due to land abandonment). In Paranaíta, agricultural involution was characterized by the switch from crop production to grazing. Although ranchers have always preferred to buy cleared land for pasture, the scarcity of available deforested land in Paranaíta led ranchers to buy forested parts of colonists' plots, which made such plots smaller and increased the fraction of deforested land to total plot area. These are the plots that ended up in the northwest quadrant.

Could a large number of small farmers cause as much deforestation as a few large ones? During the first years of a colonization project, this is likely to happen because most of the land is equitably distributed among colonists in small parcels that generally do not exceed 100 hectares. Over time, however, the initial configuration of land allocation changes, as land is transacted and more successful farmers buy out small ones. When the first survey was carried out in 1981, projects had been recently established in Mato Grosso and were approximately ten years old in Pará. It is likely, therefore, that in 1981 small farmers hold most of the total land and most of the deforested area. In 1991, however, sufficient time had elapsed for the land market to develop, which would probably lead to a different allocation of land within projects. As time passes, for several reasons, small farmers are unlikely to hold most of the total land and deforested area in colonization projects:

- unlike large farmers, small farmers in most projects, especially the poorer ones, produce little or no surplus, given binding financial and physical constraints in technology, mainly labor (but also given problems of access to credit, inadequate transport facilities), thus keeping production and marginal deforestation (the additional land cleared each year *after* the initial high deforestation undertaken to claim property rights) to relatively low levels, i.e., the minimum required to support household consumption;
- unlike large farmers, for small farmers, clearing dense forestlands is an expensive labor-intensive activity. Because household labor is the only

source of labor available, any deforestation undertaken by a small farmer draws heavily on household consumption (since there is no savings), as work effort is diverted from subsistence crop production to land clearing;

- for small farmers, collective action to deforest larger shares of their plots is infeasible because there is no surplus labor in newly opened colonization areas to assist them in undertaking this activity; helping a neighbor to deforest could impose a stringent reduction on household consumption;

- in view of serious financial constraints, it is unfeasible for small colonists to contract outside labor from distant places to clear land.

Figures 8.6 through 8.11 show, for each sample, the evolution of farm sizes and deforestation during the 1981–91 period. Each figure displays two diagrams. In each diagram, plots were stratified along the horizontal axis in several categories, ranging from very small to very large. In the upper diagram, the bars show the cumulative percentage of plot sizes. In Figure 8.6 for Anapu/Pacajá, for example, in 1981 zero percent of plots are less than 50 hectares, 73 percent are less than 100 hectares, 93 percent are less than 150 hectares, and all are less than 200 hectares. By 1991, only 40 percent are less than 100 hectares, only 60 percent are less than 150 hectares, and only 70 percent are less than 200 hectares. Thus, plots are larger. In the same diagram, the lines connect dots showing the cumulative percentage deforested in each category, in 1981 and in 1991. In 1981, 68 percent of the total deforestation was carried out in farms of less than 100 hectares, 95 percent in farms of less than 150 hectares and all deforestation was carried out in farms less than 200 hectares. In 1991, only 35 percent of the total deforestation was carried out in farms of of less than 100 hectares, only 58 percent in farms of less than 150 hectares, and only 65 percent of the total deforestation was carried out in farms of less than 200 hectares.

This implies that a considerable share of deforestation was carried out in farms larger than 200 hectares. Deforestation is, therefore, a positive function of plot size. In the lower diagram, deforestation is measured in cumulative hectares rather than percentages. Together, the two diagrams show a typical characteristic of the Amazon frontier: a place where land is readily available, rewarding extensive agricultural practices and, consequently, deforestation.

With the exception of Monte Alegre, which is a project located in a very old frontier, most of the sampled projects experienced extraordinary growth of plot size and deforestation between 1981 and 1991. In 1981, cumulative plot area and deforested area approached the 100 percent mark much 'faster' (at smaller plot sizes) than in 1991, i.e., the slopes of the

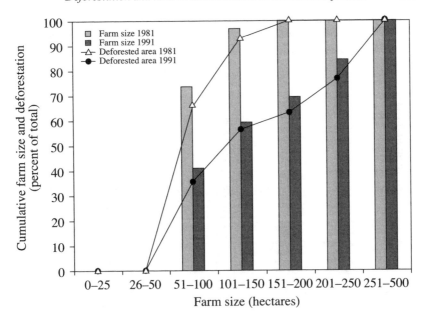

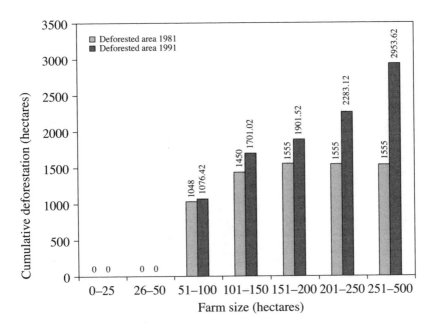

Figure 8.6.   *Anapul/Pacajá: land and deforestation, cumulative distributions (1981 and 1991)*

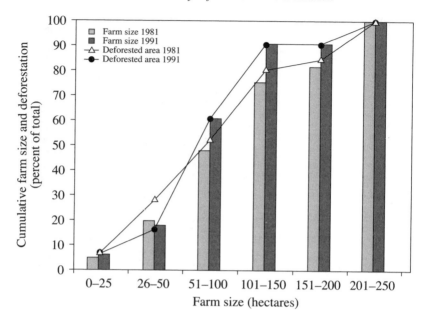

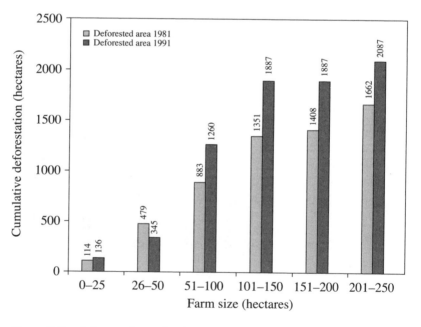

*Figure 8.7.   Monte Alegre: land and deforestation, cumulative
               distributions (1981 and 1991)*

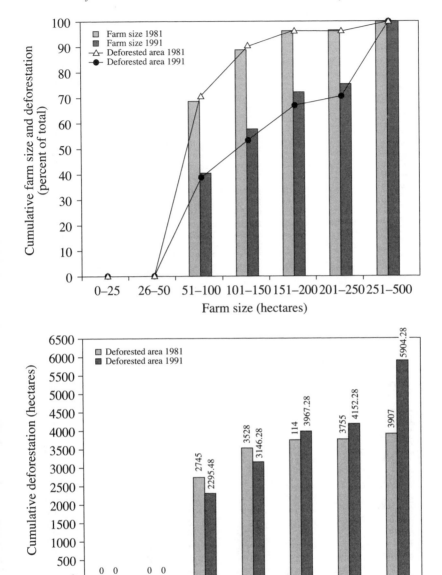

Figure 8.8.   Pacal: land and deforestation, cumulative distributions (1981 and 1991)

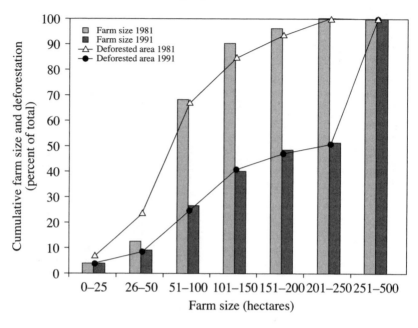

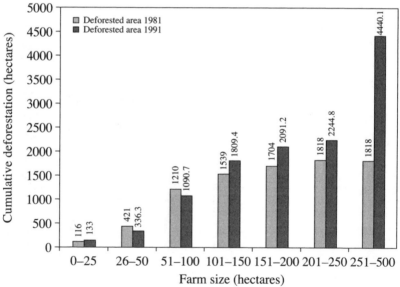

Figure 8.9.   Alta Floresta: land and deforestation, cumulative distributions (1981 and 1991)

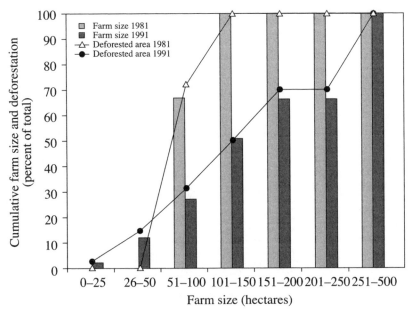

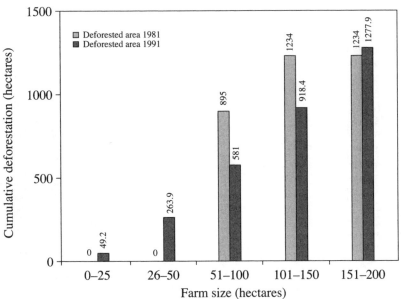

Figure 8.10. *Paranaíta: land and deforestation, cumulative distributions (1981 and 1991)*

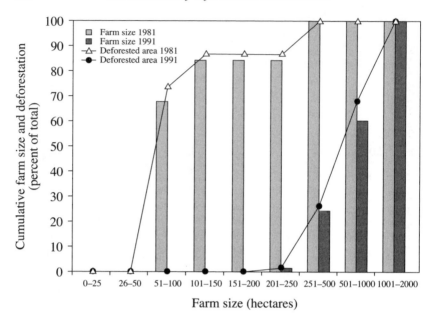

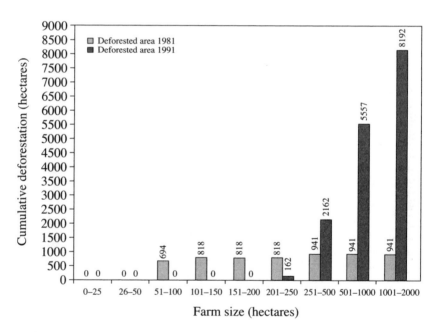

*Figure 8.11.   Mutum: land and deforestation, cumulative distributions
              (1981 and 1991)*

cumulative distributions of land size and deforestation in 1981 are steeper than in 1991.

To put it another way, in 1981 small plots with small deforested areas accounted for most of the sample; by 1991 neither of these claims was any longer true. Table 8.2 summarizes these data. In the overall sample, the third entry shows that 76 percent of the farms in the overall sample were small (less than 100 ha). By 1991, however, the situation had reversed, as small farms represented only 57 percent of the sample. The figures above show that not only was the percentage deforestation higher in 1991, but also the total hectares deforested. When the second survey was carried out in 1991, plots had become larger, accumulating most of the total land and most of the deforested area in the sample.

Table 8.2 can be used with Figures 8.6 to 8.11 to illustrate the relationship between farm size and deforestation between 1981 and 1991. For example, from Table 8.2 we know that in Anapu/Pacajá in 1981, 76 percent of the plots were smaller than 100 hectares. From Figure 8.6 we know that the cumulative area associated with plots of that size or smaller accounted for 73 percent of the total area in that sample. Furthermore, the cumulative deforestation associated with plots of that size or smaller accounted for 65 percent of the total deforested area. From Table 8.2, in 1991 only 57 percent of the plots in the sample are 100 hectares or smaller (a reduction of 19 percent compared to the same size category in the 1981 sample). Figure 8.6 shows that in 1991, plots in that size category account for only 40 percent of the total area in the sample (a reduction of 33 percent relative to 1981), and for only 35 percent of the total deforestation in the sample (a reduction in 30 percent relative to 1981).

The purpose of this section is to highlight the importance and the impact that plot growth has on deforestation and, further, to show that the two issues cannot be separated. As we have seen in Chapter 5, these relationships are crucial to the turnover hypothesis. The hypothesis, however, associates these factors with the behavior of newcomers. Such behavior is analyzed in future sections of this chapter.

8.5. LORENZ CURVES

One way to quantify the extent of land re-concentration is to observe how the Lorenz curves of the samples behaved over time. Figure 8.12 depicts projects in two periods: 1981 and 1991. The 45-degree line in the diagrams is the equality line that depicts an equal distribution of land among all colonists in the sample.

Table 8.2. *Cumulative percentage of farms per category of size*

Farm sizes (has)	Anapu/ Pacajá		Monte Alegre		Pacal		Alta Floresta		Paranaíta		Mutum		Overall sample	
	1981	1991	1981	1991	1981	1991	1981	1991	1981	1991	1981	1991	1981	1991
0–25	0	0	15	18	0	0	13	15	0	12	0	0	4	7
26–50	0	0	48	42	0	0	32	30	0	38	0	0	12	16
51–100	76	57	73	79	75	57	81	58	70	62	78	0	76	57
101–150	98	78	91	97	94	79	96	73	100	82	94	0	96	75
151–200	100	85	94	97	99	90	98	79	100	91	94	0	98	82
201–250	100	93	100	100	99	92	100	81	100	91	94	5	99	85
251–500	100	100	100	100	100	100	100	100	100	100	100	44	100	96
501–1000	100	100	100	100	100	100	100	100	100	100	100	78	100	99
1001–2000	100	100	100	100	100	100	100	100	100	100	100	100	100	100

114

Five of the six projects displayed land re-concentration to varying degrees during the inter-survey period. The exception is Monte Alegre, due to the fact that this project was an old frontier when the first survey was carried out and, as early as 1981, land allocations had already reached equilibrium. Thus, the 1981 and 1991 curves almost coincide.

Judging by the shapes of the 1981 Lorenz curves, government agencies and private colonization companies truly attempted to distribute land equitably among initial colonists, as land allocations in several projects approached the equality line. Reasonably equitable allocation can be observed in Anapu/ Pacajá, Paranaíta and Pacal, where the 1981 Gini indices were, respectively, 0.04, 0.05 and 0.09. However, the situation was quite different ten years later. The shapes of the 1991 Lorenz curves in 1991 justify a more in-depth analysis of land re-concentration in colonization projects.

The degree of land re-concentration observed in the Lorenz curves can be measured by the change in the Gini indices between 1981 and 1991. Table 8.3 ranks projects according to this change.

Table 8.3.   Change in Gini indices: 1981 and 1991

Projects ranked according to change in Gini	Change in Gini indices (Gini 91–Gini 81)
Monte Alegre	–0.04
Mutum	0.14
Pacal	0.16
Anapu/Pacajá	0.17
Alta Floresta	0.18
Paranaíta	0.42

The larger the change in the Gini indices between the two periods, the greater the extent of re-concentration. According to the information presented in this table, projects can be divided into three groups: (i) no re-concentration (Monte Alegre); (ii) moderate re-concentration (Mutum, Pacal, Anapu/Pacajá and Alta Floresta); and (iii) high land re-concentration (Paranaíta).

This section provides clear evidence that land re-concentration is occurring to different extents in the surveyed projects. However, it still needs to be assessed whether one of the main tenets of the turnover hypothesis holds, i.e. whether it is becoming re-concentrated because of the newcomers. While this section dealt with land re-concentration, the following section will investigate the linkages between growth in plot size and deforestation.

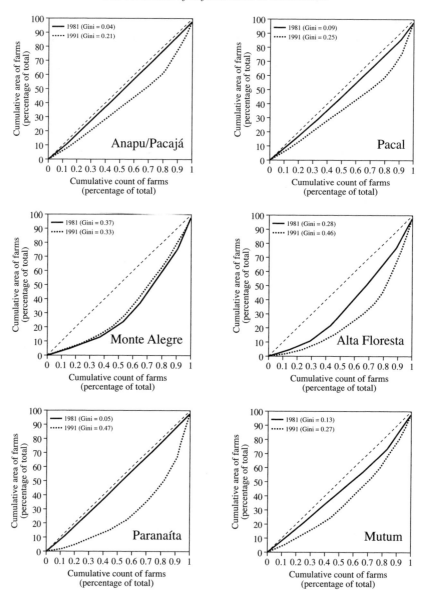

Figure 8.12. Lorenz curves and Gini indicators

8.6. DECOMPOSING THE CHANGE IN DEFORESTATION INTO SIZE EFFECT AND INTENSITY EFFECT

While the previous section showed that land distribution is indeed a problem that warrants attention from the socio-economic standpoint, this section models the linkages between land re-concentration and deforestation from an empirical perspective. This section shows that land re-concentration is an environmental problem (which is the focus of this study) as much as it might be a distributive problem (which is *not* the focus of this study). Thus, the purpose of this section is to measure that part of deforestation that is associated with an increase in farm size between 1981 and 1991, and isolate it from the overall increase in deforestation in that period.

The total increase in deforestation between 1981 and 1991 can be represented by H^{TOT}, which is calculated as follows:

$$H^{TOT} = \sum_{i \in S,N} (L_{91}^i.D_{91}^i - L_{81}^i.D_{81}^i) \tag{8.1}$$

where, as in Chapter 5, i indicates the plot, L is the size of the plot in hectares, D is the fraction of the plot deforested, S is the set of plots occupied by survivors, and N is the set of plots occupied by newcomers. Equation (8.1) can be decomposed as follows:

$$H^{TOT} = \underbrace{\sum_{i \in S,N} D_{81}^i.(L_{91}^i - L_{81}^i)}_{Size\ Effect} + \underbrace{\sum_{i \in S,N} L_{91}^i.(D_{91}^i - D_{81}^i)}_{Intensity\ Effect} \tag{8.2}$$

The first term of (8.2) is the *size effect*, which says that part of the increase in total deforestation between 1981 and 1991 is due to increase in plot size and *not* to change in the rate of deforestation. The second term of (8.2) is the *intensity effect*, which states that another part of the increase in total deforestation in that 10-year period is due to an increase in the rate of deforestation and *not* to change in the size of the plot.

Figure 8.13 illustrates equation (8.1) using the field evidence used in this study. This figure displays the total hectares that had been deforested by 1991 as the total deforestation that was carried out from the early days of colonization through 1981 plus the increase in deforestation during the 1981–91 period (H^{TOT}). H^{TOT} for each project is represented by different patterns and represents 57 percent of the total deforestation carried out by 1991.

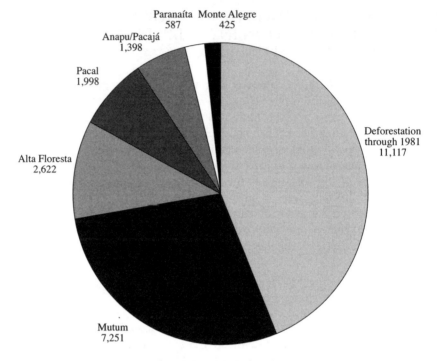

Figure 8.13.   Total deforestation in 1991 (ha)

Similarly, Figure 8.14 disaggregates total deforestation into two parts: that carried out up until 1981 and H^{TOT}. The first three bars represent projects in Pará; the other three represent projects in Mato Grosso. This figure is different from Figure 8.14 because it disaggregates 1981 deforestation by project. In Pará, most of the deforestation had taken place prior to 1981. The most outstanding H^{TOT} is observed in Mutum.

Figure 8.15 illustrates equation (8.2), which decomposes H^{TOT} into size effect and intensity effect. This figure reveals that the size effect was larger than the intensity effect in three projects: Pacal, Alta Floresta and Mutum. In Mutum, the increase in farm size is mainly due to the shift from the cultivation of rice to soybean during the inter-survey period. While the cultivation of rice is typical of small farmers, soybean production exhibits economies of scale and is cultivated by large farmers who demand more deforested land to carry out this type of activity.

Figure 8.16 further disaggregates the results shown in Figure 8.15 by type of agent (newcomers and survivors). In Monte Alegre, the size effect is not observed either for newcomers or survivors, meaning that the contribution of plot size increases to H^{TOT} is nonexistent regardless of the

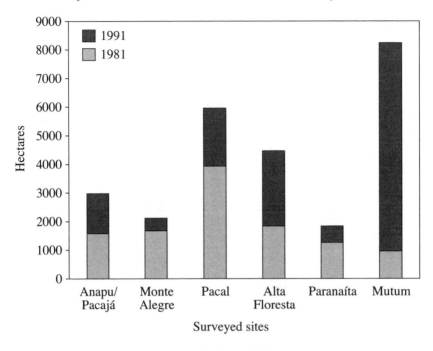

Figure 8.14. Total deforestation, 1981 and 1991

farmer category. In Paranaíta, the size effect among newcomers is negative, while in Anapu/Pacajá it is nonexistent. In Pacal and Mutum, the size effect is larger among survivors than newcomers, a result that is counter-intuitive for the turnover hypothesis.

The intensity effect among survivors is noticeably higher than for newcomers only in Mutum. Given that in this project survivors have a higher size effect and intensity effect than newcomers, it is unlikely that the turnover hypothesis will hold in this particular project. In Pacal, the intensity effect among newcomers is nonexistent. In other projects, there is no apparent difference in the intensity effect among survivors and newcomers.

Figure 8.17 decomposes the size and intensity effects of H^{TOT} in terms of the average hectares deforested by newcomers and survivors. Newcomers in Anapu/Pacajá and Alta Floresta have larger average size and intensity effects than survivors. This result is consistent with what is expected of the average newcomer according to the turnover hypothesis.

Although Figure 8.16 indicates that in Mutum the survivor's size effect contributes the most to H^{TOT}, Figure 8.17 shows that the *average* size effect of newcomers in this location is higher. Although the deforestation carried out by the average newcomer in Mutum during the inter-survey

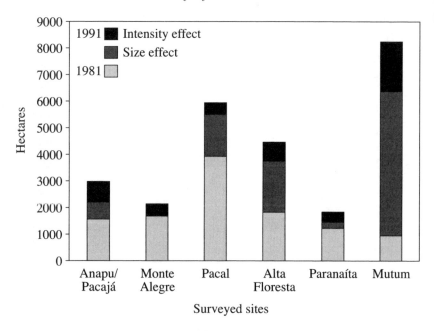

Figure 8.15.   Decomposition of deforestation: size effect and intensity effect

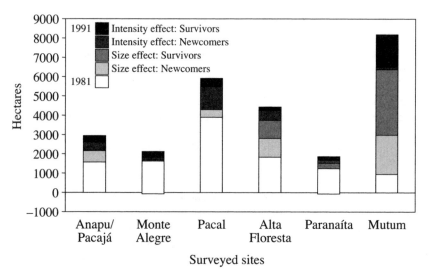

Figure 8.16.   Decomposition by newcomers and survivors

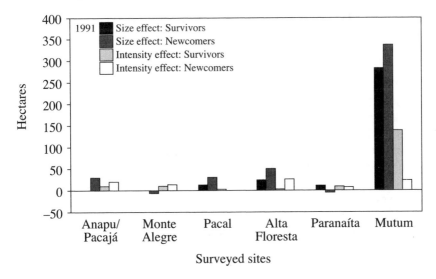

Figure 8.17.   Decompostition by newcomers and survivors (averages)

period is due mostly to the size effect, newcomers were not in sufficient numbers to account for most in H^{TOT}.

Table 8.4 summarizes the results of this section, showing whether it is the size effect or the intensity effect that dominates H^{TOT} in each project. The size effect dominates the intensity effect in most projects, suggesting that the change in deforestation during the inter-survey period was due to increases in plot size rather than increases in the rate of deforestation. Except for Anapu/Pacajá and Alta Floresta, change in deforestation due to increase in plot size was more common among survivors than newcomers. The fact that deforestation is most likely to be associated with the behavior of survivors provides an initial argument to challenge the turnover hypothesis.

Table 8.4. H^{TOT}: *Size effect and intensity effect, newcomers and survivors (totals and averages)*

Project	Size effect		Intensity effect	
	Newcomer	Survivor	Newcomer	Survivor
Anapu/Pacajá	X			
Monte Alegre				X
Pacal		X		
Alta Floresta	X			
Paranaíta		X		
Mutum		X		

8.7.   PLOT SIZES AND DEFORESTATION IN 1981: BASELINE INDICATORS

Plot sizes in 1981 is a baseline indicator against which all changes in farm sizes will be assessed. Figure 8.18 compares, for each project, the distribution of plots that turned over between 1981 and 1991 (Newc) and those which did not (Surv) with respect to what these plots looked like in 1981 in terms of size. The shapes of the distributions provide corroborating evidence that colonization projects were fairly equitable in terms of land allocation among initial settlers, as projects were very similar, each displaying plot medians of, at most, 100 hectares, regardless of whether projects were public or private. None of the differences (between newcomers and survivors) within projects are statistically significant.

The discrepancy observed in Monte Alegre between plots that turned over and those that did not is due to the fact that this project was not originally part of a directed colonization program. Settlement in that site dates back to the 1920s, and INCRA's role was to regularize titling and not to redistribute land among settlers. INCRA's policy of allocating 100 hectares of land to colonists started in the 1970s and did not affect older projects, such as Monte Alegre.

Deforestation in 1981 is a baseline indicator against which all changes in land clearing will be evaluated. Figure 8.18 shows how deforestation in 1981 was distributed in different projects in 1981. Within any project, the medians are approximately the same for plots where turnover occurred (Newc) as for those where it did not (Surv). Furthermore, none of the projects displays statistically significant difference between the two groups.

8.8.   GROWTH AND DEFORESTATION IN PLOTS THAT TURNED OVER

This section assesses the extent to which plots prior to turnover (under the ownership of the pioneer farmer) are actually smaller than after turnover occurs (under the ownership of the newcomer). Then it will explicitly show the relationship between farm growth and deforestation.

Figure 8.19 shows the distribution of plot sizes in two periods: 1981 (before turnover) and 1991 (after turnover). The most outstanding difference in farm growth is observed in Mutum, where half of the newcomers owned plots of between 625 and 1500 hectares in 1991; these are the same plots that, without exception, had been only as large as 100 hectares in 1981. This extraordinary growth is statistically significant and is due to Mutum's

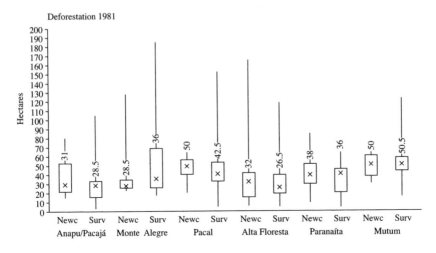

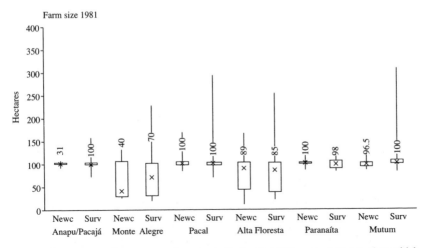

Notes: The presence of a common character indicates that differences between plots which turned over (Newc) and those which did not (Surv) are statistically significant at the 1 percent level (a), 5 percent level (b) and 10 percent level (c). The absence of a character indicates that no differences were found at the 10 percent level. (See Tables 8.15 and 8.19.)

Figure 8.18. Farm size and deforestation in 1981: newcomers and survivors

becoming one of the largest producers of soybeans in Mato Grosso and, more recently, in Brazil. Since soybean cultivation offers economies of scale and requires large land holdings, the growth of plots in this sample is a consequence of this particular land use.

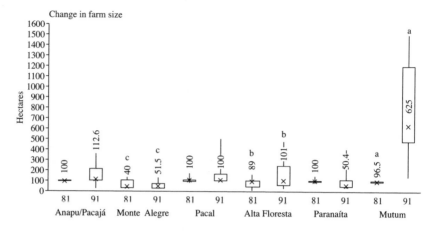

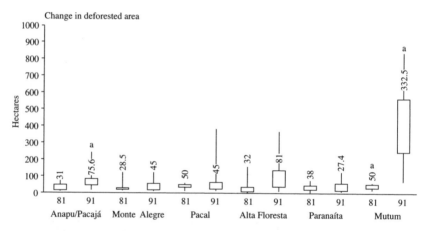

Notes: The presence of a common character indicates that differences between 1981 and 1991 are statistically significant at the 1 percent level (a), 5 percent level (b) and 10 percent level (c). The absence of a character indicates that no differences were found at the 10 percent level. (See Tables 8.13 and 8.17.)

Figure 8.19.   Change in farm size and deforested area during the 1980s: newcomers

The other two projects in Mato Grosso behave differently from each other. While plots in Alta Floresta display statistically significant growth between 1981 and 1991, in Paranaíta, contrary to the conceptual framework of the turnover hypothesis, the median farm size among newcomers actually dropped during the decade, but the change was not statistically significant. In Pará, the median size of farms where plots turned over increased in Anapu/Pacajá and in Monte Alegre; in Pacal, the medians remained the same. The only project in Pará in which the median increase is statistically significant (at the 90 percent level) was Monte Alegre.

In terms of deforestation, Figure 8.19 shows that, once again, Mutum stands out. Deforestation in Mutum is particularly exceptional (and the difference is statistically significant) because as farmers increased the planted area of soybeans, they also deforested at very high rates. In other locations, median growth in deforestation is observed in Anapu/Pacajá, Monte Alegre and Alta Floresta, although only Anapu/Pacajá displays statistically significant change.

Mutum would be the 'best candidate' for the hypothesis if turnover rates in this project were higher. However, this is not the case. The turnover hypothesis seems to be holding well in Anapu/Pacajá and Alta Floresta. These are the two projects that simultaneously exhibit relatively high turnover (see Chapter 7) associated with high farm growth and deforestation (Figure 8.19). This suggests behavioral differences in the way newcomers use and clear land relative to previous owners.

Since newcomers' plots are highly heterogeneous in terms of the 1991 sizes and deforestation, Figure 8.20 shows the same information in percentage terms. It is worth noting both positive and negative changes in plot size and deforestation. Positive changes indicate that land was incorporated into the original plot either through acquisition, lease or invasion of public or private lands. Negative changes indicate that a part of the original plot was sold, rented or abandoned. When land transactions occur, it is generally the deforested parts of the plots that are bought, sold or leased. This happens because in consolidated frontiers, deforested land is a scarce resource highly demanded by ranchers to raise cattle. Therefore, the negative percentage changes in deforestation displayed in Figure 8.20 reflect variation in the ratio of cleared to uncleared land due to land transactions, and is not necessarily due to forest regrowth.

Except for Mutum, Alta Floresta and Anapu/Pacajá, the median percentage change in farm size and the median percentage change in deforestation are very low. However, an interesting result arises: in projects that display positive growth, the percentage growth in deforestation is a multiple of the percentage growth in plot size. This result leads to an important conclusion, which is the key point of the turnover hypothesis: *change in deforestation is a convex function of the change in plot size.* Therefore, among newcomers, the larger the plot gets, the larger is the ratio of cleared to uncleared land. This result provides an even stronger case for the turnover hypothesis in Anapu/Pacajá and Alta Floresta, where newcomers have a different agenda for land clearing and, consequently, a different behavior in regard to deforestation than did their predecessors.

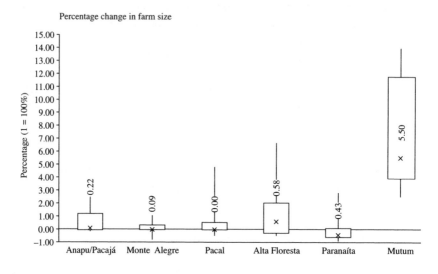

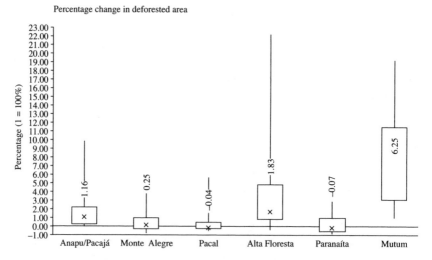

Figure 8.20.　Percentage change in farm size and deforested area during the 1980s: newcomers

The results presented so far do not provide any evidence to support the argument that newcomers' plots were substantially larger than those where plots had not changed owners by 1991. The transition matrices displayed in Figure 8.21 show that, except for Mutum, Anapu/Pacajá and Alta Floresta, which exhibit a higher number of newcomers who bought small plots and transformed them into large farms, in all other projects, not more than 27 percent of the small plots ended up as part of large farms. Furthermore, only Anapu/Pacajá and Alta Floresta exhibit high turnover associated with high growth and high deforestation. Table 8.5 ranks projects according to turnover rates and shows, for each site, the percentage of the plots that were small (under the ownership of the pioneer farmer) and that, later in the decade, became large (under the ownership of the newcomers).

Several conclusions can be drawn from this section. First, the evidence presented leads to the rejection of the turnover hypothesis in most projects, as the hypothesized relationship between turnover, plot growth and deforestation is often not observed. In fact, the expected outcome linking the three pillars of the turnover hypothesis – i.e., high turnover, high deforestation and high farm growth – was observed in Anapu/Pacajá and Alta Floresta only, which ranked second and third in both turnover and farm growth, respectively; it is also observed that deforestation by newcomers in these locations was quite high. However, differences in Anapu/Pacajá are not statistically significant in terms of plot size, although it is highly significant for deforestation. Second, only one project had plots exhibiting extraordinary growth and deforestation (both statistically significant) among newcomers during the inter-survey period (Mutum); turnover in this project, however, was relatively low. Finally, the evidence from the other projects shows that growth and deforestation are either not occurring (Pacal, Paranaíta), or are rather modest (Monte Alegre).

Table 8.5.   Turnover and change in farm size

Rank in Turnover Rates	Project	Turnover Rates (%)	Rank in Farm Growth (% of plots which became part of large farms)
First	Paranaíta	44.2	20.00 (Fifth)
Second	Anapu/Pacajá	40.5	63.16 (Second)
Third	Alta Floresta	35.9	42.11 (Third)
Fourth	Mutum	33.3	100.00 (First)
Fifth	Monte Alegre	24.3	0.00 (Sixth)
Sixth	Pacal	12.7	27.27 (Fourth)

How many of the newcomers are actually becoming large landholders? The projects' transition matrices below depict changes in plot areas between 1981 (before turnover) and 1991 (after turnover). Plots in both periods were classified into two categories, small and large. A plot is considered small when its has 100 hectares or less (the baseline), and large otherwise.

Alta Floresta

Frequency Percent		1991		Total
		Small	Large	
1981	Small	6 31.58	8 42.11	14 73.68
	Large	3 15.79	2 10.53	5 26.32
	Total	9 47.37	10 52.63	19 100

Notes:

In Alta Floresta, approximately 73 percent of the plots were small in 1981. Of these, only 31 percent remained small, i.e. 42 percent had become large by 1991.
Total change in land held by newcomers: 1531 ha
Change in land held by newcomers who became large: 999 ha
Total change in deforestation by newcomers: 1529 ha
Change in deforestation by newcomers who became large: 863 ha

Paranaíta

Frequency Percent		1991		Total
		Small	Large	
1981	Small	8 53.33	3 20	11 73.33
	Large	3 20	1 6.67	4 26.67
	Total	11 73.33	4 26.67	15 100

Notes:

In Paranaíta, approximately 73 percent of the plots were small in 1981. Of these, only 53 percent remained small, i.e. 20 percent had become large by 1991. It is interesting to observe that in this sample of the four farms that started out large (in 1981), three became small during the inter-survey period.
Total change in land held by newcomers: –100 ha
Change in land held by newcomers who became large: 169 ha
Total change in deforestation by newcomers: 102 ha
Change in deforestation by newcomers who became large: 133 ha

Figure 8.21.   Transition matrices (newcomers): small (81) to large (91)

Anapu/Pacajá

Frequency Percent		1991		Total
		Small	Large	
1981	Small	4 21.05	12 53.16	16 84.21
	Large	1 5.26	2 10.53	3 15.79
Total		5 26.32	14 73.68	19 100

Notes:
In Anapu/Pacajá, about 84 percent of the farms were small in 1981. Of these, only 21 percent remained small, i.e. over 63 percent had become large by 1991.
Total change in land held by newcomers: 1294 ha
Change in land held by newcomers who became large: 1202 ha
Total change in deforestation by newcomers: 1042 ha
Change in deforestation by newcomers who became large: 913 ha

Mutum

Frequency Percent		1991		Total
		Small	Large	
1981	Small	0	6 100	6 100
	Large	0	0	0
Total		0	6 100	6 100

Notes:
In Mutum, all plots were considered small in 1981. By 1991, all had become large.
Total change in land held by newcomers: 4299 ha
Change in land held by newcomers who became large: 4299 ha
Total change in deforestation by newcomers: 1529 ha
Change in deforestation by newcomers who became large: 1529 ha

Figure 8.21. continued

Monte Alegre

Frequency Percent		1991 Small	Large	Total
1861	Small	5 62.50	0	5 62.50
	Large	2 25	1 12.50	3 37.50
Total		7 87.50	1 12.50	8 100

Notes:
In Monte Alegre, 62.5 percent of the plots were small in 1981. By 1991, the situation had remained the same. It is also interesting to observe that of the three large farms surveyed in 1981, two had become small by 1991.
Total change in land held by newcomers: –24 ha
Change in land held by newcomers who became large: 0
Total change in deforestation by newcomers: 89 ha
Change in deforestation by newcomers who became large: 0

Pacal

Frequency Percent		1991 Small	Large	Total
1861	Small	5 45.45	3 27.27	8 72.73
	Large	1 9.09	2 18.18	3 27.27
Total		6 54.55	5 45.45	11 100

Notes:
In Pacal, approximately 72 percent of the plots were small in 1981. Of these, 45 percent remained small, i.e. over 27 percent had become large by 1991.
Total change in land held by newcomers: 566 ha
Change in land held by newcomers who became large: 538 ha
Total change in deforestation by newcomers: 377 ha
Change in deforestation by newcomers who became large: 381 ha

Figure 8.21. continued

8.9.   NEWCOMERS AND SURVIVORS IN 1991

The small plots that newcomers buy from colonists are only partially deforested, since labor constraints decrease the likelihood that a small farmer will deforest his entire plot. When newcomers re-concentrate small plots into large farms, they can clear the remainder of the forest area if they choose to do so, since they are less constrained by labor supply. The purpose of this section is to assess whether newcomers have re-concentrated more land relative to survivors during the inter-survey period (condition (8.2)) and to observe whether deforestation has increased accordingly (condition (8.4)).

Figure 8.22 compares the sizes of newcomers' and survivors' plots in 1991. In Mutum, farms are outstandingly large, regardless of whether colonists are survivors or newcomers. In fact, the median farm size among survivors in this sample is higher than among newcomers, although this difference is not statistically significant. Therefore, in this particular project, land re-concentration in the hands of newcomers is not occurring. Like newcomers, survivors in Mutum invested heavily in soybeans for export, and the large size of farms overall in this project reflects this tendency.

In other projects, differences in plot size between newcomers and survivors were rather modest. In fact, the outcome predicted by the turnover hypothesis is only observed in Anapu/Pacajá and Alta Floresta, as newcomers in these projects have larger farms than survivors in 1991 and, moreover, these samples display differences that are statistically significant. These two projects provide strong corroborating evidence for the underlying hypothesis, especially considering that turnover rates in these locations are quite high (40 percent in Anapu/Pacajá and 36 percent in Alta Floresta).

In terms of deforestation, Figure 8.22 shows identical trends. In Mutum, deforestation is very high both among newcomers and survivors. Anapu/ Pacajá and Alta Floresta continue to support the turnover hypothesis. Further, the differences observed in the medians between newcomers and survivors are statistically significant both for farm size and deforested area. Other samples do not support the turnover hypothesis.

8.10.   RATES OF CHANGE: SURVIVORS AND NEWCOMERS

The cornerstone of the turnover hypothesis is the assumption that the behavior of newcomers is different from the behavior of survivors with regard to deforestation. In order to detect differences in behavior between

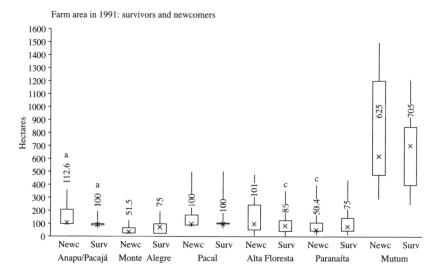

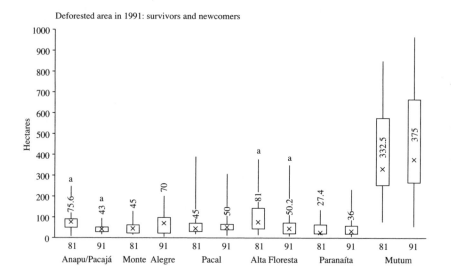

Notes:
The presence of a common character indicates that differences between survivors and newcomers
are statistically significant at the 1 percent level (a), 5 percent level (b) and 10 percent level (c).
The absence of a character indicates that no differences were found at the 10 percent level.
(See Tables 8.16 and 8.20.)

Figure 8.22.   Farm size and deforestation in 1991: newcomers and survivors

the two groups, this section will analyze rates of change (percentages) rather than absolute numbers.

For each project, Figure 8.23 shows the percentage change in farm size during the 1981–91 period for plots that turned over (Newc) and for those that did not (Surv). The first diagram in the figure shows that plots which experienced turnover grew at higher rates than those which did not in Anapu/Pacajá, Monte Alegre, Alta Floresta, and Mutum, although the difference between the two groups is statistically significant only in Anapu/ Pacajá. Thus, different behaviors between newcomers and survivors with regard to rate of change in plot size were observed only in Anapu/Pacajá.

The second diagram in Figure 8.23 shows the rates of change in deforestation between plots that experienced turnover and those that did not. These rates did not take into account change in plot size, but only the change in hectares deforested on any given plot (the next section will take into account changes in plot size by computing the differences in the percentage of the plot that has been deforested). In Figure 8.23, the percentage change in deforestation was measured as follows:

$$RATE = (L_{91}.D_{91} - L_{81}.D_{81})/L_{81}.D_{81}$$

where, as in Chapter 5, L is the size of the plot in hectares and D is the fraction of the plot deforested.

Deforestation in plots that turned over grew at higher rates than among plots that did not in Anapu/Pacajá, Monte Alegre, Alta Floresta and Mutum. However, these differences were statistically significant only in Anapu/Pacajá and Alta Floresta.

The Pacal sample displayed an interesting outcome that runs counter to the intuition of the turnover hypothesis. For the first time in the analysis, plots that *did not* turn over display statistically significantly higher rates of deforestation than plots that *did* turn over. This presents a challenge to the turnover hypothesis: *survivors* may be deforesting the Amazon at higher rates than newcomers. The reasons why this may be the case are discussed in Chapter 9.

Figure 8.24 displays 'static' pictures of the percentages of the total plot areas that were deforested when the first and second surveys were carried out. It is worth emphasizing that, in 1981, all farmers were pioneer settlers. However, it is important to split the sample between plots that turned over (Newc) and those which did not (Surv) in order to check whether those who left and passed on their plots to newcomers had different behavior relative to those who stayed. Given that all pioneer farmers had very similar exogenous characteristics and faced the same site-specific constraints and problems, the outcome displayed in the first diagram in Figure 8.24 was not

Percentage change in farm size: 1981–1991

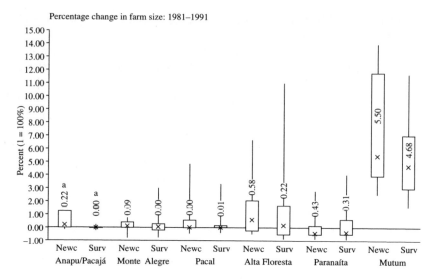

Percentage change in deforestation: 1981–1991

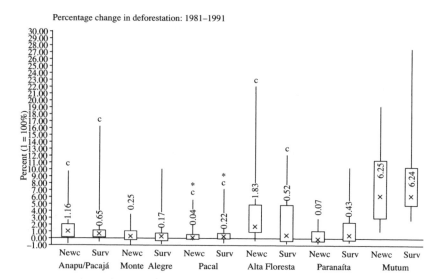

Notes:
The presence of a common character in the whisker indicates that differences between survivors and newcomers are statistically significant at the 1 percent level (a), 5 percent level (b) and 10 percent level (c). The absence of a character indicates that no significant difference was found at the 10 percent level. An asterisk (*) indicates that the statistical difference is counter-intuitive. (See Tables 8.21 and 8.22.)

Figure 8.23.   Percentage change in farm size and deforestation in the 1980s: newcomers and survivors

surprising: all farmers on any given project had similar behaviors in 1981, as none of the projects displayed statistically significant differences. However, in Anapu/Pacajá, Pacal and Mutum, plots that turned over between 1981 and 1991 display a larger median than the ones that did not.

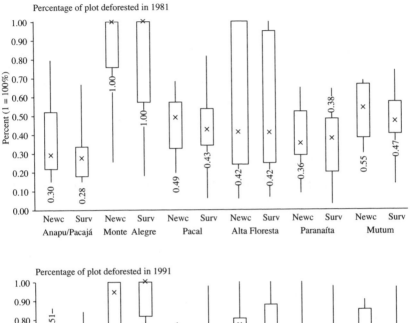

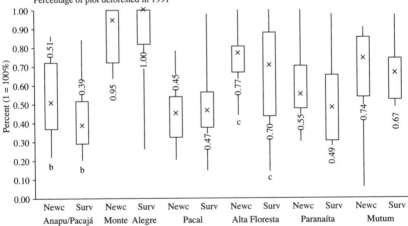

Notes: The presence of a common character in the whisker indicates that differences between survivors and newcomers are statistically significant at the 1 percent level (a), 5 percent level (b) and 10 percent level (c). The absence of a character indicates that no significant difference was found at the 10 percent level. (See Tables 8.23 and 8.24.)

Figure 8.24.   Percentage of plot deforested in 1981 and 1991: newcomers and survivors

The second diagram shows that in 1991 newcomers had a larger fraction of their plots deforested in Anapu/Pacajá, Alta Floresta, Paranaíta and Mutum. Only the Anapu/Pacajá and Alta Floresta samples display differences that are statistically significant.

In summary, the difference in behaviors between survivors and newcomers suggested by the turnover hypothesis do not seem to hold well in most projects. Only two samples displayed the expected outcomes of land re-concentration and deforestation: Anapu/Pacajá and Alta Floresta. In three other projects, namely Monte Alegre, Paranaíta and Mutum, survivors and newcomers seem to have the same behavior in terms of land size and deforestation. Pacal provides statistically supported evidence that it is survivors and not newcomers who are responsible for most of the deforestation.

8.11.　CHALLENGING THE TURNOVER HYPOTHESIS

While the rates of deforestation computed in the previous section depicted important similarities in the behavior of newcomers and survivors in most samples, such rates did not take into account changes in plot size. Therefore, the linkage between deforestation and plot growth was not observed directly. Using the same notation as before, in Figure 8.25, the change in deforestation is measured as the change in the fraction of the plot that has been deforested:

$$RATE = (L_{91} \cdot D_{91})/L_{91} - (L_{81} \cdot D_{81})/L_{81}$$

The turnover hypothesis assumes that plots that turned over display larger rates of deforestation than plots that did not. This difference would entail distinct behaviors between newcomers and survivors. The way rates of deforestation were measured in this section provides conclusive results.

According to Figure 8.26, the turnover hypothesis can be rejected in most samples. Between 1981 and 1991, plots that turned over (Newc) displayed larger medians that those that did not (Surv) only in Alta Floresta and Paranaíta, although these differences were not statistically significant. In all other samples, newcomers deforested as much as survivors (Anapu/Pacajá) or less (Monte Alegre, Pacal and Mutum). The hypothesis can definitely be rejected in Pacal, where the difference in the fraction of deforestation in plots that did not turn over was statistically higher than in plots where turnover occurred.

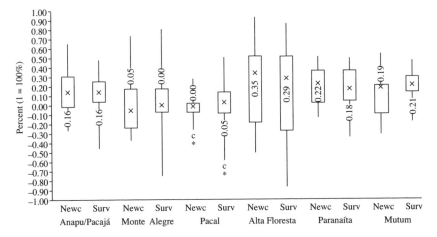

Notes: The presence of a common character in the whisker indicates that differences between survivors and newcomers are statistically significant at the 1 percent level (a), 5 percent level (b) and 10 percent level (c). The absence of a character indicates that no significant difference was found at the 10 percent level. An asterisk (*) indicates that the statistical difference is counter-intuitive to the turnover hypothesis. (See Table 8.25.)

Figure 8.25.   *Difference in the percentage of the plot deforested between 1981 and 1991: newcomers and survivors*

Table 8.6 summarizes the results of this chapter. The turnover hypothesis fails to be rejected in two locations only: Anapu/Pacajá and Paranaíta. Everywhere else it can be rejected.

8.12. THE TURNOVER HYPOTHESIS IN ANAPU/ PACAJÁ AND ALTA FLORESTA

The results of this chapter indicate that the turnover hypothesis fails to be rejected in two locations only: Anapu/Pacajá and Alta Floresta. An OLS regression was used to observe the impact of a newcomer on how much land was deforested between 1981 and 1991 in these locations. The change in deforestation in that period is represented by Δ and was regressed on the size of the plot in 1981 (SIZE81), the area deforested in 1981 (DEF81) and on a dummy variable (INTN) that assumes the value of one when the farmer interviewed in 1991 was a newcomer. The regression equation is:

$$\Delta^{i,j} = \alpha_0^{i,j} + \alpha_1^{i,j}SIZE81 + \alpha_2^{i,j}DEF81 + \alpha_3^{i,j}INTN + \varepsilon_{i,j} \qquad (8.23)$$

where i = Plot; j = Location (Anapu/Pacajá or Alta Floresta).

Table 8.6. *Summary results: the turnover hypothesis*

Conditions of the Turnover Hypothesis	Anapu/ Pacajá	Pará Monte Alegre	Pacal	Alta Floresta	Mato Grosso Paranaíta	Mutum
a) Excessive turnover (higher than national indices)	Y	Y	Y	Y	Y	Y
b) In plots that turned over, plot size in 1991 were larger than in 1981	Y	Y[c]	N	Y[b]	N	Y[a]
c) Plot size among newcomers are larger than survivors	Y[a]	N	N	Y[c]	N	N
d) Larger percentage change in farm size among newcomers	Y[a]	Y	N	Y	N	Y
e) Larger percentage change in fraction of plot deforested among newcomers	Y[c]	Y	N[c]	Y[c]	N	N
f) In plots that turned over, deforested area was larger in 1991 than in 1981	Y[a]	Y	N	Y[b]	N	Y[a]
g) In plots that turned over, deforested area was larger among newcomers	Y[a]	N	N	Y[a]	N	N
Fail to reject the TH	X			X		
Rates of turnover	40.5%	24.3%	12.7%	35.9%	44.2%	33.3%
Rank of turnover	2	5	6	3	1	4

Notes:
Y = Yes, N = No
Superscripts indicate level of statistical significance: 1% (a), 5% (b), 10% (c)

138

Table 8.7 displays the estimated coefficients and the standard errors.

Table 8.7.   Regression results: change in deforestation 1981–91 (Δ)

	Anapu/Pacajá	Alta Floresta
Constant	77.6181	4.5937
	(66.1136)	*(23.7002)*
SIZE81	–0.6167	0.5086
	(0.7038)	*(0.3032)*
DEF81	–0.0929	–0.3558
	(0.3671)	*(0.4503)*
INTN	41.8740	48.6338
	(13.1211)	*(22.5964)*
No. of observations	47	53
Adjusted R^2	0.1770	0.0789

The values of the coefficients show that the fact of being a newcomer (INTN) in Anapu/Pacajá and Alta Floresta had a large, positive and statistically significant impact on Δ. In Anapu/Pacajá, an inverse relationship was found between initial plot size (SIZE81) and initial deforestation (DEF81) and Δ. These coefficients, however, are not statistically significant. In Alta Floresta, while SIZE81 is positively correlated with Δ, DEF81 displays an inverse relationship with the dependent variable. Both coefficients, however, are not statistically significant. It is worth emphasizing that the purpose of this regression is *not* to model deforestation; therefore, the value of the adjusted R^2 is irrelevant.

To determine the magnitude of the newcomers' contribution to the change in the area deforested between 1981 and 1991 (H^{TOT}), Equation (5.7) can be rewritten as:

$$H^{TOT} = \mathbf{N} \, (\bar{H}^i_{91,N} - \bar{\hat{H}}^i_{91,S}) \qquad (8.4)$$

where, as in Chapter 5, $\mathbf{N}$ represents the number of plots that turned over, $\bar{H}$ is the average area deforested by a newcomers, and $\hat{H}$ is the predicted average area that would have been deforested on a plot that turned over, had this plot been owned by a survivor instead of a newcomer. While H^{TOT}, $\mathbf{N}$ and $\bar{H}$ are observable, $\bar{\hat{H}}$ for plot i is estimated as follows:

$$\bar{\hat{H}}^i_{91,S} = \frac{(L^i_{91,N} - L^i_{81,N})}{L^i_{81,N}} \cdot D^i_{81,S} \qquad (8.5)$$

where, as in Chapter 5, L represents size of the plot in hectares, and D represents the fraction of the plot that was deforested. While Equation (8.5) allows plot i to turn over and grow between 1981 and 1991, it imposes on it the deforestation behavior of the previous owner.

Table 8.8 compares the counter-factual (H^{TOT}) with the factual deforestation ($H^{FACTUAL}$) in each project. The last column of the table shows that the turnover hypothesis explains 60.4 percent and 76.4 percent of the factual deforestation in Anapu/Pacajá and Alta Floresta, respectively.

Table 8.8.   Counter-factual and factual deforestation in Anapu/Pacajá and Alta Floresta

	N	$\bar{H}$ (ha)	$\bar{\bar{H}}$ (ha)	$H^{TOT} = N.(\bar{H} - \bar{\bar{H}})$ (ha)	$H^{FACTUAL}$ (ha)	$H^{TOT} / H^{FACTUAL}$ (%)
Anapu/Pacajá	19	54.8	12.9	796.1	1041.2	76.4
Alta Floresta	19	80.5	31.9	923.4	1529.5	60.4

8.13. DEFORESTATION IN THE LARGEST FARMS: REVISITING THE LORENZ CURVES

Most samples provide only weak evidence of land re-concentration and higher deforestation among newcomers. If the hypothesized relationship between land re-concentration and deforestation holds, and if newcomers cannot be held responsible for either land re-concentration or deforestation in most projects, then two possibilities arise:

(i)   survivors are responsible for re-concentrating land and deforesting, or

(ii) a mix of survivors and newcomers are responsible for re-concentrating land and deforesting.

In either case, the turnover hypothesis does not provide an adequate framework of analysis to explain the relationships between turnover, land re-concentration and deforestation in Amazonian colonization projects. Based on the evidence presented here, the hypothesis only holds in special cases (only two projects in Table 8.6 have 'YES' all the way down the columns for all conditions of the turnover hypothesis).

In order to evaluate the two possibilities above, the Lorenz curves are revisited in this section. For each project, farms in the top quartile of the

1991 curves were analyzed independently from the rest of the sample, in order to answer the following questions:

- What is the proportion of newcomers and survivors in the largest farms?
- How much land does each farmer group hold?
- How much deforestation is associated with each group?

Table 8.9 provides the answers to these questions.

The proportion of newcomers ranged from 12 percent (Monte Alegre) to 83 percent (Anapu/Pacajá). In most projects, newcomers do not seem to hold most of the largest farms. An exception is observed in Anapu/Pacajá, where newcomers hold 88 percent of the total land in the top quartile, which represents 38 percent of the total sampled area. Another exception was observed, although to a much lesser extent, in Alta Floresta, where newcomers and survivors hold approximately the same amount of land. Further, these are locations with high turnover rates, which provides corroborating evidence for the central condition of the turnover hypothesis, i.e. that turnover is high. Elsewhere, the numbers displayed in Table 8.9 do not support the hypothesis either because newcomers do not own a significant share of the total land (Paranaíta, Pacal and Monte Alegre), or, where they do (Mutum), because turnover is relatively low.

In terms of deforestation, the conclusions are more or less the same. The hypothesis seems to be holding only in Anapu/Pacajá and, to a lesser extent, in Alta Floresta. Newcomers in Anapu/Pacajá are responsible for 91 percent of the total area deforested in the largest farms, which is equivalent to 42 percent of the project's total sampled area. In Alta Floresta, newcomers' lands account for 41 percent of the deforestation in the largest farms, which correspond to 24 percent of the project's total. In other projects, the results presented in Table 8.9 do not support the turnover hypothesis.

Taking into consideration the exceptions of Anapu/Pacajá and Alta Floresta, this section provides quite definitive results regarding the turnover hypothesis:

1. the number of newcomers is not large among the largest quartile of farms;
2. newcomers do not cause most of the deforestation in the largest farms; survivors do;
3. although the out-migration of small farmers may be associated with deforestation in new frontiers, this relationship does not hold in consolidated frontiers.

Table 8.9. Land sizes and deforestation in the 25 percent largest farms in 1991

Project (ranked from high to low turnover rates)	Turnover rates (% who left)	Number of farms in top quartile (% in quartile)		Total farm area in top quartile (ha) (% in quartile) [% in sampled total]		Total hectares deforested in top quartile (% in quartile) [% in sampled total]	
		Newc	Surv	Newc	Surv	Newc	Surv
Paranaíta	44.2%	3 (67%)	6 (33%)	753 (33%) [20%]	1536 (67%) [41%]	403 (38%) [22%]	656 (62%) [36%]
Anapu/Pacajá	40.5%	10 (83%)	2 (17%)	2265 (88%) [38%]	314 (12%) [.05%]	1253 (91%) [42%]	131 (8%) [.04%]
Alta Floresta	35.9%	6 (43%)	8 (57%)	2037 (49%) [30%]	2132 (51%) [31%]	1086 (41%) [24%]	1545 (59%) 1[35%]
Mutum	33.3%	2 (40%)	3 (60%)	2850 (45%) [21%]	3395 (55%) [25%]	1690 (47%) [20%]	1915 (53%) [23%]
Monte Alegre	24.3%	1 (12%)	8 (88%)	131 (12%) [5%]	981 (88%) [42%]	114 (11%) [.05%]	884 (89%) [42%]
Pacal	12.7%	5 (23%)	17 (77%)	1153 (21%) [9%]	4367 (79%) [37%]	1081 (37%) [18%]	1869 (63%) [32%]
Total		27 (38%)	44 (62%)	9189 (42%) [21%]	12725 (58%) [29%]	5627 (45%) [22%]	7000 (55%) [27%]

8.14. CONVEXITY

Figure 8.26 displays scatter diagrams showing the percentage change in plot size on the horizontal axis and the percentage change in deforestation on the vertical axis. Survivors are mostly above and to the right of newcomers. In other words, except for Anapu/Pacajá and Alta Floresta, the diagrams confirm that plots that did not experience turnover (survivors) were the ones which displayed the largest growth and deforestation rates, contrary to the argument of the turnover hypothesis.

From the diagrams, change in deforestation seems to be a convex function of plot size. The diagonal line in each diagram functions as would a 45-degree line if the diagrams were drawn to scale. Points above that line indicate that the percentage change in deforestation was greater than the percentage change in plot size, a typical case for convexity. Points that lie along the line display a slope of one, indicating that percentage changes in deforestation and plot sizes were the same. Points below the 45-degree line represent plots where the percentage increase in deforestation was less than the percentage increase in plot size.

Table 8.10 takes stock of the points above the 45-degree line. The table shows that 56 percent of the total sample exhibit convex behavior, ranging from 30 percent in Monte Alegre to 78 percent in Mutum. There are two results that emerge from this discussion:

1. In most cases, deforestation is not associated with turnover on plots;
2. Percentage change in deforestation is mostly a convex function of percentage change in plot size.

Table 8.10. Plots that exhibit convex behavior

	Total number of plots in Fig. 8.26	Number of plots that exhibit convex behavior (above the 45-degree line)	Number of 'convex' plots excluded from Fig. 8.26 due to negative growth	Total number of 'strictly convex' plots in Fig. 8.26
Anapu/Pacajá	47	35 (74.4%)	0	35 (74.4%)
Monte Alegre	33	10 (30.3%)	0	10 (30.3%)
Pacal	87	51 (58.6%)	0	51 (58.6%)
Alta Floresta	53	34 (64%)	8	26 (49%)
Paranaíta	34	26 (76.5%)	9	17 (50%)
Mutum	18	14 (78%)	0	14 (78%)
Total	272	170 (62.5%)	17	153 (56%)

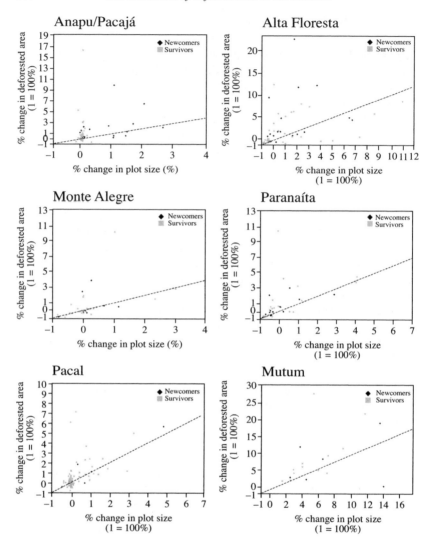

Figure 8.26.   Scatter diagram: percentage change in plot size by percentage change in deforested area during the 1980s

8.15. CONCLUSION

For at least two decades, most of the literature on Amazonian development has argued that deforestation is a consequence of the frequent out-migrations of small farmers from old to new frontiers and the arrival of newcomers as frontiers consolidate. The out-migrations of small farmers are considered the result of demographic instability among the rural poor and assumed to be rooted in the failure of agriculture in colonization projects. It is argued that the unsuitability of rain forest soils coupled with the lack of support for family farming condemn frontier agriculture to failure, forcing settlers to sell out their lands to newcomers and move further into the forest.

The turnover hypothesis argues that the arrival of newcomers on the frontier is marked by the re-concentration of land, as these farmers acquire and consolidate neighboring plots that once belonged to small colonists. When a newcomer buys a plot, it is generally small and only partially deforested, since the previous owner received or bought the land from the government under land settlement programs. Original settlers are often constrained by labor supply, which prevents them from deforesting their plots beyond the point that allows them to acquire property rights (high initial deforestation in new frontiers) and support family consumption (low marginal deforestation in consolidated frontiers). These plots are ultimately incorporated into large farms owned by a newcomer. Since newcomers are large farmers unconstrained by labor supply, they finish deforesting the plots in order to undertake commercial agriculture and cattle ranching. By consolidating small properties into large ones, newcomers cause an increase in deforestation practices, which makes deforestation a convex (i.e., positive and growing) function of plot size.

This chapter challenges these hypothesized relationships and draws its conclusions from field surveys undertaken in colonization projects in the Amazon region. It shows that the distributive effects of directed colonization are more long-lasting than was once believed, as much of the land in colonization areas is still in the possession of the initial settlers. These are also the farmers who are the largest deforesters. This conclusion leads to the rejection of the turnover hypothesis in most projects.

An important policy implication arises from the results presented in this chapter. The Brazilian government has recently begun carrying out a large agrarian reform program, much as it did in the 1970s. Settlement schemes have re-emerged, becoming a governmental priority and consuming large amounts of government resources. These programs are distributing subsidized land to settlers, but still do very little to contain deforestation in the areas where projects are established. The government actually expects some deforestation to take place when a project is established; after all, migrants are farmers. The government must act upon the fact that deforestation in areas designated for settlement is in excess of what is legally intended and, possibly, socially optimal.

Many politicians are voicing the demands of the rural poor, asking for government action to establish small farmers on the land. However, the

Table 8.11.   Summary table: turnover, land re-concentration and deforestation

What does the turnover hypothesis argue?	What does the field evidence show?	What are the main implications for deforestation?
• The frequent out-migrations of pioneer farmers and the arrival of newcomers into colonization projects promote land re-concentration and deforestation. • Deforestation among pioneer settlers is initially high in new frontiers (deforestation to obtain property rights) and marginally low as frontiers mature (deforestation to support family consumption). When plots are sold, they are only partially deforested. • Newcomers incorporate original colonization plots into larger farms, which are then deforested at higher	• While in 1981 small farms accounted for most of the total land in the samples, in 1991 large farms held most of the land; • Although land was equitably distributed among pioneer colonists upon arrival, some degree of re-concentration is observed in five projects (except for Monte Alegre) during the inter-survey period; • Between 1981 and 1991, only two projects exhibit simultaneously high turnover and growth in farms owned by newcomers (Alta Floresta and Anapu/Pacajá); • The project that exhibits the most pronounced growth in the sample (Mutum) is the one in which the turnover rate is not very high, i.e., survivors' and newcomers' farms experienced about the same growth between 1981 and 1991; • Except for two projects (Anapu/Pacajá and Alta Floresta), newcomers' farms are not larger than survivors' in 1991, which implies that, over time, land	• While in 1981 most of the deforestation was undertaken in small plots, in 1991 the situation reversed and large farms account for most of the total land cleared for agriculture; • Deforestation in the Amazon is a convex function of farm size; • Although land re-concentration and deforestation is happening among newcomers, both are more pronounced among survivors. • The behavior of survivors and

rates given that they are not constrained by labor.
- Turnover among small farmers occurs because of the unsuitability of rain forest soils to sustain agriculture and the lack of sufficient government support for family farming (this is discussed in Chapter 9).
- Deforestation is a positive function of the plot size; thus as newcomers' farms grow, so does deforestation.

in colonization areas is not becoming re-concentrated in the hands of newcomers;
- Analyzing the 25 percent largest farms in each project, in four of them (Mutum, Paranaíta, Pacal and Monte Alegre) newcomers do not own most of the land in 1991; in fact, survivors do.
- In one project with relatively high turnover (Alta Floresta), survivors and newcomers hold approximately equal amounts of land in the largest farms.
- Two projects exhibit statistically significant growth among survivors (Pacal and Mutum); however, turnover rates were low, re-enforcing the evidence that it is the survivors, and not the newcomers, who are responsible for re-concentrating land in these sites;
- Except for one project (Monte Alegre), in all others deforestation increased as farms became larger;
- In one project (Anapu/Pacajá), newcomers hold most (91%) of the deforested area in the largest farms. In all other projects, the shares of deforestation in plots that turned over were rather modest.
- Only one project (Anapu/Pacajá) unambiguously supports the turnover hypothesis;
- Except for one project (Anapu/Pacajá), survivors hold most of the deforested area in the largest farms.

newcomers w.r.t. the fraction of the plot that each group deforests is not different in most samples.
- It is true that deforestation is a positive function of plot size in most projects; however, it is not associated with turnover.
- Deforestation is a convex function of plot size.

results of this chapter show clearly that 'fixing' farmers on the land may reduce migrations and deforestation elsewhere; the drawback effect is that it may increase deforestation on the current site, once it is recognized that the survivors cause most of the damage to the forest. In view of these results, agrarian reform programs, as well as other programs aimed at curbing Amazonian migrations and alleviating social pressures, must also be accompanied by sound environmental policy.

The most serious deforestation problem occurs when colonists are given land, deforest it, grow crops for a few years until the soil is exhausted of its nutrients, then abandon the land and move on to a new frontier to farm another plot. Abandoning the land is far worse than selling it to newcomers for two reasons: (1) colonists do not get any payment for it (a distributive issue) and (2) the land is not put to productive use. Although this study does not intend to say whether a hectare of Amazonian forest is worth more (socially) than a hectare of pasture, clearly a hectare of forest must be worth more than a hectare of land that has been deforested and abandoned.

The main results of this chapter are summarized in Table 8.11.

STATISTICAL PROCEDURES

Part of the analysis of this chapter was based on descriptive statistics of the variables of interest. The samples' distributions were often skewed and normality was not assumed to carry out hypothesis testing. The purpose of this section is, first, to show the results of the normality test performed in the 1981 and 1991 samples with regard to plot size and deforestation. Second, it provides the results of the non-parametric tests used to test the hypotheses of this chapter.

Normality Test

Table 8.12 shows the Shapiro-Wilk statistic for a test of normality for plot sizes and deforestation for the 1981 and the 1991 samples. The first number in each cell is the test statistic (W). The second number, in italics, is the probability that the observed distribution comes from a normally distributed population. From the information provided in the table, it is clear that normality does not hold.

Non-parametric Tests (Wilcoxon Scores)

Since normality cannot be assumed and a functional form is not known for the respective distributions, a non-parametric approach was chosen for hypothesis testing. The method used was the Wilcoxon scores. The scores

Table 8.12. Normality test

	1981				1991			
	Farm Size		Deforestation		Farm Size		Deforestation	
	Newcomers	Survivors	Newcomers	Survivors	Newcomers	Survivors	Newcomers	Survivors
Para								
Anapu/	0.8016	0.7152	0.8960	0.8463	0.5758	0.5758	0.8146	0.9333
Pacajá	*0.0008*	*0.0001*	*0.0412*	*0.0006*	*0.0029*	*0.0001*	*0.0013*	*0.0841*
Monte	0.8010	0.8578	0.5779	0.7899	0.8589	0.8897	0.8382	0.9082
Alegre	*0.0307*	*0.0020*	*0.0001*	*0.0001*	*0.1197*	*0.0104*	*0.0742*	*0.0279*
Pacal	0.6498	0.5140	0.9295	0.8973	0.6211	0.5267	0.5557	0.6220
	0.0002	*0.0001*	*0.3879*	*0.0001*	*0.0001*	*0.0001*	*0.0001*	*0.0001*
Mato Grosso								
Alta	0.9422	0.8341	0.7015	0.7662	0.8317	0.8185	0.8217	0.7215
Floresta	*0.2967*	*0.0001*	*0.0001*	*0.0001*	*0.0027*	*0.0001*	*0.0018*	*0.0001*
Paranaíta	0.6494	0.9709	0.9662	0.9523	0.7213	0.7494	0.7926	0.7409
	0.0001	*0.7824*	*0.7623*	*0.4374*	*0.0003*	*0.0001*	*0.0026*	*0.0001*
Mutum	0.8372	0.4429	0.8866	0.8762	0.8727	0.9285	0.9481	0.8784
	0.1150	*0.0001*	*0.2978*	*0.0748*	*0.2331*	*0.3426*	*0.7442*	*0.0798*

are the rank of the observations. For two-sample data, the Wilcoxon scores method produces the rank sum statistic of the Mann-Whitney-Wilcoxon test. For the type of data at hand, this method has several advantages:

1. *It is powerful for small samples:* Although the overall sample is large, some of the individual project samples are not very large, especially for the respective newcomers' groups;
2. *It is appropriate for this type of data:* The sample distributions for both newcomers and survivors are often skewed, sparse and tied around certain values for the variables of interest (e.g., median and mode farm size in 1981 is 100 hectares for most locations);
3. *It can be used regardless of whether distributions are normal or not:* Even in cases where project samples are normally distributed (e.g., Mutum), this method can be used, as it gives normal approximations;
4. *It is more suitable than the median scores:* The median scores method was not used because it is most powerful for distributions that are symmetric and heavy tailed, which is not the case here.

Hypothesis Testing

Hypothesis testing is carried out using paired comparisons. Since there are two periods and two farm categories, the tests were performed in two steps, as follows:

1. *Fixed time/across groups:* Here, newcomers and survivors were compared in a given year. First, newcomers and survivors were compared in terms of land size and deforestation in 1981. Then, newcomers and survivors were compared in terms of land size and deforestation in 1991. In this step, *the 1981 and the 1991 samples are considered independent.*
2. *Variable time/within group:* In this step, newcomers and survivors were considered separately, allowing for comparisons over time for each group. First, newcomers' land size and deforestation in 1981 were compared to their 1991 values. Then, the test is repeated, this time considering the survivors' sample. Here, *newcomers and survivors are considered independent.*

In the tables that follow, Z is the normal approximation for the Mann-Whitney-Wilcoxon test statistic. P denotes the significance of the normal approximation test statistic. T is the t-test approximation significance. KW is the Kruskall-Wallis test, which is the one-way ANOVA statistic produced by the Wilcoxon scores method.

The results of the following tables were incorporated into the footnotes of each figure presented in the main text. Appropriate references to the tables were made in each figure.

Farm Size

Paired comparison: variable time/within group

Table 8.13. Hypothesis testing on differences of farm size between 1981 and 1991 among newcomers

Group: Newcomers
Variables: *Farm Size in 1981* and *Farm Size in 1991* (probabilities reflect one-tail test)

Project	N 1981	N 1991	Sum of scores 1981	Sum of scores 1991	Expected under H0	St. Dev.	Mean score 1981	Mean score 1991	Wilcoxon Normal Approx. S	Z*	Pr>|Z|	t-approx.	KW χ^2	DF	Pr>χ^2
Para															
Anapu-Pacajá	19	19	348.5	392.5	370.5	32.95	18.34	20.65	348.5	−0.65	0.2570	0.2590	0.4457	1	0.2522
Monte Alegre	8	8	52	84	68	9.48	6.5	10.5	52	−1.63	0.0511	0.0615	2.8444	1	0.0458
Pacal	11	11	125	128	126.5	15.07	11.36	11.63	125	−0.06	0.4735	0.4738	0.0099	1	0.4603
Mato Grosso															
Alta Floresta	19	19	299.50	441.50	370.50	34.20	15.70	23.20	299.50	−2.06	0.0196	0.0232	4.3075	1	0.0189
Paranaita	15	15	232	233	232.5	23.95	15.46	15.53	232	0	0.5	0.5	0.0004	1	0.4916
Mutum	6	6	21	57	39	6.2	3.5	9.5	21	−2.82	0.0024	0.0083	8.4255	1	0.0018

Table 8.14. Hypothesis testing on differences of farm size between 1981 and 1991 among survivors

Sample Group: Survivors
Variables: *Farm Size in 1981* and *Farm Size in 1991* (probabilities reflect one-tail test)

Project	N		Sum of scores		Expected under H0	St. Dev.	Mean score		Wilcoxon Normal Approx.			t-approx.	KW		
	1981	1991	1981	1991			1981	1991	S	Z^*	Pr>|Z|		χ^2	DF	Pr>χ^2
Para															
Anapu-Pacajá	28	28	697	899	798	60.53	24.89	32.10	697	−1.66	0.0484	0.0513	2.7837	1	0.0476
Monte Alegre	25	25	589.5	685.5	637.5	51.45	23.58	27.42	589.5	−0.92	0.1780	0.1802	0.8700	1	0.1754
Pacal	76	76	6210.5	5417.5	5814	268.26	81.71	71.28	6210.5	1.47	0.0699	0.0710	2.1846	1	0.0697
Mato Grosso															
Alta Floresta	34	34	936.5	1409.5	1173	80.76	27.54	41.45	936.5	−2.92	0.0017	0.0023	8.5756	1	0.0017
Paranaita	19	19	329	412	370.5	32.94	17.31	21.68	329	−1.24	0.1066	0.1105	1.5872	1	0.1038
Mutum	12	12	79	221	150	17.26	6.58	18.41	79	−4.08	0.00005	0.0002	16.914	1	0.00005

Paired comparison: fixed time/across groups

Table 8.15. Hypothesis testing on differences of farm size between newcomers and survivors in 1981

Sample Groups: Survivors and Newcomers
Variable: *Farm Size in 1981* (probabilities reflect two-tail test)

Project	N		Sum of Scores		Expected under H0		St. Dev.	Mean Score		Wilcoxon Normal Approx			t-approx.	KW		
	Newc.	Surv.	Newc.	Surv.	Newc.	Surv.	Surv.	Newc.	Surv.	S	Z	Pr>|Z|	Pr>|Z|	χ^2	DF	Pr>χ^2
Para																
Anapu-Pacajá	19	28	445	683	456	672	44	23.42	24.39	445	−0.23	0.8114	0.8125	0.0624	1	0.8026
Monte Alegre	8	25	129.5	431.5	136	425	23.77	16.18	17.26	129.5	−0.25	0.8007	0.8023	0.0747	1	0.7845
Pacal	11	76	490	3338	484	3344	76.30	44.54	43.92	490	0.07	0.9425	0.9427	0.0061	1	0.9373
Mato Grosso																
Alta Floresta	19	34	538.5	892.5	513	918	53.72	28.34	26.25	538.5	0.46	0.6417	0.6436	0.2252	1	0.6350
Paranaíta	15	19	294	301	262.5	332.5	28.53	19.6	15.84	294	1.08	0.2774	0.2853	1.2183	1	0.2697
Mutum	12	6	129	42	114	57	10.36	10.75	7	42	−1.39	0.1618	0.1798	2.0947	1	0.1478

Table 8.16. Hypothesis testing on differences of farm size between newcomers and survivors in 1991

Sample Groups: Survivors and Newcomers
Variable: *Farm Size in 1991* (probabilities reflect one-tail test)

Project	N		Sum of Scores		Expected under H0		St. Dev.	Mean Score		Wilcoxon Normal Approx			*t*-approx.	KW		
	Newc.	Surv.	Newc.	Surv.	Newc.	Surv.	Surv.	Newc.	Surv.	S	Z	Pr>|Z|		χ^2	DF	Pr>χ^2
Para																
Anapu-Pacajá	19	28	635.5	492.5	456	672	45.51	33.44	17.58	635.5	3.93	0.00005	0.0001	15.554	1	0.00005
Monte Alegre	8	25	119.5	441.5	136	425	23.71	14.93	17.66	119.5	-0.67	0.2499	0.2524	0.4840	1	0.2433
Pacal	11	76	496	3332	484	3344	76.50	45.09	43.84	496	0.15	0.4402	0.4404	0.0246	1	0.4377
Mato Grosso																
Alta Floresta	19	34	590.5	840.5	513	918	53.85	31.07	24.72	590.5	1.42	0.0763	0.0793	2.0712	1	0.0750
Paranaíta	15	19	241.5	353.5	262.5	332.5	28.80	16.10	18.60	241.5	-0.71	0.2383	0.2408	0.5315	1	0.2329
Mutum	12	6	109.5	61.5	114	57	10.64	9.12	10.25	61.5	0.37	0.3535	0.3558	0.1787	1	0.3362

Deforestation

Paired comparison: variable time/within group

Table 8.17. Hypothesis testing on differences of deforested area between 1981 and 1991 among newcomers

Sample Group: Newcomers

Variables: *Deforested Area in 1981* and *Deforested Area in 1991* (probabilities reflect one-tail test)

Project	N		Sum of scores		Expected under H0	St. Dev.	Mean score		Wilcoxon Normal Approx.			t-approx.	KW		
	1981	1991	1981	1991			1981	1991	S	Z	Pr>|Z|		χ^2	DF	Pr>χ^2
Para															
Anapu-Pacajá	19	19	258	483	370.5	34.21	13.57	25.42	258	−3.27	0.0005	0.0011	10.811	1	0.0005
Monte Alegre	8	8	58.5	77.5	68	9.5	7.31	9.68	58.5	−0.94	0.1719	0.1794	0.9983	1	0.1588
Pacal	11	11	107	146	126.5	15.2	9.72	13.27	107	−1.24	0.1053	0.1127	1.6433	1	0.0999
Mato Grosso															
Alta Floresta	19	19	371.5	369.5	370.5	34.24	19.55	19.44	371.5	0.01	0.4942	0.4942	0.0008	1	0.4883
Paranaita	15	15	215.5	249.5	232.5	24.09	14.36	16.63	215.5	−0.68	0.2467	0.2494	0.4979	1	0.2402
Mutum	6	6	21	57	39	6.24	3.5	9.5	21	−2.80	0.0025	0.0086	8.3077	1	0.0019

Table 8.18. *Hypothesis testing on differences of deforested area between 1981 and 1991 among survivors*

Sample Group: Survivors
Variables: *Deforested Area in 1981* and *Deforested Area in 1991* (probabilities reflect one-tail test)

Project	N 1981	N 1991	Sum of scores 1981	Sum of scores 1991	Expected under H0	St. Dev.	Mean score 1981	Mean score 1991	Wilcoxon Normal Approx. S	Z	Pr>|Z|	t-approx.	χ^2	KW DF	Pr>χ^2
Para															
Anapu-Pacajá	28	28	660.5	935.5	798	61	23.58	33.41	660.5	−2.24	0.0123	0.0144	5.0802	1	0.0121
Monte Alegre	25	25	646.5	628.5	637	51.50	25.86	25.14	646.5	0.16	0.4344	0.4348	0.0305	1	0.4306
Pacal	76	76	4720	6908	5814	271.29	62.10	90.89	4720	−4.03	0.00005	0.00005	16.261	1	0.00005
Mato Grosso															
Alta Floresta	34	34	997	1349	1173	81.41	29.32	39.67	997	−2.15	0.0155	0.0173	4.6731	1	0.0153
Paranaíta	19	19	310.5	430.5	370.5	34.21	16.34	22.65	310.5	−1.73	0.0410	0.0452	3.0748	1	0.0397
Mutum	12	12	78	222	150	17.31	6.5	18.5	78	−4.12	0.00005	0.0002	17.288	1	0.00005

Paired comparison: fixed time/across groups

Table 8.19. Hypothesis testing on differences of deforested area between newcomers and survivors in 1981

Sample Groups: Survivors and Newcomers
Variable: *Deforested Area in 1981* (probabilities reflect two-tail test)

Project	N Newc.	N Surv.	Sum of Scores Newc.	Sum of Scores Surv.	Expected under H0 Newc.	Expected under H0 Surv.	St. Dev. Surv.	Mean Score Newc.	Mean Score Surv.	Wilcoxon Normal Approx S	Z	Pr>|Z|	t-approx.	KW χ^2	DF	Pr>χ^2
Para																
Anapu-Pacajá	19	28	531	597	456	672	46.09	27.94	21.32	531	1.61	0.1016	0.1129	2.6472	1	0.1037
Monte Alegre	8	25	118	443	136	425	23.78	14.75	17.72	118	-0.73	0.4618	0.4672	0.5729	1	0.4491
Pacal	11	76	564.5	3263.5	484	3344	78.26	51.31	42.94	564.5	1.02	0.3067	0.3095	1.0581	1	0.3037
Mato Grosso																
Alta Floresta	19	34	537.5	953.5	513	918	53.86	28.28	26.27	537.5	0.44	0.6559	0.6577	0.2069	1	0.6492
Paranaíta	15	19	292.5	302.5	262.5	332.5	28.80	19.5	15.92	292.5	1.02	0.3058	0.3133	1.0845	1	0.2977
Mutum	12	6	116	55	114	57	10.67	9.66	9.16	55	-0.14	0.8882	0.8899	0.0351	1	0.8513

Table 8.20.   *Hypothesis testing on differences of deforested area between newcomers and survivors in 1991*

Sample Groups: Survivors and Newcomers
Variable: *Deforested Area in 1991 (probabilities reflect one-tail test)*

Project	N		Sum of Scores		Expected under H0		St. Dev.	Mean Score		Wilcoxon Normal Approx			t-approx.	KW		
	Newc.	Surv.	Newc.	Surv.	Newc.	Surv.	Surv.	Newc.	Surv.	S	Z	Pr>|Z|		χ^2	DF	Pr>χ^2
Para																
Anapu-Pacajá	19	28	621.5	506.5	456	672	46.10	32.71	18.08	621.5	3.57	0.0001	0.0004	12.886	1	0.0001
Monte Alegre	8	25	121.5	439.5	136	425	23.77	15.18	17.58	121.5	−0.58	0.2779	0.2800	0.3720	1	0.2709
Pacal	11	76	460.5	3367.5	484	3344	78.25	41.86	44.30	460.5	−0.29	0.3844	0.3847	0.0901	1	0.3819
Mato Grosso																
Alta Floresta	19	34	646	785	513	918	53.9	34	23.08	646	2.45	0.0070	0.0086	6.0867	1	0.0068
Paranaíta	15	19	259	336	262.5	332.5	28.82	17.26	17.68	259	−0.10	0.4585	0.4588	0.0147	1	0.4516
Mutum	12	6	118.5	52.5	114	57	10.67	9.87	8.75	52.5	−0.37	0.3539	0.3562	0.1778	1	0.3366

Percentages

Paired comparison: percentage change in farm size

Table 8.21.   Hypothesis testing for percentage changes in farm size between newcomers and survivors: 1981–91

Sample Groups: Survivors and Newcomers
Variable: *Percentage change in farm size during the 1980s (probabilities reflect one-tail test)*

Project	N		Sum of Scores		Expected under H0		St. Dev.	Mean Score		Wilcoxon Normal Approx.			t-approx.	KW		
	Newc.	Surv.	Surv.	Newc.	Newc.	Surv.	Surv.	Newc.	Surv.	S	Z	Pr>|Z|		χ^2	DF	Pr>χ^2
Para																
Anapu-Pacajá	19	28	623	504	456	672	45.96	32.81	18.01	623.5	3.63	0.0000	0.0000	13.279	1	0.0000
Monte Alegre	8	25	150	411	136	425	23.78	18.75	16.44	150	0.56	0.2851	0.2871	0.3465	1	0.2783
Pacal	11	76	493.5	3334.5	484	3344	77.81	44.86	43.87	493.5	0.11	0.4539	0.4541	0.0149	1	0.4514
Mato Grosso																
Alta Floresta	19	34	576	855	513	918	53.91	30.31	25.14	576	1.15	0.1232	0.1258	1.3654	1	0.1213
Paranaita	15	19	239	356	262	332	28.82	15.93	18.73	239	-0.79	0.2125	0.2153	0.6644	1	0.2075
Mutum	6	12	64	107	57	114	10.67	10.66	8.91	64	0.61	0.2712	0.2752	0.4302	1	0.2559

Table 8.22. Hypothesis testing for percentage changes in deforestation between newcomers and survivors: 1981–91

Sample Groups: Survivors and Newcomers
Variable: Percentage change in deforestation during the 1980s (probabilities reflect one-tail test): (def91–def81)/def81

Project	N		Sum of Scores		Expected under H0		St. Dev.	Mean Score		Wilcoxon Normal			t-approx.	KW		
	Newc.	Surv.	Newc.	Surv.	Newc.	Surv.	Surv.	Newc.	Surv.	S	Approx Z	Pr>|Z|		χ^2	DF	Pr>χ^2
Para																
Anapu-Pacajá	19	28	519	609	456	672	46.13	27.31	21.75	519	1.35	0.0877	0.0910	1.8651	1	0.0860
Monte Alegre	8	25	146	415	136	425	23.80	18.25	16.60	146	0.39	0.3449	0.3462	0.1764	1	0.3372
Pacal	11	76	378	3450	484	3344	78.28	34.36	45.39	378	-1.34	0.0889	0.0906	1.8335	1	0.0878
Mato Grosso																
Alta Floresta	19	34	600	831	513	918	53.91	31.57	24.44	600	1.60	0.0543	0.0573	2.6037	1	0.0533
Paranaíta	15	19	235.5	359.5	262.5	332.5	28.82	15.70	18.92	235.5	-0.91	0.1790	0.1823	0.8771	1	0.1745
Mutum	6	12	53	118	57	114	10.67	8.84	9.84	53	-0.32	0.3715	0.3735	0.1403	1	0.3539

Table 8.23. Hypothesis testing for percentage of plots deforested in 1981 between newcomers (old-timers) and survivors

Sample Groups: Survivors and Newcomers
Variable: *Percentage of total land deforested in 1981 (probabilities reflect two-tail test):* def81/land81

Project	N		Sum of Scores		Expected under H0		St. Dev.	Mean Score		Wilcoxon Normal Approx.			t-approx.	KW		
	Newc.	Surv.	Newc.	Surv.	Newc.	Surv.	Surv.	Newc.	Surv.	S	Z	Pr>|Z|		χ^2	DF	Pr>χ^2
Para																
Anapu-Pacajá	19	28	529	599	456	672	46.12	27.84	21.39	529	1.57	0.1160	0.1228	2.5051	1	0.1135
Monte Alegre	8	25	129.5	431.5	136	425	19.97	16.18	17.26	129.5	-0.30	0.7639	0.7658	0.1059	1	0.7449
Pacal	11	76	542	3286	484	3344	78.29	49.27	43.23	542	0.73	0.4627	0.4647	0.5487	1	0.4588
Mato Grosso																
Alta Floresta	19	34	520	911	513	918	53.40	27.36	26.79	520	0.12	0.9031	0.9036	0.1718	1	0.8957
Paranaíta	15	19	283	311	262	332	28.82	18.90	16.39	283.5	0.71	0.4770	0.4820	0.5307	1	0.4663
Mutum	6	12	61	110	57	114	10.67	10.16	9.16	61	0.32	0.7431	0.7471	0.1403	1	0.7079

Table 8.24. Hypothesis testing for percentage of plots deforested in 1991 between newcomers (old-timers) and survivors

Sample Groups: Survivors and Newcomers
Variable: Percentage of total land deforested in 1991 (probabilities reflect one-tail test): def91/land91

Project	N		Sum of Scores		Expected under H0		St. Dev.	Mean Score		Wilcoxon Normal Approx.			t-approx.	KW		
	Newc.	Surv.	Newc.	Surv.	Newc.	Surv.		Newc.	Surv.	S	Z	Pr>|Z|		χ^2	DF	Pr>χ^2
Para																
Anapu-Pacajá	19	28	540.5	587.5	456	672	46.12	28.44	20.98	540.5	1.82	0.0343	0.0375	3.3560	1	0.0335
Monte Alegre	8	25	123.5	437.5	136	425	22.40	15.43	17.50	123.5	−0.53	0.2961	0.2980	0.3112	1	0.2884
Pacal	11	76	441.5	3386	484	3344	78.25	40.13	44.55	441.5	−0.53	0.2957	0.2964	0.2949	1	0.2935
Mato Grosso																
Alta Floresta	19	34	593.5	837.5	513	918	53.66	31.23	24.63	593.5	1.49	0.0680	0.0710	2.2500	1	0.0668
Paranaíta	15	19	296.5	298.5	262.5	332.5	28.82	19.76	15.71	296.5	1.16	0.1216	0.1267	1.3911	1	0.1191
Mutum	6	12	58	113	57	114	10.65	9.66	9.41	58	0.04	0.4813	0.4815	0.0088	1	0.4626

162

Table 8.25. *Hypothesis testing for percentage of plots deforested in between 1981 and 1991: newcomers and survivors*

Sample Groups: Survivors and Newcomers
Variable: *Difference in Percent of Plot Deforested between 1981 and 1991 (probabilities reflect one-tail test): (def91/land91)–(def81/land81)*

Project	N		Sum of Scores		Expected under H0		St. Dev.	Mean Score		Wilcoxon Normal. Approx			t-approx.	KW		
	Newc.	Surv.	Surv.	Newc.	Newc.	Surv.		Newc.	Surv.	S	Z	Pr>|Z|	Pr>|Z|	χ^2	DF	Pr>χ^2
Para																
Anapu-Pacajá	19	28	677	451	456	672	46.13	23.73	24.17	451	-0.09	0.4611	0.4613	0.0117	1	0.4568
Monte Alegre	8	25	439	122	136	425	23.47	15.25	17.56	122	-0.57	0.2826	0.2846	0.3557	1	0.2754
Pacal	11	76	3457	371	484	3344	78.29	33.72	45.48	371	-1.43	0.0754	0.0772	2.0828	1	0.0745
Mato Grosso																
Alta Floresta	19	34	898	533	513	918	53.91	28.05	26.41	533	0.36	0.3588	0.3595	0.1376	1	0.3553
Paranaíta	15	19	319	276	262.5	332.5	28.83	18.4	16.78	276	0.45	0.3260	0.3275	0.2192	1	0.3198
Mutum	6	12	125	46	57	114	10.67	7.66	10.41	46	-0.98	0.1627	0.1696	1.0614	1	0.3029

163

9. Dispelling other myths about the Amazon

9.1. INTRODUCTION

The word 'myth' is understood here as a past context that no longer holds in the present. Some of these 'myths' had a good deal of truth in them when they were formulated. As I noted in the Preface, things change quite rapidly in the Amazon, rendering a policy context obsolete by the time it is understood. The role of subsidies, for example, has certainly been downgraded in the recent literature, but part of that downgrading arises from the removal of many of the subsidies, partly in response to the criticisms from policy makers and analysts. That being understood, the turnover hypothesis is a myth to which many authors still subscribe to explain deforestation in the Amazon.

Chapters 7 and 8 showed that low survival rates is the only tenet of the turnover hypothesis that was robust across projects. Turnover, however, is not associated with high deforestation and land re-concentration by newcomers in most projects (contrary to what the hypothesis predicted). The literature on Amazonian development assumes that turnover is the outcome of unsuccessful agriculture and is regarded as the 'fate' of colonization, as areas cleared for crops by colonists are thought to be quickly abandoned or sold and converted to pastures by newcomers. This chapter provides evidence that turnover is an economic strategy that colonists may have developed to improve their circumstances. After all, selling land that has been granted for free from the government, or acquired on favorable terms from private colonization companies, suggests rent-seeking behavior rather than 'fate'.

Turnover occurs despite the evidence of reasonably good economic success in agriculture, and independently of whether social and physical infrastructure are appropriate for farming (e.g., provision of education and health services, well-defined property rights and reasonably good access to roads and markets). This chapter introduces an economic explanation for turnover and argues that its relationship to deforestation is feeble. In fact, this chapter builds on the empirical analysis carried out in previous chapters to show that there is an inverse relationship between high turnover and high deforestation, contrary to the tenets of the turnover hypothesis.

In the following sections, the economic returns to frontier agriculture are compared to overall economic indicators. These indicators are considered the 'opportunity costs' of frontier farming. The main findings are that, during the 1980s, Amazonian farmers apparently covered their opportunity costs in the labor and financial markets, but not in the land market. Earnings were high for family labor and for family assets, compared to the overall economy, making it worthwhile to continue farming on the frontier. Returns to land, however, were apparently low compared to rapidly appreciating frontier real estate, and farmers were motivated to move on and to reap capital gains successively from each plot of land.

Those farmers who covered their opportunity costs were able to expand the farmed area and, consequently, increase deforestation. Those who did not, either abandoned or sold their plots to newcomers. The analysis carried out in Chapter 8 concluded that plots that turned over did not display larger fractions of deforested land relative to plots that remained under the same ownership.

Although turnover is not associated with deforestation in consolidated frontiers, it may be associated with deforestation in new frontiers, where migrants arrive in large numbers. The data used in this study, however, are not cut out to perform a rigorous analysis on itinerant farmers. These farmers are 'caught' in the data only when they occupy the surveyed plots and not after they have left them. In the early days of colonization, however, Chapter 8 showed that the level of deforestation carried out by the average farmer who left the plot looked no different than the deforestation carried out by the average farmer who stayed on the plot. Thus, considering that itinerant farmers *in the early stage of frontier development* (new frontiers) deforest less than survivors *in the later stage of frontier development* (old frontiers), itinerant farmers can no longer be blamed for deforestation in old frontiers. They can, at most, be responsible for opening up new ones.

Section 9.2 discusses five related studies that belie the accepted view that turnover occurs because of the failure of agriculture undertaken in unsuitable soils. These studies show that the causes of turnover are complex and go beyond the physical attributes of the land. Section 9.3 presents a way to analyze farmers' performances taking into account costs and benefits of frontier agriculture. Section 9.4 presents an empirical assessment of the main variables associated with these costs and benefits. Section 9.5 summarizes partial results from the empirical analysis. Section 9.6 discusses the changes in the uses of deforested lands during the 1980s. Section 9.7 discusses the economic rationale behind a farmer's choice on whether to sell or stay on the plot, and on whether to produce or leave his land idle. Section 9.8 summarizes and draws the final conclusions of the chapter.[1]

9.2.   RELATED WORKS

Only a few studies have analyzed empirically what is conjectured in the literature on the turnover hypothesis. Five of these studies point to the fact that high turnover is indeed occurring and land re-concentration is an undeniable fact. None of these studies, however, focuses primarily on the economics of deforestation, but rather on the socio-economic aspects of frontier agriculture in general and of turnover and land re-concentration in particular.

Moran's (1989) analysis of settlement stages warns us to expect a period of learning by doing before judging the ultimate success of settlement. A wider study by FAO/UNDP (1992) finds Amazon colonization projects economically competitive with similar projects in the South of Brazil and much more successful than in the Northeast, despite the relatively high turnover observed in Amazonian projects. An econometric study undertaken by Jones et al. (1992) in Rondônia finds no loss of incomes or yields associated with length of stay on plot, and no systematic relationship with soil classification. Schneider (1995) designs an interesting analytical framework which links turnover to the evolution of property rights in the Amazon frontier. Further, in observing the behavior of farmers in Pará in face of tenure constraints, Alston et al. (1999) provide corroborating evidence to support the results presented in the studies above. These five studies are reviewed here not because of their relevance for deforestation (none of them claims this), but because they dispel the myth that regional agriculture generates private and social (economic) losses.

Taken together, these studies show that there is a paradox with which public policy for regional development must come to grips: agricultural production in the region is economically viable, and in many places productivity shows no sign of decline over time; nevertheless, turnover and land re-concentration remain high. Since the turnover hypothesis failed to provide a good theoretical framework to establish a relationship between these issues and deforestation, this chapter undertakes such a task.

9.2.1.   Moran's 'Stages' Approach

In a review of the experience with colonization programs in Latin America, Moran (1989) emphasizes that colonization is a process of adaptation to a new environment, of learning by doing. Moran's stages approach emphasizes three important points: (i) it is inappropriate to judge the success of colonization efforts while farmers are still in the learning and adapting stage of settlement; (ii) production and equity objectives are often inconsistent; (iii) the role of government in creating settlement projects is generally negative, encouraging migrants to act on government promises, too often broken, rather than on the basis of their own information and strategies. The study also suggests that low incomes and mobility are closely related, that previous mobility is a strong predictor of future mobility, and that crop yields are negatively related to the number of previous migrations of the owner.

9.2.2.   FAO/UNDP Evaluation of Settlement Projects

In a report released in 1992, FAO/UNDP and the Brazilian Ministry of Agriculture and Agrarian Reform review the experience with land settlement projects carried out under INCRA. The report assessed projects throughout the country – not solely in the Amazon. The purpose of the report is to assess the performance of INCRA settlement projects established between 1985 and 1989. A population of 440 settlements was identified. Following stratification by state and micro-region and subsequent random selection, 44 settlements were chosen for field visits.

In terms of incomes, settlements in the North (Amazon region) generated incomes four times the minimum wage – larger than those in any region other than the South. The ability of settlers to accumulate household durable goods and productive capital (machinery, buildings, etc.) reflects these incomes, with the northern region again surpassed only by the South. Northern settlers more than tripled their initial assets (increased by 222 percent).

Although the North has the second highest rating in terms of economic performance, it has by far the lowest number of original settlers still on the land – fewer than 80 percent, compared with 97–100 percent in other regions. Even when comparing turnover and economic performance within the North, ranking the settlements in the order of 1990–91 incomes, the FAO/UNDP (1992) report finds no relationship between incomes and permanency on the plot.

9.2.3.   Jones' Study of Farming in Rondônia

Jones et al. (1992) conducted an econometric study based on a sample of 91 family farms around the city of Ouro Preto in the Amazon State of Rondônia. The sample was drawn from Ouro Preto D'Oeste, a colonization project begun in 1970 and located along the highway BR-365. Soils in the study area are primarily classified as 'good', but they range from 'moderate' to 'unsuitable' for either annual or perennial crops, and from 'good' to 'restricted' for pasture. The study found that the average farm marketed half its output, and had one third of its area in pasture and 18 percent in cultivation, leaving half uncleared. The median farm was highly diversified, with at least six income sources. Some farms had as many as ten categories of income sources. The median farmer had occupied his plot for ten years, with the longest time being 20 years.

The authors report that they have been unable to find a systematic relationship between length of time on plot and any of their measures of overall productivity. The soil classification they used predicts 20 years of 'good' yields on 'good' soils, ten years of 'good' yields on 'moderate' soils, and that yields on 'restricted' soils will decrease rapidly within ten years. Their classification also predicts that yields will be low from the very first year on the 'restricted' soils. The authors have also found scattered evidence of productivity effects on different soil types, but the effects have been crop specific and have not conformed to the rank predictions of the classification system. Per capita income is *ceteris paribus* higher on the 'restricted' soils than on the higher grades. In unreported regressions they argue that they were unable to find any relationship between gross income per cleared acre (in either crops or pasture) and time on plot, controlled for the percentage of the plot cleared for use and soil type. Dividing the sample of farms into those occupying their plots for ten years or less and for over ten years yields the same results as the full sample.

They suggest that the fact that the mean and median farmers in the sample had been on their plots for a decade belied the turnover pattern described in the literature. The authors argue that colonists' reports suggest an initial, entry effect that involved extensive clearing; what the reports do not suggest is the possibility that initial clearing was accompanied by learning through trial and error, as Moran (1989) argued in his study. However, their data yield a zero simple correlation between length of time on plot and percentage of the plot cleared, which belied the pattern of clearing three hectares a year, abandoning previously cleared land, until the entire plot is cleared and abandoned. Instead, an initial period of rapid deforestation may be followed by a calmer period, closer to an equilibrium pattern of farming practices, during which some reforestation and regeneration of damaged soils occurs.

9.2.4. Schneider's Property Rights Approach

Schneider (1995) proposes an interesting analytical framework to look at transience on farming plots in the Amazon. Schneider's main contribution is that he draws on the evolution of property rights to explain turnover and, consequently, deforestation in the frontier.

Schneider argues that the relationship between the emergence of economic rent to land (and deforestation) and the emergence of the demand for some form of government is nearly perfect. On earlier frontiers, clarifying and enforcing property rights is one of the earliest functions of emerging government action. The need for collective action to enforce property rights increases with an increasing value of land as the frontier moves forward.

Schneider provides an insightful economic definition of the frontier as the point at which the marginal laborer is as well off as he would be in his best alternative employment. It is at this point that the marginal laborer begins to integrate the national economy into previously unexploited areas. Since he only manages to cover his opportunity cost, he is relatively indifferent with respect to his ownership of the land. Since he has no competitors for land (he himself is the marginal laborer), he can farm unimpeded by concerns over land security. As roads improve, transportation costs fall, and markets grow, the potential value of this settler's land begins to increase. Its net present value now exceeds both his opportunity cost and that of other low-opportunity cost settlers. Competition for land begins to emerge. Since formal government is weak or nonexistent, the rules to manage this competition are established locally. For example, as long as the potential income stream is perceived as being low relative to the opportunity costs of potential settlers, the initial settler may need to mark his cleared area. To an incoming migrant (e.g., a squatter) the land isn't worth a fight – he can always settle on the plot next door. As transportation continues to improve, however, so do returns to agriculture, and the difference between opportunity costs and potential income streams grows – relative land scarcity and true economic rent emerge, and land becomes an item worth fighting over.

With competition for land intensifying, colonists must strengthen their claim to land. Cutting timber marks claims clearly and increases the visibility of squatters should they attempt to invade. It is expensive, however, and results in a dissipation of some portion of the economic rent that was beginning to emerge. The more valuable the land becomes, the more competition arises, and the more expensive it becomes for established settlers to protect ownership. With the arrival of formal government, which, in a way, enforces property rights, the pioneer settlers become seriously disadvantaged if they choose to stay. The human capital attributes that select the marginal laborers (pioneer colonists) are precisely those which limit their ability to take advantage of government – illiteracy becoming a serious handicap. This is the point at which pioneer colonists must weigh their alternatives and make a decision about whether to sell out or stay. Schneider (1995) recognizes that the decision to sell is prompted by fundamental demographic and economic forces and argues that, without government policy initiatives to counteract these forces, turnover will hardly be contained.

Schneider's property-rights approach is an insightful theoretical framework to analyze turnover. The study uses secondary sources of information to perform forecasts on returns to agriculture under several different scenarios, ranging from gains to farmers under nonexistent government and unspecified property rights, to the existence of formal government and well-defined rights.

9.2.5.   Alston et al. (1999) Study on Titles, Conflicts and Land Use

Alston et al. (1999) have the most coherent framework to address a few of the key issues that also pertain to this study. The authors examine the institutional development involved in the process of land use and ownership in the Amazon and show how this phenomenon affects the behavior of economic actors. Their work complements Schneider's (1995) study and explores the way in which the absence of well-defined property rights in the Amazon has led to both economic and social problems, including lost investment opportunities, high costs in protecting claims, and especially violence. The study offers a unique opportunity to observe a rare instance where institutional change can be empirically observed. This allows the authors to study property rights as they emerge and evolve, and to analyze the effects of development on the regional economy.

Although their study is not about deforestation *per se*, the main contribution of Alston et al. (1999), so far as this book is concerned, is that in briefly touching upon the issue of turnover, the authors find that the number of moves a farmer makes is constrained by life-cycle behavior. They argue that farmers will move from place to place only until they accumulate sufficient capital to cover their opportunity costs; this is the point at which a subsequent move would not pay off. The authors offer an invaluable piece of corroborating evidence to support the results presented in this book.

9.3.   BENEFITS AND COSTS OF FRONTIER AGRICULTURE

This chapter attempts to take as much real world variation into account as possible in explaining the performance of small farmers in the Amazon and its association with deforestation. Given the variety of conditions in the Amazon, the evaluation of performance, based on the calculation of benefits and costs, is perhaps as important as the framework of analysis, that is how these costs and benefits are defined, measured and analyzed.

9.3.1. Private Benefits of Frontier Agriculture

In order to assess the private benefits of frontier agriculture, colonists' performance must be compared to the opportunity costs they face in three factor markets: labor, capital and land. These opportunity costs are calculated as follows:

Labor market   As half the Brazilian urban labor force earns less than a minimum wage (in real terms, approximately US$1,000 per year, varying with the annual inflation rate), the minimum wage is a reasonable upper-bound proxy for small farmers' opportunity cost in this factor market. In these terms, small farmers cover this opportunity cost if income from family labor is at least one minimum wage per worker.

Capital market   The only financial instrument widely available to small savers is the savings certificate (*caderneta de poupança*), which paid in 1991 a real interest rate of 0.5 percent per month. If this is used as a proxy for the opportunity cost in the capital market, then colonists cover this opportunity cost if the accumulation rate of all physical and financial assets is at least 0.5 percent per month.

Land market   The price per hectare of land is a straightforward variable. Colonists cover their opportunity cost in this market if the rate of return to the use of the land is at least equal to the percentage variation in the price of the land during the same period.

9.3.2. Private and Environmental Costs of Frontier Agriculture

In broad terms, the total costs of frontier agriculture include both private costs and environmental externalities. Private costs comprise current and start-up costs, which include conventional fixed costs plus the farm-level costs of deforestation. Relatively open-access conditions tend to reduce these costs, as access to forested land tends to be cheap in new frontiers relative to established areas. Other private costs of settlement are related to uncertainty and lack of information, which introduce considerable variance into expected returns on any one piece of land.

Environmental costs (externalities) arise with improper farming and mismanagement of nonrenewable resources. These costs include, among others, the loss of biodiversity, sedimentation of rivers, increase in the occurrence of floods and soil erosion. Although it is not within the scope of this work to measure environmental costs, we can identify conditions in which they are reduced. For example, cost reductions per unit of benefit occur when, for any given hectare deforested, agricultural production or grazing become more intensive, the ratio of harvested to total cleared area increases, or the number of harvests prior to turning land to fallow increases.

Very often there is interplay between low private and high environmental costs (a *win-lose* scenario). By providing cheap access to forested lands, frontier open-access conditions are thought to induce a wasteful use of soils, which are cleared for extensive agricultural practices and ranching, increasing the environmental costs of settlement (as discussed in Chapter 6). Although deforestation may be in excess of what the government expected, the evidence provided in this chapter shows that, in most sampled projects, deforested land is put to some form of economic use. Therefore, deforested lands are not being wasted, at least not to the point at which deforestation yields no social returns at all.

9.4. EMPIRICAL EVIDENCE

9.4.1. Wage Rate

In each survey, the opportunity cost in the labor market was taken to be the minimum wage, US$1,000 per year. As mentioned previously, since roughly half the urban labor force in Brazil earns less than this, a lower value might provide a better comparison. Nonetheless, the minimum wage is the most widely accepted indicator in Brazil and was therefore adopted here.

Payments to family labor can be approximated by measuring the value of monetary and non-monetary yearly consumption per household and dividing this figure by the number of full-time workers. The result is an estimate of how much families were remunerating their own labor, which can be compared to the going wage rate in the labor market.

On average, there appears to have been a sharp increase in imputed remuneration to family labor over the 1980s, from 1 minimum wage in 1981 to 3.2 minimum wages in 1991 (Table 9.1). These wages seem to be higher in private colonization projects than in public ones. The imputed wage is relatively higher in Pacal (3.54 minimum wages) and significantly higher in Mutum (19.54 minimum wages).

The dollar value of the average annual wage also grew. Throughout the 1980s, exchange rate devaluation was smaller than the loss in real value of the minimum wage, so the change from 1981 to 1991 is actually smaller than it appears in Table 9.2 relative to Table 9.1. Differences among locations remain roughly the same. In this case, only Mutum, with its outstanding value (US$19,000) differed significantly from the rest.

On average, family workers earned around US$4,000 per year (approximately US$333 per month), which is about four times the yearly minimum wage. Even those in the lowest income groups self-remunerated above the minimum wage. Although much of the sample was very poor by international standards, it did better than average by domestic standards, given stringent conditions in the Brazilian labor market. Using this criterion, therefore, frontier farming covered its opportunity cost in the labor market.

9.4.2. Interest Rate

In the financial market, the opportunity cost of frontier farming is the interest rate paid on the most widespread saving instrument for small and medium savers in Brazil, the *caderneta de poupança*. In 1991, this certificate paid 0.5 percent per month plus monetary correction (an indexation measure to make up for inflation).

The rate of accumulation is the average monthly percentage increase in net worth since arrival on the plot. It is measured by comparing all real and financial resources brought to the frontier with the value of net worth in 1991. This concept is different from the rate of return, which shows how much net income was earned on farmers' real assets over time. The accumulation rate is an alternative measure of asset appreciation.

Table 9.3 shows that the average monthly real rate of accumulation was very high, about 2.3 per cent, or more than four times the interest rate. Mutum, once again, had the highest figures. Although there were slight variations across locations, these were statistically insignificant and small compared to variations in imputed wages.

The rate of accumulation, as measured, does not imply net additions to productive capacity, but merely additions to net asset values. Land is an important part of farmers' net worth (about 50 percent on average), and rising land prices have contributed in large measure to land appreciation (approximately 80 percent, on average). So capital gains have inflated accumulation rates by approximately 30 percent, meaning real rates of accumulation were around 30 percent lower than those shown in Table 9.3. Even so, these real rates would still be at least double the interest rate. Farming, therefore, was very good business all over the frontier and covered its opportunity cost in the financial market.

9.4.3. Price of Land

In the land market, the opportunity cost of land is the price of land per hectare. This can be measured by weighting the micro-regional prices of forested areas, permanent or temporary crop areas, pasture areas, and fallow areas by the number of hectares devoted to each of these uses. Subsequently dividing the result by total land area gives one overall price per plot. This is the value the farmer would get by selling land under current market conditions. In this way, the change over time in the price of land can be compared to the rate of return gained from farming it.

Table 9.4 shows that, during the 1980s, the price of land rose considerably in most of the frontier. As we have seen, tax and credit incentives, large-scale colonization and titling programs, the laying down of physical and social infrastructure, and an inflationary economy all boosted demand for frontier land. As people moved into the region, and more and more land became private property, the frontier land market began to operate dynamically, and real estate appreciated far more here than in the rest of the economy.

The same table shows that, during the inter-survey period, average land prices seem to have appreciated in all projects, with the exception of Alta Floresta and Paranaíta. The highest rate of increase was in Anapu/Pacajá (19.5 percent), where land prices had been the lowest. The next highest were Pacal (9 percent) in the state of Pará, and Mutum (8 percent) in the state of Mato Grosso. In Alta Floresta and Paranaíta, however, land values declined (–4.3 percent).

Across locations, land prices followed no trends. They sometimes rose with agricultural productivity, as in Mutum and Pacal, but they could appreciate despite declining productivity, as in Anapu/Pacajá. Nor do land prices necessarily reflect the amount or quality of infrastructure or government services available, as argued by Schneider (1995). Alta Floresta, known as the 'jewel' of colonization and rated most highly for physical and social infrastructure among all locations surveyed, witnessed declining land prices. Anapu/Pacajá, one of the most neglected areas along the Transamazon Highway, displayed sharply rising land prices. It appears, therefore, that exogenous factors contribute to variations in land prices in the Amazon frontier. Many determinants in widely varying weights are active in different places, and any generalization would be simplistic, as land markets are so poorly integrated on the frontier.

Land prices should be compared to the returns to land in agriculture in each location to ascertain whether colonists are covering the opportunity cost of frontier farming in the land market. Unfortunately, it is difficult to measure the return to land, because factor remuneration is mixed with land rent. Open access conditions on a frontier further complicate the issue, as the price of land in relatively remote locations is, theoretically, zero. An added problem is that landed property rights have traditionally been poorly defined or poorly enforced in the Amazon. Much of the basin has been exploited under ambiguous titling concessions by activities that are focused less on the land than on the forest covering it. This, of course, is the case in extraction, whether in forests (for example, rubber tapping, gathering and logging) or rivers (prospecting, fishing and so forth). The patchwork effect of haphazard land titling has only confused matters even further, making it practically impossible to measure directly the real productive returns to land at the frontier. The next section, therefore, will look at indirect indicators of such returns.

9.4.4.   Productivity, Land Use, and Agricultural Prices

The returns to land depend on the fertility of the soil, the intensity of land use, the productivity of other factors, and prices of agricultural products (see Tables 9.4 to 9.9). Total quantum productivity (Table 9.5) adds together kilograms of all crops and divides by harvested area. In the course of this study, however, this measure has been considered flawed as an indicator of land productivity, because Pacal's extremely high average productivity, largely based on its production of sugar cane, an extremely bulky product, distorts total averages. The distribution of annual yields of rice, corn and coffee (Table 9.6), however, indicates interesting variations in productivity. Overall, productivity increased, with the greatest increases in Pacal (especially coffee) and Mutum, although there were some declines in Anapu/Pacajá and Alta Floresta-Paranaíta (rice). In several cases, considerable gains occurred over the ten-year period, even in temporary crops. Such gains may indicate that, as farmers gain experience, they learn to identify the best soil in their properties and acquire seeds and adopt technologies most suitable for local conditions. Productivity gains are to be expected, of course, for perennial crops, such as coffee or cocoa, as trees mature. The significance of the general increase is considerable. It shows that, contrary to widespread belief, productivity has *not* tended to decline in the sampled locations.

The average productivity of the sample also compared well with national averages. The few cases of constant or declining productivity, such as in Alta Floresta, Paranaíta or Anapu/Pacajá, indicate a decrease in farming activity, the eradication of perennials (mainly coffee in Alta Floresta), and the conversion of most of the deforested land to pasture. Elsewhere, as in Monte Alegre, slash-and-burn shifting agriculture left behind low productivity crops and expanding fallow areas to which farmers rarely, if ever, returned.

Table 9.7 shows the low overall percentage of deforested land used for temporary and permanent crops in 1991 (32.5 percent). The highest intensity of land use was in Mutum (84.7 percent), followed by Pacal (39.8 percent), with the lowest in Monte Alegre (18.4 percent), where many very old plots have already been totally deforested and abandoned by their owners.

Table 9.4 indicates that agricultural prices during the 1980s were stagnant for basic temporary crops (rice and corn) and drastically declined for the main perennial (coffee). These figures are less than half those quoted at the international level, reflecting high transport costs to ports and to regional and national markets, as well as monopsonized frontier markets.

Thus during the 1980s, rates of return to land in the Amazon seem to have been rather poor in the face of strongly rising land prices. Agricultural prices were so low that, except for showcase locations, such as Pacal and Mutum, many farmers gave up on agriculture, sold their land, reaped capital gains, and moved on. Some went to other frontiers; others went to urban centers where they set themselves up in business with the proceeds of their land sales. In fact, many of the most successful colonists in the sample had done exactly the same in the past. They had moved from frontier to frontier, as had their parents and grandparents before them, buying and selling land as they went, in a process of itinerant accumulation. The less successful were even more likely to sell out, as rising land prices increased the opportunity cost of their low productivity farming.

9.5.   SUMMARY: LABOR, FINANCIAL AND LAND MARKETS ON THE FRONTIER

In the 1980s, frontier farming does not seem to have covered its opportunity cost in the land market, but these costs were covered in the labor and financial markets. The combination of high returns to capital and labor and low returns to land reduced the advantage to a farmer of remaining long on a specific plot of land, but not the advantage of continuing to farm in the frontier. Thus, high capital gains spurred turnover in old frontiers and financed the opening of new frontiers. Colonists who covered their opportunity costs in the land market seem to have done well during the inter-survey period (Pacal and Mutum). These farmers were the highly successful, who ploughed back their profits into expanding farms and, consequently, into deforestation.

Therefore, farmers who covered their opportunity costs were the very successful ones who invested in their farms, increased the size of their plots, and deforested at relatively high rates. Those who were not able to cover their opportunity costs sold their plots to newcomers and moved either to nearby villages or further into the forest in search of a place to continue farming and, consequently, deforesting at relatively low rates.

9.5.1. Who are the Newcomers?

There seems to be a two-stage process of frontier occupation in directed colonization projects that is not unlike the traditional frontier process in the rest of Brazil. Many original family farmers deforest, produce, leave, and are replaced by other farmers. Many are substituted by newcomers who are generally city dwellers looking for investment opportunities. Many others sell their lands to successful neighbors who are seeking to expand their holdings.

There is still much work to be done to identify who the newcomers are, where they came from, what their motives were for buying up frontier lands that had already appreciated significantly, and whatever other distinguishing characteristics they may have had when they bought the land. Tables 9.8 and 9.9 suggest that these newcomers, embedded in the 1991 total, were younger and significantly wealthier than survivors in high turnover locations (Anapu/Pacajá, Alta Floresta and Paranaíta). During the field research, it became evident that many were not farmers at all, but rather merchants, public servants, and other city dwellers.

9.5.2. Overall Performance of Colonists in the 1980s

In general, Amazonian colonists did well during the 1980s, not only in terms of being able to cover their opportunity costs in the labor and financial markets, but also in terms of the absolute values of their net worth (Table 9.9), which increased significantly from 1981 to 1991. Most (71 percent) expressed the opinion that they had improved their lot in life (*melhorou de vida*) by migrating to the frontier (Table 9.10), with the highest ratings occurring in low turnover locations (Mutum, Pacal, and Monte Alegre). An even higher proportion (76 percent) planned to stay on their present plots (Table 9.11), though only 41 percent planned to invest further in these plots (Table 9.12).

This apparent inconsistency – planning to stay on, but not willing to invest in agriculture – may indicate that in 1991 these farmers did not expect much from agriculture and planned to diversify into other activities. In fact, as Table 9.4 indicates, the evolution of agricultural prices during the 1980s was not promising. Except where agriculture was most productive (Mutum), gross agricultural income (Table 9.13) covered less than half of total household expenditures (Table 9.14). Many farmers, therefore, diversified into non-agricultural activities, such as wage employment, businesses, rents, and so on, to the extent that non-agricultural income (Table 9.15) became generally larger than agricultural income. In Alta Floresta and Paranaíta (higher turnover locations), agricultural income practically disappeared in 1991. This represents a drastic change from the previous decade, when nonagricultural income was, on average, 10 percent of total income. Non-monetary, or subsistence income was measured by imputing local market prices to all goods and services produced for purposes of family consumption or production, agricultural or non-agricultural (Table 9.16). This value also grew as a percentage of gross income (Table 9.17), from roughly 20 percent in 1981 to roughly 35 percent in 1991 (Ozório de Almeida 1992, Chapter 16).

Once current household consumption and productive expenditures were met, current net income levels (Table 9.18) were lower in Pará (sometimes negative) than in Mato Grosso projects. Net current income, in this sense, is somewhat meaningless, as it is net not only of productive expenditures, but also of household expenditures. Solvent farmers have positive net current income, and insolvent farmers have negative net current income, which, in turn, indicates whether there is net debt or net investment. High net income figures in Mato Grosso, in the face of declining crop area during the 1980s, indicate that these colonists were no longer mainly farmers, another important change relative to the past. Tables 9.19, 9.20 and 9.21 show, respectively, that one-quarter of the sample had owned land elsewhere before coming to the present location; all had farmed in at least one place before arrival; and the parents of 86 percent of the colonists had been farmers. Yet, as noted in Table 9.12, less than half of these farmers still intended to invest in their present plots either because plots were not sustaining family farming (negative net incomes imply indebtedness) or because the farmers were already thinking of moving on.

Investment is difficult to analyze, as it refers to dynamic decisions that go beyond current production. Net investment (Table 9.22) is defined as investment (all expenditures intended to increase net worth, after the current agricultural year) minus disinvestments (sale of all durables, reduction in stocks of physical and financial assets, and so on). Thus measured, investment turns out to be negative or very small in most of Pará's projects, but quite large in Mato Grosso's projects. This result is consistent with Pará's projects' negative and Mato Grosso's projects' positive net incomes. These differences in investment help explain the pattern of deforestation that was occurring in each location.

The major investment cost item in the Amazon frontier was deforestation. Chapter 8 showed that, in many projects, total deforestation by 1991 had eaten up more than 50 percent of total land held. In the public projects of Pará, total deforestation was less than in Mato Grosso's private projects. In the latter, the largest plots and the largest deforesters, by far, were located in Mutum, where much more land had been cleared than in any other sampled project by 1991. The pace of deforestation varied widely from place to place in 1991 alone (Table 9.23), being larger in private projects (64.15 hectares) than in public ones (6.93 hectares).

In sum, colonists with lower net agricultural incomes (as was generally the case in Pará), had less left over for investment and deforested less; colonists with higher net agricultural incomes (as was generally the case in Mato Grosso) had more left over for investment and deforested more. The source of income apparently matters, as farmers with relatively high non-agricultural income (as was the case in Alta Floresta) deforested less, despite the fact that they did have positive balances left over for investment.

Interestingly enough, fully 83 percent of Mutum's colonists, who deforested the most, declared that forest conservation is important (Table 9.24). Yet, only 4 percent of them perceived that loss of soil fertility might become a problem (Table 9.25), contrary to the rest of the sample (43 percent), and none of them practiced any kind of conservation technique, such as crop or area rotation, compared to 21 percent overall (Table 9.26). Those who were least worried about soil fertility and conservation were located in projects with the highest turnover: Anapu/Pacajá and Paranaíta. In Anapu/Pacajá, initial low soil fertility, rather than eventual loss of soil fertility, may have had an important association with the exodus observed in these locations and the ensuing high deforestation by newcomers. Elsewhere this is not observed.

Market conditions may also have had an important influence on colonists' performance. Insufficient storage facilities generally led farmers to sell 82 percent of their product during the first three months after harvest (Table 9.27). Distance to market (Table 9.28) and insufficient transportation facilities led them to sell 53 percent of total farm output at the farm gate (Table 9.29). Mutum and Monte Alegre, however, due to active cooperatives, sold only around 10 percent at the farm gate. For the same reason, agricultural credit was also greatest for Monte Alegre and especially for Mutum (Table 9.30).

Loans add to current resources if incoming flows are greater than debt repayment on former loans. If repayment burdens are greater, then current account resources must be used to service outstanding debt. Chronic indebtedness leads to dependence on local merchants and to various debt-peonage[2] conditions that frequently lead colonists to sell out and creditors to move in. This is perhaps the most important motive for turnover and, definitely, the hardest one to observe empirically, as farmers are loath to reveal their debts and their creditors. For this reason observed indebtedness is deceivingly small (Table 9.31). Negative net current incomes are a better indicator of indebtedness, as they indicate that farmers are covering their current expenditures either through borrowing from themselves (e.g., selling durable goods, such as cattle), or through borrowing from others. In either case the farmer is insolvent.

The capacity to escape informal sector indebtedness depends mainly on titled property ownership of the land (Table 9.32). One hundred percent of the colonists in Mutum held such title, as did 84 percent in the whole sample, certainly a much higher percentage than is typical of Amazonian small farmers.

Although many farmers had low absolute income levels, they still earned more than did half the labor force in Brazil. Their net worth, rates of accumulation, access to credit, productivity, and other economic indicators set them off as part of a small 'elite' within the Amazon. Since such benefits are attributable to the fact that they were in directed colonization projects, colonization may deserve re-evaluation for its social and distributive impact. Yet the resulting natural resources degradation due to Amazon colonization is considerable. It contributes to deforestation directly among the most successful colonists, and, indirectly, is a source of instability among the less successful farmers, spurring turnover on such plots.

9.6. CHANGES IN THE USE OF DEFORESTED LANDS DURING THE 1980s

It is unquestionable that the main cause of deforestation in the Amazon during the 1980s was not turnover, but either the high economic return to agriculture associated with particular land uses, or hoarding. The objective of this section is to show how deforested land was used in the sampled locations during the inter-survey period. Figure 9.1 shows the percentage changes in the use of deforested land during the 1980s. In Pará, there was an unambiguous decline in temporary subsistence crops (rice, corn and beans), and a simultaneous increase in permanent cultures (mainly coffee and cocoa). The percentage of deforested land occupied in pastures rose considerably in Anapu/Pacajá and in Pacal. Monte Alegre displays a decline in grazing activities during the inter-survey period. The land in *capoeira* (fallow, a secondary growth that consists of rough and shrubby vegetation) increased quite a lot in Monte Alegre, as large parts of the plots were abandoned, given that slash-and-burn agriculture caused irreversible damage to the soils (nutrient mining). Monte Alegre presents a worst-case scenario where deforestation does not pay off in the long run.

Except for Mutum, the inter-survey period in Mato Grosso was characterized by agricultural involution and an outstanding increase in

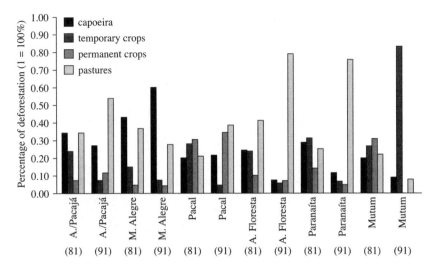

Figure 9.1. Deforestation and land use

grazing activities in the north. In Alta Floresta and Paranaíta, coffee plantations were burnt down and replaced by pastures. The area in *capoeira* and those previously destined for temporary and permanent crops were mostly converted to pasture. In Mutum, the area in *capoeira* decreased and permanent crops (mainly rice) disappeared, as land was completely converted into large soybean farms. While cattle ranching became a common activity all over the frontier, the amount of soybean planted in the Amazonian *cerrados* cannot be underestimated (Figure 9.2).

9.7. FARMERS' ECONOMIC DECISION-MAKING IN THE 1990s: RETAIN OR RELINQUISH THE PLOT?

Given the conditions described throughout this chapter, small farmers in the frontier must constantly make decisions on whether to sell or to keep their land and whether to hoard or to farm the soil. Much of the literature deals with the farmers' discount rate as an important determinant in their patterns of resource use. This section, however, discusses concrete economic factors upon which farmers base their decisions. It is not the intent here to analyze how expectations are formed; rather this section describes how such expectations inform the farmer's decision to continue or cease to farm his plot.

A frontier farmer in the Amazon faces three choices in a sales decision about his land: he may choose not to sell his farm and instead to use it

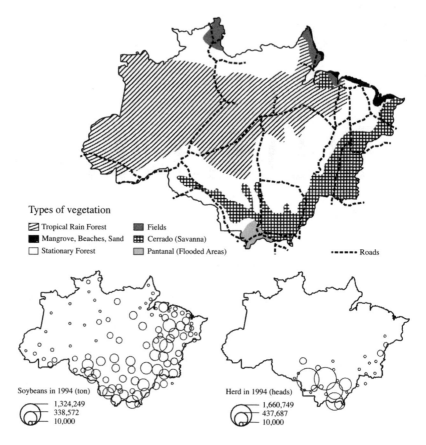

Figure 9.2.   Cattle and soybean by phytophysiognomy

productively; he may choose not to sell, but leave his plot idle, keeping it only as a store of value; or he may choose neither to farm nor to hoard, but to sell his land at the going market price. To deal with this variety of choices, the farmer must be able to discount, at the moment of his decision, the expected payoff of his choice. Thus his decision depends on the net present value of agricultural income (NPVA) and the discounted salvage value of land (NPVL).

The NPVA is the value today of the future income stream that can be generated by agricultural production, discounted according to the interest rate. The discounted salvage value of land, NPVL, is the value today of the land price per hectare at some future date, discounted at the appropriate rate. Farmers take past experience into account in their expectations regarding the evolution of land prices in the future. Therefore, in computing the net present value of land in 1991, it is assumed that farmers used the same yearly rate of increase in prices that had occurred during the 1980s. The NPVA and NPVL were thus computed for a ten-year period – the 1990s – by discounting agricultural income and current land prices by the relevant rate. In this case, the opportunity cost of capital (the interest rate on savings certificates) was taken to be the appropriate discount rate.

Table 9.33 displays interesting results. By adding both NPVA and NPVL, the farmer can determine the overall net present value of his plot (NPV) and compare it to the going market price of land. If the NPV is higher than the value of his plot, the farmer is likely to keep the plot; otherwise, he will probably sell it.

Comparing the NPV to the going market price of land, in half the projects farmers would be better off selling the land. Not surprisingly, this would occur only in locations where the NPVL exceeds the NPVA, that is, where returns to agriculture are not keeping up with land prices. Comparing the NPVA to survival rates on plots yields the following result: survival rates are lower in areas of relatively low NPVA. Therefore, high turnover on plots is likely to be associated with low returns to farming.

In Mato Grosso, land sales peaked in Alta Floresta and Paranaíta, both areas of agricultural 'involution', encroaching pastures, rapid urbanization and rapidly appreciating land prices. In Pará, land sales peaked in Anapu-Pacajá. In that particular location, the NPVA and NPVL were approximately the same, US$33 and US$31, respectively. The average price of land in Anapu-Pacajá was US$59 per hectare, making NPV only slightly higher than the price of land (US$64 compared with US$59, respectively). As land prices continue to appreciate rapidly in this area, farmers are, in fact, selling out.

For those farmers who choose not to sell, that is, whose NPV exceeds the going price of land, the question is whether to produce. A farmer is likely to produce only if the NPVA exceeds the NPVL, meaning that his discounted income stream from agriculture is greater that his expected returns from keeping his land idle. In this case, the farmer has motivation to produce; otherwise his plot will remain idle. The results of this section are summarized in the following matrix:

Factors that inform a farmer's decision to retain or relinquish his plot

	NPV>P	NPV<P
NPVA>NPVL	Keep land productive	Sell the land
NPVA<NPVL	Keep land idle (hoard)	Sell the land

This simple exercise confirms that farming in the Amazon is unlikely to be successful unless land productivity and, consequently, agricultural income keep up with land prices. In high turnover locations, the NPVA is not sufficiently large to keep farmers on their plots and motivate production. In other words, the price of land is still higher than the expected income stream from agriculture.

Throughout the 1990s, therefore, the rational behavior of many frontier farmers in the Amazon have would been to sell the land at the going market price. This is probably what happened, since intraregional out-migrations of the rural population increased during the decade. The implication of this result for the conservation of unoccupied areas of rain forest is evident. Policies should aim at keeping the net present value of agricultural income level with and prices. If the gap between agricultural incomes and land prices becomes too large due to rising land values, the NPVL is likely to rise beyond the NPVA, in which case it will pay not to produce anything at all but only to keep land as a store of value (i.e., in areas where NPV>P). This would further fuel the speculation under way in the frontier land market, accelerate migrations to new frontiers and, consequently, increase deforestation in unopened areas.

9.8. CONCLUSION

The relationship between turnover and deforestation is not a widespread phenomenon as claimed in the literature. In colonization projects originally intended for the poor, many small farmers leave because they can reap capital gains from selling their land. Those who sell the land and move may not be poor at all. Rather, they may be farmers who view itinerancy as a means to accumulate capital. Deforestation is a part of this strategy, as private economic benefits are unquestionable given the government policies discussed in Chapter 3 (e.g., clearing land is one of the means that farmers can secure title; deforested lands are worth more than forested areas).

Although farmers may cover their opportunity costs in the labor and capital markets and consume at a level three or four times that of the minimum wage, this does not mean that the majority of them are well off in any absolute sense. Houses are rustic, health care is dismal, schooling is minimal, and transport and communications are sorely insufficient. Even if they are better off than the majority of the Brazilian labor force at the same skill level, most farmers are still poor and will only settle down in their current plots if it becomes worthwhile to do so, that is, if they cover their opportunity cost in the land market.

Given the pressure of inflated real estate markets on the frontier, covering the opportunity costs of frontier agriculture becomes possible only if land becomes highly productive. During the 1980s, although turnover was high in all sampled projects (compared to indicators in the rest of Brazil), high productivity frontiers displayed relatively higher survival rates. Conversely, low and/or declining productivity frontiers had low survival rates. Even some colonists with relatively high incomes and net worth withdrew from agriculture and converted their lands into pasture or sold their plots and moved away. Frontier land markets fueled high turnover among all but the best farming communities. It is worth noting that even in view of the economic bust of the 1980s, particularly for the agricultural sector, the data provides no generalized evidence of deforested lands being completely wasted (except for Monte Alegre where fallow increased substantially during the 1980s). The economic use of deforested lands signals the resilience and economic viability of Amazonian agriculture and ranching.

In high turnover locations, those who moved in, and those who remained behind, became disenchanted with agriculture. Low agricultural prices, poor marketing, scarce credit facilities and weak institutions led them to diversify into pasture and non-farming activities. They showed concern about soil fertility, professed to practice some conservation techniques, planted little, and deforested little (about 3 percent of their holdings per year). In low turnover locations, agriculture boomed, with little concern about conservation or loss of soil fertility. Farm sizes expanded by incorporation of new areas, credit was available, and deforestation proceeded at around 20 percent per year. Thus, on the one hand, high turnover rates in most places are associated with low deforestation, the withdrawal from agriculture and the conversion of deforested lands to pasture. On the other hand, low turnover seems to be associated with agricultural expansion and increasing deforestation.

In 1991, the price of land in many locations was higher than the overall net present value (NPV) of potential earnings in any given plot, prompting farmers to sell. Where the NPV was higher than land prices, but returns to land (NPVL) were still higher than returns to agricultural production (NPVA), a farmer kept his plot but did not farm it, holding it as a store of value. Land sales (which occur when NPV is lower than land values) and speculation (which occurs when NPV is higher than land values, but the NPVA is lower than the NPVL) seem to be the essential causes of high turnover in Amazonian settlements.

Thus, the private benefits of colonization (indicated by relatively more intensive agriculture and falling turnover) per unit of environmental loss (indicated by the number of hectares deforested) evolved differently throughout the frontier. In low-productivity projects, farming was not intensive and turnover was high. In these projects, however, the environmental cost of settlement may be considered relatively low, as only small areas were deforested (despite the extensive practices). On the other hand, in high-productivity projects, farming was relatively more intensive and turnover was relatively low. Deforestation, however, rose at high rates (despite the intensive practices).

The evidence presented in this chapter indicates that in most places deforestation is the outcome of high productivity farming and is not associated with turnover. Therefore, while improved farming may reduce turnover, it accelerates deforestation in the current location.

Finally, it is worth comparing these results with the five studies discussed early in the chapter. The chapter provides corroborating evidence for Moran's (1989) argument that productivity is negatively related to turnover. It does not support the findings of FAO/UNDP's (1992) study which reports that incomes and the permanence of farmers on plots are unrelated. So far as the Jones et al. (1992) study is concerned, this chapter does not support the argument that there is no relationship between length of stay on plot and productivity. Further, it does not support Schneider's (1992) and Alston et al.'s (1999) argument that turnover is associated with the lack of formal property rights, as most of the farmers in the sample had definitive title to the property and turnover occurred in spite of this.

NOTE

1. Most of this chapter was drafted during the years I spent at the World Bank and, later, at the University of Texas. I am grateful for the support I received from colleagues at both institutions.
2. When colonists are 'locked' into debt with creditors. Colonists generally pay this debt with labor or give up their plots for creditors.

DESCRIPTIVE TABLES

Table 9.1.   Imputed wages (average number of minimum wages)

	1981	1991
Para	1.1	2.76
Anapu-Pacajá		2.49 [a]
Monte Alegre		1.19 [a]
Pacal		3.54 [a]
Mato Grosso		3.83
Alta Floresta		1.69 [a]
Paranaíta		1.28 [a]
Mutum		19.54 [a]
Total	1.1	3.23

Note: Lowercase letters: The presence of a common letter superscript indicates that there is no difference at the 10 percent level of significance between locations (within columns).

Table 9.2. *Annual wage per family worker (average amount of US dollars – thousands)*

	1981	1991
Para	1.7	4.3
Anapu-Pacajá		2.2 [a]
Monte Alegre		1.0 [a]
Pacal		7.0 [a b]
Mato Grosso		3.5
Alta Floresta		1.5 [a]
Paranaíta		1.3 [a]
Mutum		19.0 [b]
Total	1.7	3.9

Note: The presence of a common letter superscript indicates that there is no difference at the 10 percent level of significance between locations (within columns).

Table 9.3. *Monthly accumulation (percent)*

	1981	1991
Para	2.0	2.3
Anapu-Pacajá		2.4
Monte Alegre		1.9
Pacal		2.4
Mato Grosso		2.3
Alta Floresta		2.5
Paranaíta		1.5
Mutum		2.8
Total	2.0	2.3

Table 9.4.　*Prices for crops and land (crops: average US dollars/kg; land:*
average US dollars/ha)

	Rice		Corn		Coffee		Land	
	1981	1991	1981	1991	1981	1991	1981	1991
Para	0.13	0.12	0.09	0.14	1.13	0.17	80	131
Anapu-Pacajá	0.13	0.12	0.09	0.14	0.90	0.17	20	59
Monte Alegre	0.14		0.10				70	87
Pacal	0.14	0.14	0.09	0.14	1.16	0.17	130	248
Mato Grosso	0.13	0.11	0.10	0.09	0.38	0.29	290	308
Alta Floresta	0.13	0.10	0.10	0.09	0.38	0.29	460	258
Paranaíta*		0.14						
Mutum	0.14	0.11	0.13	0.08			220	398
Total	0.13	0.12	0.10	0.12	0.76	0.23	190	219

Note:* With one exception, all Paranaíta means are included in Alta Floresta means.

Table 9.5.　*Total agricultural productivity in 1991 (thousands of kg/ha)*

	1991
Para	22.1
Anapu-Pacajá	0.6
Monte Alegre	15.4
Pacal	36.7
Mato Grosso	0.8
Alta Floresta	0.3
Paranaíta	1.5
Mutum	1.8
Total	14.1

Table 9.6.   Annual yields (average kg/ha)

	Rice 1981	Rice 1991	Corn 1981	Corn 1991	Coffee 1981	Coffee 1991
Para	1077	1402	844	1301	307	1816
Anapu-Pacajá	1068	1007	704	902	415	658
Monte Alegre	1010	1359	941	1500		
Pacal	1097	1765	859	1500	200	2975
Mato Grosso	1352	1671	1255	1824	550	741
Alta Floresta	1541	1390	1527	1573	696	933
Paranaíta*		1683				
Mutum	1244	1861	1230	2400	485	
Total	1166	1502	1005	1563	396	1278

Note: * With one exception, all Paranaíta means are included in Alta Floresta means.

Table 9.7.   Deforested land used for agriculture in 1991 (percentage)

	1991
Para	29.8 [x]
Anapu-Pacajá	23.2 [a]
Monte Alegre	18.4 [b]
Pacal	39.8 [a]
Mato Grosso	36.2 [y]
Alta Floresta	26.7 [ab]
Paranaíta	24.7 [ab]
Mutum	84.7 [ab]
Total	32.5

Note: The presence of a common letter superscript indicates that there is no difference at the 10 percent level of significance between locations or states (within columns); a,b: between locations; x,y: between states.

Table 9.8. Age of head of household (years)

	1981 Total	1991 Survivors	1991 Total
Para	45 A	53 x	50 A
Anapu-Pacajá	45 a	52 a	47 ab
Monte Alegre	48 a	54 a	52 a
Pacal	44 b	52 a	51 a
Mato Grosso	42 A	49 y	47 A
Alta Floresta	42 ab	50 ab	48 ab
Paranaíta*	45 a	53 a	47 ab
Mutum	36 b	41 b	42 b
Total	44 A	51 B	49 AB

Note: *Uppercase letters*: The presence of a common letter superscript indicates that there is a difference at the 10 percent level of significance in the following cases (within columns): A: 1981 total compared with 1991 total; B: 1991 Survivors compared with 1991 Total.
Lowercase letter: The presence of a common letter superscript indicates that there is no difference at the 10 percent level of significance in the following cases (within columns): a,b: between locations; x,y: between states.

Table 9.9. Net worth (thousands of US dollars)

	1981 Total	1991 Survivors	1991 Total
Para	29.5 b	40.7 x	45.8 x
Anapu-Pacajá	15.0 b	15.3 c	36.6 c
Monte Alegre	37.0 bc	42.8 bc	33.5 c
Pacal	38.1 cd	50.1 bc	57.7 c
Mato Grosso	78.0 A	164.5 y	176.5 Ay
Alta Floresta	54.0 Acd	64.1 bc	106.3 Acd
Paranaíta*	39.3 Acd	63.4 bc	106.0 Abc
Mutum	264.2 Aa	564.1 a	513.0 Aa
Total	51.6 A	93.7	101.4 A

Note: *Uppercase letter*: The presence of a common letter superscript indicates that there is a difference at the 10 percent level of significance in 1981 total compared with 1991 total (within columns).
Lowercase letter: The presence of a common letter superscript indicates that there is no difference at the 10 percent level of significance in the following cases (within columns): a,b: between locations; x,y: between states.

Table 9.10.   Perceived improvement in quality of life in 1991 (percentage)

	1991
Para	75 [x]
Anapu-Pacajá	72 [ab]
Monte Alegre	90 [a]
Pacal	70 [ab]
Mato Grosso	66 [y]
Alta Floresta	63 [ab]
Paranaíta	50 [b]
Mutum	91 [a]
Total	71

Note: The presence of a common letter superscript indicates that there is no difference at the 10 percent level of significance between locations or states (within columns); a,b: between locations; x,y: between states.

Table 9.11.   Farmers who planned to remain on the same plot, 1991 (percentage)

	1991
Para	81 [x]
Anapu-Pacajá	82 [ab]
Monte Alegre	93 [a]
Pacal	76 [ab]
Mato Grosso	69 [y]
Alta Floresta	65 [b]
Paranaíta	63 [b]
Mutum	96 [a]
Total	76

Note: The presence of a common letter superscript indicates that there is no difference at the 10 percent level of significance between locations or states (within columns); a,b: between locations; x,y: between states.

Table 9.12.   Farmers who planned to invest on the plot, 1991 (percentage)

	1991
Para	43
Anapu-Pacajá	58
Monte Alegre	26
Pacal	39
Mato Grosso	37
Alta Floresta	33
Paranaíta	37
Mutum	39
Total	41

Table 9.13.   Gross income from agriculture in 1991 (thousands of US dollars)

	1991
Para	2.9 [x]
Anapu-Pacajá	1.8 [b]
Monte Alegre	2.7 [b]
Pacal	3.8 [b]
Mato Grosso	8.1 [y]
Alta Floresta	0.9 [b]
Paranaíta	0.4 [b]
Mutum	43.3 [a]
Total	5.1

Note: The presence of a common letter superscript indicates that there is no difference at the 10 percent level of significance between locations or states (within columns); a,b: between locations; x,y: between states.

Table 9.14.   Total expenditures (thousands of US dollars)

	1991
Para	8.9
Anapu-Pacajá	2.8 [a]
Monte Alegre	16.9 [a]
Pacal	9.5 [a]
Mato Grosso	15.3
Alta Floresta	9.5 [a]
Paranaíta	9.2 [b]
Mutum	47.2 [a]
Total	11.7

Note: The presence of a common letter superscript indicates that there is no difference at the 10 percent level of significance between locations (within columns).

Table 9.15.   Net nonagricultural income (thousands of US dollars)

	1991
Para	4.4 [x]
Anapu-Pacajá	3.5
Monte Alegre	3.1
Pacal	5.5
Mato Grosso	27.8 [y]
Alta Floresta	13.0
Paranaíta	34.9
Mutum	71.8
Total	14.7

Note: The presence of a common letter superscript (x,y) indicates that there is difference at the 10 percent level of significance between states.

Table 9.16.　Net subsistence income in 1991 (thousands of US dollars)

	1991
Para	0.4
Anapu-Pacajá	−0.05
Monte Alegre	−0.8
Pacal	1.1
Mato Grosso	11.5
Alta Floresta	23.8
Paranaíta	−2.1
Mutum	4.4
Total	5.5

Table 9.17.　Gross income in 1991 (thousands of US dollars)

	1991
Para	12.2 [x]
Anapu-Pacajá	9.4 [a]
Monte Alegre	9.6 [a]
Pacal	15.2 [a]
Mato Grosso	67.1 [y]
Alta Floresta	57.5 [ab]
Paranaíta	46.0 [a]
Mutum	156.5 [b]
Total	36.5

Note: The presence of a common letter superscript indicates that there is no difference at the 10 percent level of significance between locations or states (within columns); a,b: between locations; x,y: between states.

Table 9.18.   Net income in 1991 (thousands of US dollars)

	1991
Para	-1.4^x
Anapu-Pacajá	2.5
Monte Alegre	-12.0
Pacal	0.8
Mato Grosso	32.2^y
Alta Floresta	28.2
Paranaita	24.1
Mutum	72.3
Total	14.0

Note: The presence of a common letter superscript (x,y) indicates that there is no difference at the 10 percent level of significance between states.

Table 9.19.   Farmers who have been landowners in the past (prior to 1991) (thousands of US dollars)

	1991
Para	22^x
Anapu-Pacajá	35^a
Monte Alegre	7^b
Pacal	20^{ab}
Mato Grosso	30^y
Alta Floresta	34^{ab}
Paranaíta	31^{ab}
Mutum	25^{ab}
Total	26

Note: The presence of a common letter superscript indicates that there is no difference at the 10 percent level of significance between locations or states (within columns); a,b: between locations; x,y: between states.

Table 9.20. *Itinerancy (prior to 1991) (number of stops prior to arrival on current plot)*

	1991
Para	1.4 [x]
Anapu-Pacajá	1.7 [abc]
Monte Alegre	0.8 [c]
Pacal	1.3 [bc]
Mato Grosso	2.2 [y]
Alta Floresta	2.3 [a]
Paranaíta	2.1 [ab]
Mutum	1.6 [abc]
Total	1.7

Note: The presence of a common letter superscript indicates that there is no difference at the 10 percent level of significance between locations or states (within columns); a,b,c: between locations; x,y: between states.

Table 9.21. *Farmers whose parents were farmers (1991) (percent)*

	1991
Para	86
Anapu-Pacajá	89
Monte Alegre	84
Pacal	85
Mato Grosso	82
Alta Floresta	82
Paranaíta	92
Mutum	96
Total	86

Table 9.22.   Net investment in 1991 (thousands of US dollars)

	1991
Para	−1.3 [x]
Anapu-Pacajá	2.5
Monte Alegre	−11.8
Pacal	0.9
Mato Grosso	32.4 [y]
Alta Floresta	28.4
Paranaíta	24.2
Mutum	72.8
Total	14.1

Note: The presence of a common letter superscript (x,y) indicates that there is no difference at the 10 percent level of significance between states.

Table 9.23.   Deforestation in current year (1991) (hectares)

	1991
Para	6.93 [x]
Anapu-Pacajá	3.88 [b]
Monte Alegre	3.72 [b]
Pacal	9.75 [b]
Mato Grosso	64.15 [y]
Alta Floresta	3.95 [b]
Paranaíta	3.46 [b]
Mutum	244.05 [a]
Total	25.63

Note: The presence of a common letter superscript indicates that there is no difference at the 10 percent level of significance between locations or states (within columns); a,b: between locations; x,y: between states.

Table 9.24.   Farmers who reported that forest conservation is good (1991)
(percent)

	1991
Para	68 [x]
Anapu-Pacajá	82 [ab]
Monte Alegre	56 [b]
Pacal	64 [ab]
Mato Grosso	82 [y]
Alta Floresta	76 [ab]
Paranaíta	89 [a]
Mutum	83 [a]
Total	74

Note: The presence of a common letter superscript indicates that there is no difference at the 10 percent level of significance between locations or states (within columns); a,b: between locations; x,y: between states.

Table 9.25.   Farmers who reported loss in soil fertility (1991) (percent)

	1991
Para	35 [x]
Anapu-Pacajá	31 [bc]
Monte Alegre	40 [ab]
Pacal	35 [b]
Mato Grosso	54 [y]
Alta Floresta	67 [a]
Paranaíta	60 [ab]
Mutum	4 [c]
Total	43

Note: The presence of a common letter superscript indicates that there is no difference at the 10 percent level of significance between locations or states (within columns); a,b,c: between locations; x,y: between states.

Table 9.26. Farmers who reported employing environmental conservation agricultural techniques in 1991 (percent)

	1991
Para	20
Anapu-Pacajá	14 bc
Monte Alegre	23 bc
Pacal	23 bc
Mato Grosso	20
Alta Floresta	16 bc
Paranaíta	25 b
Mutum	0 c
Total	20

Note: The presence of a common letter superscript indicates that there is no difference at the 10 percent level of significance between locations or states (within columns); a,b,c: between locations; x,y: between states.

Table 9.27. Product sold after first harvest (1991) (percent)

	1991
Para	82
Anapu-Pacajá	79
Monte Alegre	68
Pacal	86
Mato Grosso	81
Alta Floresta	83
Paranaíta	78
Mutum	77
Total	82

Table 9.28.   Distance to nearest market center in 1991 (minutes)

	1991
Para	32.0 [x]
Anapu-Pacajá	33.3 [ab]
Monte Alegre	46.7 [a]
Pacal	24.5 [bc]
Mato Grosso	25.2 [y]
Alta Floresta	24.3 [bc]
Paranaíta	27.9 [bc]
Mutum	30.9 [abc]
Total	29.2

Note: The presence of a common letter superscript indicates that there is no difference at the 10 percent level of significance between locations or states (within columns); a,b,c: between locations; x,y: between states.

Table 9.29.   Product sold at farm gate in 1991 (percentage)

	1991
Para	58 [x]
Anapu-Pacajá	53 [a]
Monte Alegre	11 [b]
Pacal	76 [a]
Mato Grosso	44 [y]
Alta Floresta	60 [a]
Paranaíta	67 [a]
Mutum	9 [b]
Total	53

Note: The presence of a common letter superscript indicates that there is no difference at the 10 percent level of significance between locations or states (within columns); a,b: between locations; x,y: between states.

Table 9.30.   Farmers who received agricultural credit in 1991 (percentage)

	1991
Para	3 [x]
Anapu-Pacajá	0 [c]
Monte Alegre	7 [bc]
Pacal	3 [c]
Mato Grosso	11 [y]
Alta Floresta	1 [c]
Paranaíta	3 [c]
Mutum	52 [a]
Total	7

Note: The presence of a common letter superscript indicates that there is no difference at the 10 percent level of significance between locations or states (within columns); a,b,c: between locations; x,y: between states.

Table 9.31.   Net debt in 1991 (thousands of US dollars)

	1991
Para	0.08
Anapu-Pacajá	0.03
Monte Alegre	0.2
Pacal	0.02
Mato Grosso	0.2
Alta Floresta	0.2
Paranaíta	0.007
Mutum	0.5
Total	0.1

Table 9.32.   Farmers who have title to the plot (1991) (percentage)

	1991
Para	82
Anapu-Pacajá	75 ab
Monte Alegre*	–
Pacal	86 b
Mato Grosso	87
Alta Floresta	82 ab
Paranaíta	86 ab
Mutum	100 a
Total	84

Notes:
The presence of a common letter superscript indicates that there is no difference at the 10 percent level of significance between locations.
*Data not available.

Table 9.33.   Net present values and land values in 1991, and survival rates
(average kg/ha)

	NPVA	NPVL	NPV	Land values	Survival rates
Para	89.2	69	158.2	131	77.2%
Anapu-Pacajá	33	31.1	64.1	59	59.5%
Monte Alegre	131.7	45.8	177.5	87	75.7%
Pacal	176.4	130.6	307	248	87.3%
Mato Grosso	145	162.2	160	258	61.9%
Alta Floresta	24.1	135.9	160	258	64.1%
Paranaíta*					55.8%
Mutum	376.8	209.6	586.4	398	66.7%
Total	129.6	115.3	244.2	219	71.3%

Notes:
NPVA and NPVL are calculated using data from Tables 9.13 (income from agriculture) and 9.4 (land values), respectively. The NPVA was obtained by dividing agricultural incomes by total farmed area; the result is shown in dollars per hectare, then dividing that ratio by $(1+r)t$ for each year over the 1981–91 time span. The discount rate used was 0.06 (the yearly interest rate on savings certificate, which is the farmer's opportunity cost in the financial market). NPVL is the salvage value of the plot at the end of the period under consideration. From Table 9.4 $[(price91/price81)/t] \times 100 - 100 = g$, the average geometric growth rate of land prices during the 1980s. Then, $NPVL = (price91 \times g)/(1+r)t$.
*Mean land prices in Paranaíta are included in Alta Floresta's.

10. Policy implications and recommendations

10.1. INTRODUCTION

How many of the assumptions that we rely on at a very deep level in theorizing about Amazonian deforestation are truly essential and how many of them can be relaxed and still potentially yield a world that appears close to ours? This book argues that most of the current assumptions about Amazon deforestation today are fundamentally driven by what is known and assumed to be known about the past, which do not necessarily reflect the forces behind current deforestation dynamics. The pace at which the agricultural frontier moves is very fast and the understanding of the factors that may have triggered deforestation in any one period is very likely to become obsolete before policy to contain it is designed and implemented. Therefore, the actions to contain deforestation in the Amazon have always been a step behind current developments.

This book has looked into the turnover hypothesis and has rejected it as an important cause of deforestation. Although government-induced inter-regional migrations to the Amazon were associated with the opening of new frontiers during the 1970s, during the 1980s this ceased to exist. By the end of the 1980s, intra-regional migrations of small farmers continued, but the bulk of deforestation was carried out by a stable core population of large farmers. Turnover of colonization plots is, therefore, overemphasized as a root cause of deforestation in the literature.

This study also argues that during the 1980s, deforestation was greater than expected, given that policy incentives enhanced the private benefits to clear land. The combination of high private benefits among large farmers associated with the high social costs of excessive deforestation has led to a *win-lose* scenario. Current deforestation rates will slow down only if economic policies for forest conservation are focused on changing the behavior of large and successful farmers in consolidated frontiers.

10.2.   LESSONS LEARNED

For a long time, policy makers and analysts have theorized that deforestation was of the type *lose-lose*, in which turnover would be the result of low private benefits that were accrued at the expense of the forest. This study provides evidence that private economic returns to agriculture in the Amazon are quite high, although these returns are associated with relatively high social costs in terms of excessive deforestation among large farmers. Therefore, deforestation is of the type *win-lose*.

This finding in itself may not seem surprising *today* as we can easily observe large-scale agriculture eating up the rain forest. However, there is no previous record in the literature that can safely claim that a *win-lose* scenario goes back to the early days of colonization. For decades, we have believed that the assumptions of the turnover hypothesis were correct without ever questioning them. The findings of this study show that policies to contain deforestation and turnover chased the wrong targets for more than two decades: low agricultural income, bad soils, land re-concentration and bad infrastructure were assumed to expel small farmers from their plots and lead to the bulk of deforestation.

Turnover on farming plots was seen as the 'fate' of peasant farmers and not understood as a rational behavior of economic agents. The decision to deforest or conserve and migrate or stay was as rational during the 1980s as it is today and has always depended on the relative economic returns (measured in this book by the opportunity costs of farmers in capital, labor and land markets). While, on the one hand, the private economic gains from deforestation emerged from positive rent and speculation in land markets, on the other hand, the lack of policy enforcement (and the absolute certainty of impunity) greatly reduced transaction costs to farmers. The combination of these elements is the true source of deforestation that policy makers and opinion formers need to address to deal with the *win-lose* scenario.

The prevalence of a *win-lose* scenario requires a shift in policy paradigm. Deforestation, or rather, the use of deforested lands, is a highly profitable business. This study shows that deforestation rewards larger landowners, as lands cleared of forests are attributed a higher value than those with standing trees regardless of whether the deforested lands are used or not. In theory, the current legislation and changes on the land taxation systems for unused deforested land has removed these perverse incentives. In practice, however, the main threat to farmers with regard to unoccupied forested land is invasion by the landless and the anticipated possibility of expropriation for agrarian reform. Law enforcement or the tax system are secondary because government is known as a lethargic entity and taxes are easily evaded (since land taxes are based on the size of the property *declared* by the farmers). Here is the point where strong institutions that shape private behavior (rules that effectively guarantee property rights and enforce contracts) are necessary for long-lasting conservation efforts.

There are very few examples in the literature that show that Amazon deforestation is of the type *win-lose*. Margulis (2001) and Chomitz and Thomas (2001) demonstrate that this scenario holds in the case of cattle ranching, almost entirely because of the low transaction costs involved in clearing land. Ozório de Almeida and Campari (1996) and Schneider (1995) recognize the *win-lose* scenario among Amazonian farmers and validate the hypothesis that they behave as rational economic agents that capitalized on agricultural and land markets. This study hopes to contribute to this scarce literature by arguing that unless old approaches to regional development are dismissed entirely, that is, a *lose-lose* situation, and a new paradigm is internalized by analysts and policy makers, that is a *win-lose* scenario, current trends in deforestation are unlikely to be reversed.

10.2.1. The Turnover Hypothesis

Although turnover rates varied a lot across the colonization projects analysed in this book, these rates were all quite high compared to the ones reported for the rest of Brazil. While some aspects of the turnover hypothesis held well in two locations (Anapu-Pacajá and Alta Floresta), turnover did not seem to be associated with land re-concentration and high deforestation in most projects. In fact, most pioneer settlers have demonstrated relatively good performance in agriculture over time; however, deforestation among them occurred at an accelerated pace. The relative success of pioneer colonists challenges the turnover hypothesis, which predicted a somewhat bleak future for them, where a form of low-level production/deforestation equilibrium would take place. In that regard, the economic benefits of colonization for pioneer settlers are more long-lasting than was once believed, although it remains questionable whether the environmental costs associated with deforestation, if internalized, would justify such benefits. This study shows that, contrary to widespread belief, a considerable share of the deforested lands are being used productively and not being wasted.

10.2.2. Turnover, Land Markets and Deforestation

Small farmers in the Amazon have typically farmed along many migratory stops. Many were squatters and tenants who moved from farm to farm, living off lands that were never theirs. Some were landowners who bought, deforested, sold and profited from successive plots. Relatively high returns to household labor and capital, and relatively low returns to land, have kept small farmers moving, shifting the frontier forward.

During the 1980s, land prices in consolidated frontiers rose beyond the growth of agricultural productivity mainly because of an inflationary economy in general and a prospering urban frontier economy in particular (in 1991, two-thirds of the Amazonian population was urban). Physical and social infrastructure increased, while local public and private sectors grew rapidly. Rising land prices set off different reactions among farmers. Many original colonists sold their plots, reaped capital gains and moved from old to new frontiers within the Amazon, which they proceeded to deforest and quit once again. Others held on to their lands, but diversified out of agriculture. The more urban groups held on to land as a hedge against inflation. Finally, highly successful farmers neither moved out of their lands nor abandoned agriculture. On the contrary, they expanded their holdings and increased their agricultural production. They also deforested their lands at an accelerated pace. Thus, the more successful farmers tended to continue to deforest where they were, while the less successful ones possibly deforested wherever they relocated. Meanwhile, some of the land originally cleared of forest for farming was added to the net worth of a non-farming urban middle class.

10.2.3.   Productivity, Agricultural Income, Turnover and Deforestation

During the 1980s, projects that displayed constant or declining productivity were associated with high turnover, though deforestation was rather low. Only in those projects with increasing productivity was turnover low, but deforestation was high. There are different underlying motives for deforestation that change in different circumstances. In projects that exhibited productivity gains during the 1980s, farmers were able to cover their opportunity costs in land, labor and capital markets. Increasing agricultural income in these projects, then, should stimulate the demand for land, rewarding extensive agriculture (given the availability of land, it wouldn't pay to intensify its use) and increase deforestation; increasing land prices should decrease the demand for land and reduce deforestation. In frontiers that exhibited productivity losses, speculative motives for holding land dominated productive ones. In these places, farmers did not cover their opportunity costs, which would lead to inverse outcomes. Increasing agricultural income in face of productivity losses would reduce deforestation, and increasing land prices would stimulate deforestation.

10.2.4. Market and Institutional Failure

Frontier institutions and market structures seem to have stimulated deforestation and discouraged good farming practices. Land distribution agencies (Institute of Colonization and Agrarian Reform and state-level agencies) have not proven capable of handling titling needs or choosing suitable places to establish colonization projects. Marketing of Amazonian agricultural products and transport facilities have been poor, markets incipient and concentrated, and agricultural prices depressed. Availability of credit to large landholders during the 1980s, although declining, still made forest clearing less costly, because the value of land prices rises with such clearing, meaning that collateral subsequently increases. Taxation on deforestation, or on the capital gains derived from land speculation, is practically non-existent. Therefore, the economic conditions necessary to contain deforestation and promote stability among the rural population are not there. Yet, considering the same data set used for this study, Ozório de Almeida and Campari (1996) show that settlers have proven to be sensitive to economic conditions, as their response to agricultural income and land prices accounts for most of the variation in deforestation in colonization projects.

Ozório de Almeida and Campari (1996) also show that total deforestation (since arrival on plot) depends significantly on farmers' backgrounds: where they came from, the value of initial capital, whether their parents were farmers, whether they were landowners before, and how many migratory stops they made prior to their arrival on the current site. Current deforestation (during 1991, after a frontier consolidates) depends significantly on the characteristics of farmers' present locations: whether they are on a public or a private project, how distant they are from markets, and what their market and storage conditions are. It is reported that individual variations, such as age, family size, time on plot, attitudes and plans and expectations, seem to matter much less, in terms of total or current deforested area, than background and location characteristics. Thus, policies that reduce deforestation on the frontier would do so differently among different migrant groups, according to their prior experiences and current location characteristics (new or consolidated frontiers).

10.3. ENVIRONMENTAL POLICY: THE ROLE OF *LEGAL RESERVES* AND *PERMANENTLY PROTECTED AREAS*

In order to understand why deforestation is 'excessive' and why environmental policy is inefficient, the reader must be minimally familiar with forest legislation in Brazil. Environmental policy in Brazil is too often (mis)understood as defining legislation. The result is that policy often focuses on the 'written law' as an end in itself and not as an enabling tool for government to change the behavior of economic agents. Therefore, environmental law, as sound as it may be, rarely finds continuity in the executive branch of government. This means that the normative approach based on command and control and therefore on strong government enforcement action, is unrealistic in its application, given governmental constraints. Thus, the relevance that the normative approach could have for forest conservation becomes secondary to the government ineptitude in dealing with the environment.

A good example of good legislation and poor enforcement is the Forest Code (Law 4771/65 of 15 September 1965) that embodies the Brazilian forest legislation (Milaré, 2004). The Forest Code was amended by a Provisional Measure in 2001 (Medida Provisória 2166/67 of 24 August 2001) which enhanced the role that command and control has usually (ineffectively) played on forest conservation. The Forest Code specifies two special categories for forest protection in rural properties in Brazil: *legal reserves* and *permanently protected areas*. Legal reserves are areas within a given rural property that must be set aside and destined for the sustainable use of natural resources, the conservation and rehabilitation of ecological processes, the conservation of biodiversity and the protection of native flora and fauna (Milaré 2004). Permanently protected areas are defined as areas covered with native or non-native vegetation that have the following functions: to preserve hydrological resources, to preserve the landscape, to maintain geological stability, to protect biodiversity, to ensure the genetic flow of fauna and flora, to protect the soil and to assure the well-being of the human population (Milaré 2004). Furthermore, the legal reserve area must not coincide with the permanently protected area. The consequences of these legal concepts for the Amazonian farmer are illustrated below.

Any privately held rural property in the Amazon rainforest must contain a legal reserve that represents 80 percent[1] of the property area. Until 2001, the size of the legal reserve used to be 50 percent of the property area, but this was increased to 80 percent in that year by a Provisional Measure (a presidential decree). The remaining 20 percent of the property area can be cleared provided that the following are fully preserved: riparian vegetation, slopes above 45 degrees and inundated areas.[2] These areas are the *permanently protected areas*. Therefore, Amazonian producers must: (a) set aside 80 percent of their property for conservation (which can only be used when there is a management plan certified by the environmental authority) and (b) fully protect the permanently protected areas, which must not coincide with the legal reserve. The land in any private property that can actually be deforested is, therefore, at most 20 percent of the total property area. Furthermore, any agricultural activity (aside from small family farming) must be fully licensed. This is much ado about nothing because despite the legislation that regulates forest use, institutions are not sufficiently strong and resourceful to enforce the law in each property. The outcome, as we have seen in Chapter 8, is excessive total deforestation.

In order to control human settlement in environmentally sensitive areas, the Ministry of the Environment (MMA) and the Institute of Colonization and Agrarian Reform (INCRA) jointly signed, in 1999, an Executive Order (Portaria 88/99) prohibiting settlements in areas of primary and secondary dense forests. This Executive Order was incorporated into the Provisional Measure (Art. 37-A, paragraph 6) mentioned above, so that it must be enforced as law. However coherent these policies may sound, INCRA continues to clear forests for human settlement in the Amazon.

The gap between legislation on paper and its enforcement has left behind a clear record of 'excessive' deforestation. Since the early 1990s, Brazil has been losing approximately 0.5 percent of this area annually. On average, this figure corresponds to 17 000-18 000 square kilometers (Toni and Kaimowitz, 2003). This happened because the enforcement of such policies depends on the strength of government institutions which, in the Amazon, fail to enforce policies in a way that does justice to the very clever legislation. There is the possibility that forest policy is overly strict, in which case its implementation would lead to economic inefficiencies, but before anyone can make a claim with regard to such inefficiencies, there is the need for serious research conducted on hypotheses associated with optimal non-compliance.

We can claim, though, that legislation without enforcement was clearly unable to reduce excessive deforestation. We can also claim that command and control mechanisms that regulate land use on individual properties have not been effective. It would not be any easier to rely solely on market-based instruments, such as Pigouvian taxes or tradeable permits, given that the underlying assumptions for their functioning would be institutional strength, the existence of well-defined and enforceable property rights, and competitive markets, all of which are non-existent (in new frontiers) or very poorly developed (in consolidated frontiers). A hybrid solution that mixes command and control with market-based instruments may be the most appropriate until (a) institutions become sufficiently strong to enforce price-induced mechanisms (such as Pigouvian taxes) and (b) property rights are well-defined and enforced and markets are competitive; only then are market-based instruments likely to lead to efficient outcomes. As Snowareski (2003)[3] points out the environmental authority must be willing to migrate from widely used command and control instruments to ones that fully use market-based solutions. The adoption of such instruments must find the political space for development; for decades the Brazilian government has relied on command and control as the sole approach to environmental policy.

Two issues must be brought to the foreground in policy making for controlling deforestation in the Amazon. The first is institutional change, understood as the formal and informal rules of the game for example the law and norms as well as cultural traits and consciousness, respectively – that shape the behavior of economic agents (North, 1990). The second is the development and proper functioning of competitive factor and output markets. The association of these two issues is intrinsic because it is the institutional framework that sets the preconditions in which markets will function. In Brazil, as in many other developing countries, formal rules (legislation) are way ahead of enforcement of contracts, and therefore the individuals' readiness (and willingness) to comply is reduced because the certainty of impunity greatly reduces transaction costs (and increases net private benefits).

10.3.1.   The Role of Government and Levels of Government Intervention

Steff Proost[4] (1995) offers interesting insights that could provide guidance to government on positive behavior in environmental management. Proost explores the full gradient of possibilities for government action and economic outcomes in different scenarios. He finds that optimal solutions do not depend so much on the engagement of government, as on the set of assumptions, constraints and government organization that underlie the choice of policy. He observes, for example, that under certain conditions optimal outcomes do arise in the absence of government (private solutions).

In dealing with the Amazon, there is an underlying assumption among policy makers and policy analysts that *the* solution to deforestation must be sought through government action. While it is likely that a strong government could make a difference in reducing deforestation through policy enforcement, what happens when the hand of the state is feeble? Unlike legislation, policy enforcement cannot be created on paper. There is no continuum between legislation and enforcement because the legislative and the executive branches of government (federal, state, municipal) fail terribly to coordinate actions with regard to environmental policy. In the Amazonian context, the presence of the federal government is weak, state governments are institutionally fragile and municipal governments are not interested in containing deforestation because the opportunity costs involved in keeping areas of standing forests are too high (that is, foregone revenues from deforestation and the agricultural activities that ensue).

Furthermore, the incompatibilities observed between what is on paper (regulation) and actual practice (enforcement) of environmental policy in the Amazon is mostly due to an unclear definition of roles and responsibilities among levels of government and their respective executive agencies. These conflicting roles can be observed in three levels:

- Federal *versus* federal government agencies;
- Federal *versus* state government agencies;
- State *versus* state government agencies.

In briefly outlining the conflicts below, it will become evident that the one service that the Brazilian government could provide to society would be the implementation of an environmental system of cooperative federalism, resolving the pending issues of roles and responsibilities among federal, state and municipal governments.

10.3.1.1. Federal versus federal government agencies

In Brazil, the Ministry of the Environment (MMA) is the government body responsible for proposing policies for environmental management. Within the MMA, the Secretariat for the Coordination of Amazonian Affairs has the prerogative of establishing policy priorities and defining strategies for environmental conservation in the Amazon region. The government's environmental enforcement agency is the Brazilian Institute for Renewable and Non-renewable Natural Resources (IBAMA).

For a long time, before MMA was created, IBAMA (and its predecessor IBDF – the Brazilian Institute for Forest Development) was responsible for recommending, prioritizing and enforcing environmental policy. Later, after the Ministry was created, the unclear division of responsibilities between the two institutions led to inter-institutional rivalry and the ineffective enforcement of environmental policy at the federal level.

IBAMA is an enforcement agency that often abuses its prerogative of using coercive instruments (fines) to deal with environmental management in the Amazon. The main problems with IBAMA in enforcing environmental policy reside in four areas: (i) the rules established by the headquarters are not generally pursued by the institution's regional offices in the Amazon; (ii) due to institutional failure, penalties are rarely collected, rendering ineffective the command and control instruments used by the agency (ceilings on deforestation); (iii) enforcement is arbitrary and unsupervised, with the aggravating factor that field staff are insufficiently trained to undertake their tasks, which frequently leads to mishandling of forms so that offences are not prosecuted; (iv) the combination of institutional failure, arbitrary methods and unqualified individuals with low salaries opens the way to widespread misconduct on the part of federal agents. This has strongly affected the credibility of the federal government in the public's eyes in enforcing environmental legislation.

The conflicting roles of MMA and IBAMA are not the only challenge for the federal government with regard to environmental management in the Amazon. The Ministry of Agrarian Development (MDA) and its executive branch that responds to agrarian reform issues – the Institute for Colonization and Agrarian Reform (INCRA) – face similar conflicts. Despite the existence of stringent legislation prohibiting human settlement or agrarian reform in areas of primary and secondary dense forests (except for agro-extractivist projects), INCRA continues its titling procedures and land distribution programme in such areas. Besides the conflicting intra-ministerial roles, there has been much uncoordinated action between the MMA and the MDA.

Furthermore, Brazil is currently facing an 'agricultural divide': large (agribusiness) and family farmers are handled by two different ministries that do not coordinate actions internally. While the Ministry of Agriculture (MA) deals with the large productive sector that propels the Brazilian economy (and is responsible for much of the deforestation), the Ministry for Agrarian Development (MDA) deals with family farming and agrarian reform (which, as we have seen in this book, are only marginal to the bulk of deforestation). There is no evidence that government attempts to promote the coexistence of the large and small or to coordinate actions between the two Ministries. While agribusiness representatives use the argument of efficiency and revenues from export of grains and cotton, family farmers would like to see a 'revolution' in the field, where family agriculture would be the solution to Brazil's unequal land distribution.

Since agriculture is the main driver of deforestation in the Amazon, it would only make sense for the federal government to coordinate the actions of these two ministries through the Ministry of the Environment. As much as this would make sense, it simply does not happen.

Environmental compliance depends on the consistency of enforcement. Until government agencies (Ministry of the Environment and the Ministries of Agriculture and Agrarian Development) come to a clear definition of roles and responsibilities regarding the enforcement of environmental legislation, the Amazon can have no hope for a governmental solution to the problem of rural settlement and deforestation. Without institutional modernization and reform, the current scenario poses a threat to the Amazonian rain forest.

10.3.1.2.   Federal versus state government institutions

In each of the Brazilian states, IBAMA has one or more regional offices that, in practice, function independently and often in conflict with the norms established by the headquarters. In each state of the Legal Amazon, there is also a state-level government institution that proposes and enforces environmental policy. The responsibilities of IBAMA's regional offices often collide with those of the state governments. In the case of issuing permits to deforest, for example, it is common for the two to have different and overlapping rules. A firm or individual that submits a request for a license to deforest and, for some technical reason, has it denied by one agency, can always turn to the other agency in order to obtain approval. If a routine inspection takes place by the agency that denied the license, penalties are unlikely to be applied because the supposed 'outlaw' holds documentation from the other government body authorizing the operation. This example does not represent an exception; rather, it happens quite frequently in the case of IBAMA and state-level environmental institutions. Like IBAMA, INCRA also has regional offices in the states, whose level of integration with state-level environmental authorities is dismal. Once again, until federal and state-level institutions define their roles and responsibilities, the enforcement of environmental legislation will continue to be precarious and excessive deforestation will continue to happen.

10.3.1.3. State versus state government
While INCRA's state offices oversee land distribution in lands that belong to the Union, each state of the Legal Amazon has its own land distribution authority that is responsible for colonization in state lands. In most states, the actions of land and environmental institutions are poorly integrated, which promotes the occupation of fragile environments whose carrying capacity do not generally support human settlement and agricultural production in the long run.

10.3.2. Proposing Coherent Policy Instruments to Contain Deforestation

Given the institutional failure and the pervasive market imperfections facing the Amazon region, designing an appropriate policy 'package' to contain deforestation is a challenging task. Rather than prescribing policy, this section recommends policy instruments that should be considered in the light of the discussions and results presented in this study. Whatever combination of policy instruments is used, the simultaneous goal must be to reduce excessive deforestation, promote best management practices in agriculture and penalize speculation and deforestation, in view of institutional failure and incipient markets.

10.3.2.1. Zoning and the Green VAT
There is an appropriate role for zoning and promoting settlement only where the land is sufficiently productive to sustain farming income. However,

as zoning cannot by itself control the intra-regional forces that promote deforestation, it should be accompanied by a redesign of regional fiscal policy by federal and state governments. Some states have successfully redesigned the legislation to redistribute part of the value-added tax income to municipalities based on the area that the municipality chooses to devote to conservation and on other ecological criteria. The objective of this ingenious mechanism is to pay for the environmental services provided by such municipalities. Many poor municipalities in the Amazon have adopted the 'Green VAT' (ICMS-Ecológico) as a source of revenue. The Green VAT has already been adopted successfully in many states of Brazil, including Paraná (in Southern Brazil), Minas Gerais (Southeast Brazil), Mato Grosso and Tocantins (Midwest) and Pernambuco (Northeast) among others.

10.3.2.2.   Taxing net worth and stumpage tax

Fiscal policy should tax net worth and capital gains from land sales, and levy a tax on deforestation on a per-hectare basis. A tax on net worth would increase the cost of deforestation undertaken only to legitimize property, since land corresponds to approximately 50 percent of a farmer's new worth. A tax on capital gains from land sales would increase the cost of speculating in the land market and improve the farming alternative. A tax on deforestation itself, such as stumpage tax, for instance, would increase the effective price of land, without exacerbating overheated land markets. To date, a system of stumpage taxes does not exist and faces strong resistance from pressure groups, mainly large Amazonian farmers.

10.3.2.3.   Improving the role of government

There is ample room for improving the role of government. The integration of federal and state-level environmental institutions is the key to reducing deforestation. A clear division of roles and coordinated actions among these institutions would reduce the uncertainty introduced by inconsistent and overlapping rules that do not allow for effective enforcement of environmental legislation and, certainly, do not support the implementation of economic instruments. The same can be said about INCRA and state land-titling agencies.

10.3.2.4.   Exploring the private solution alternative

Given pervasive market and institutional failures, command and control should not be dismissed altogether, but improved and used in combination with economic instruments. Traditional command and control, such as the 20 percent ceiling imposed by the *Medida Provisória* on the amount of land that can be cleared by farmers, have often proved to be ineffective. Market-based instruments are also difficult to implement because institutions are too weak to conduct credible monitoring of private action (deforestation). Therefore, government institutions should make adequate provision for law enforcement agents to use modern technology, such as satellite images and remote sensing techniques, to identify places where infractions have occurred. Then, based on technical field reports, the government should work closely with civil society on the public disclosure of monitoring results, and with public law officers to enforce legislation and penalize those who do not comply with the law. In doing this, government institutions would circumvent part of the problems of corruption associated with arbitrary enforcement of the law by field staff. Gradually, after a monitoring system that tracks deforestation at the individual property level is implemented, market-based instruments such as an offset system (in which farmers can trade their rights to deforest in the same ecoregion) or stumpage tax could be applied.

Some 90 percent of Brazil's land area is in private ownership and there is an urgent need for working models of private land conservation. This is especially the case in the Amazon where the concentration of private land ownership in some states is among the highest in Brazil, and where the percentage of land effectively protected (either in public or private reserves) is low.

As we have seen above, the current Brazilian legislation requires that landowners protect the 'permanently protected areas' (APPs) – gallery forests and slopes above 45 degrees of inclination, tops of hills and areas within 100 metres of the foot and the edge of plateaux. On top of that, 80 percent of the whole property, called 'legal reserve' has to be maintained undisturbed in areas of primary forest. While the APPs need restoration efforts on the part of landowners (that is, in private lands), there are several ways in which government can work with landowners to protect these lands.

Given the fact that most of the properties have been cleared almost completely due to the agriculture development incentive programs of the 60s and 70s, a few states have passed a law requiring landowners to restore forest in their properties during a 20-year period, something that in some cases is not economically interesting, nor ecologically viable. Alternatively, in some states like Mato Grosso, the legislation allows that, under certain ecological conditions, landowners acquire forestlands outside their properties as a compensation for the legal reserve that they do not wish to restore. This piece of legislation should be further supported by government to encourage landowners to buy large tracts of land jointly, thus complying with their environmental liability and at same time contributing to the conservation of large samples of ecosystems by restoring, for example, ecological viability over large areas within the same ecoregion.

Government and NGOs could help groups of farmers in two ways: (i) provide assistance to neighboring property owners to allocate their legal reserves so that, together, they form an ecological corridor where landscape fragmentation can be reversed and the ecosystem made functional again and (ii) provide assistance to farmers to acquire legal reserves outside of their properties to compensate for the environmental liabilities within their properties (only when restoration would not make ecological sense from the scientific point of view). While the concept of ecological corridors is not new and is widely accepted, the idea of compensating with legal reserves *ex-situ* is still underexploited and faces strong opposition from environmentalists. The compensation scheme would need to be designed to embrace both economic and ecological factors and enhance the gains for both. The idea is to mobilize these farmers to buy jointly a cluster of land that is ecologically relevant to offset the liabilities in their farms. There are several ways to do this. One would be for government (and NGOs interested in acquiring land for conservation) to provide financial incentives (subsidies or cost sharing) to induce farmers to compensate for their environmental liability in areas of ecological relevance. This would provide a one-time incentive for producers with an environmental liability to buy land outside their properties. The conditions under which this compensation could work are well described in Snowareski (2003).

From a purely economic standpoint, the best way to compensate for an environmental liability such as a degraded or non-existent legal reserve, would be through price-induced mechanisms based on the micro-regional value of land. In this way, liable farmers would not simply compensate elsewhere for the 80 percent of what would be their legal reserve (which is now converted to agriculture). They would compensate elsewhere an amount of land that would be equivalent in value to the 80 percent that is missing in his productive property. If there would be no market distortions in land markets (which is *not* the case in the Amazon today), then this system would assure full economic efficiency. The ambit of these trades – i.e., whether they would happen within or across micro basins or ecoregions – demands much scientific research (see Snowareski 2003 for a discussion on the topic).

10.3.2.5. Building on the path of a successful experience: the Mato Grosso pilot project

In 1999, a new approach to controlling land clearance was initiated by the State of Mato Grosso with very promising preliminary results. In the period 2000–2001, there was a 32 percent reduction in the marginal rate of deforestation compared to the period prior to the adoption of the pilot initiative (FEMA 2002). This experience deserves attention in this book because it provides a tool that enables state governments to enforce the law and therefore gain credibility. This pilot project has, therefore, the potential to help internalize the costs of excessive deforestation by large farmers, as we have observed in Chapter 8.

The idea of the project was to enforce environmental legislation on rural properties by calling on private landholders to license their operations at the State Environmental Agency. The licensing process required updated property titles and land use plans (including land conversion plans) that complied with existing environmental legislation, namely the Forest Code of 1965 and the Provisional Measure of 2001 (which revised the percentages of the land that should be set aside for conservation). Land use plans began to be monitored using satellite images and remote sensing technology, therefore reducing the likelihood of corruption. The environmental agency applied a simple command and control instrument to manage resource use, in accordance with the Forest Code. It enforced environmental legislation via the rights and obligations attached to property titles. Modern environmental economics advocates the adequate assignment and consequent enforcement of property rights as being crucial for achieving effective environmental conservation. The Mato Grosso system accommodated these principles and pioneered an innovative approach to conservation.

Decreasing land conversion rates during the project implementation phase provides evidence of success. The simultaneous increase in the state's GDP (almost 100 percent coming from grain production and ranching) suggests that the system legalized agricultural operations without compromising economic growth. The system's accomplishments have been widely recognized in the national and international media and in the scientific literature. However, state-level political support for the system decreased rapidly with the change of the Mato Grosso government in 2002; the system was fully conceived within the state government and proved to be vulnerable to political will. This system could, however, incorporate two additions that would make it work: (a) civil society, and not the government alone, should monitor deforestation and land use and (b) since there is no way of not being caught (because satellite images are processed regularly), property owners with an environmental liability should be given two choices: restore *in situ* or compensate *ex-situ* (given that the best available science will determine whether compensations may occur or not. If not, then restoration is the only option).

10.3.2.6. Improving market chains
There is also a role for improved market systems, storage, transport and roads, thus helping to break typical frontier monopsonies and monopolies to improve farmers' bargaining power in principal markets. Market chains must be improved to help small farmers – rather than large landowners – to appropriate the benefits from productivity increases. This improvement,

however, must be planned for the long run and scenarios must be developed prior to their actual undertaking. Road surfacing, for example, would certainly reduce transportation costs for grain produce on the one hand, but on the other hand, it would probably raise land prices and induce a run on land, and therefore increase deforestation. NGOs with local operations can assist government and the private sector in developing these future scenarios and offer advice on how to act so as to minimize overall social costs.

10.3.2.7.   Credit for conservation
The operation of credit and other institutions must be revised to eliminate strong incentives to deforest and offer opportunities for conservation. There are quite a few credit lines for medium and large farmers to undertake agricultural activities on the frontier, but none that finance restoration of degraded lands, for example. The transaction costs involved in obtaining micro-credit impose prohibitive constraints on small farmers.

10.3.2.8.   Conditionality clauses on federal government transfers
There must be conditionality clauses on federal government transfers to states and municipalities that would aim at environmental conservation. The *Fundo de Participação dos Estados* (FPE) and *Fundo de Participação dos Municípios* (FPM) are federal transfers from the federal government that are based on the population of each state and municipality. An environmental clause could be introduced into these transfers requiring municipalities to conserve their natural resources and enabling them to receive payment for environmental services provided.

10.3.2.9.   Decentralization
Lastly, all of the above should be developed as locally enforceable instruments, some at the state and some at the municipal levels. Since the adoption of the 1988 Constitution, democratization combined with fiscal decentralization has distributed proportionally more revenues than responsibilities. The federal government, on the one hand, is simply incapable of dealing with the complex set of policies necessary to ensure environmental conservation throughout Brazil. Local authorities, on the other hand, are now becoming politically and economically capable of taking on this task. This is especially true in the Amazon, where there is the greatest variety of local circumstances and where centralized environmental policy has not been successful. Local-level governance, however, must confront a powerful local élite (mostly composed of an urban middle class with political clout) which derives private benefits from the illegal use of the environment. Decentralization of environmental policy is a sensitive issue that warrants an in-depth analysis considering different scenarios, from one in which there is a totally corrupt

government (which would undermine decentralization efforts) to one that is fair. The involvement of civil society organizations in the decentralization process is of utmost importance to mitigate the risk of corruption.

10.3.2.10. Concluding remarks

Given the *win-lose* scenario that emerged during the 1980s, conservation policy must approach the 'carrot-and-the-stick' solution. First, government must be willing to forge strategic alliances with large farmers and provide them with incentives that would induce and reward good farming practices, such as increasing production through intensification and penalizing opening of new areas. Second, government needs to strengthen its enforcement capacity and target large farmers as excessive deforestation in the Amazon can be safely attributed to the absolute certainty of impunity. Third, civil society must strengthen its capacity to monitor land conversion and land use among large farmers and offer systematic disclosure of information on farmer behavior. Fourth, government needs to complement the traditional and ineffective command and control approach with market-based instruments that would simultaneously reduce the cost of policy enforcement and the cost of compliance.

These actions are not sufficient, but are certainly necessary to curb the pervasive market failures that have historically fostered private gains while undermining the forest resource base. They are also needed to warrant a model of regional development that makes optimal use of the forest, from an economic, social, and environmental standpoint.

These policy measures are aimed at reducing deforestation by promoting good farming practices that reward migrants for staying on the land they have already cleared, weaken their motives for speculative and unproductive deforestation in the current location, and – in places where turnover is high – reduce the economic incentives to move on to other frontiers deeper into the Amazon. Moreover, they urge for the design of development and economic policies in tune with the *win-lose* scenario discussed in this study by offering farmers a private solution such as enabling a system of compensation for the environmental liabilities in the current site.

Coordination among government institutions responsible for enforcing such policies is essential for curbing deforestation. Substantial institutional development is needed to achieve this goal. Environmental institutions must learn to use economic policy instruments to achieve environmental conservation. Economic institutions must learn to wield fiscal and pricing instruments to fulfil environmental objectives. Local governments must take on executive responsibilities previously reserved for the federal government. International organizations must broaden their objectives beyond establishing protected areas and they must contribute to improving the design and enforcement capacity of local authorities to reverse local preferences for deforesting.

There are certain obstacles to these policies that must be overcome. Designing and enforcing zoning, rural extension and improvements in marketing and credit systems will be a major undertaking. Long-term political resistance to taxes on capital gains will not disappear merely because such taxation will support conservation. Stumpage taxes have been difficult enough to levy on large-scale logging, let alone on masses of small, medium and large farmers.

One important consideration for the above policies to hold is that successful locations not be overrun by inter-regional migrants in a perverse demonstration effect. The evidence presented in Chapters 2 and 3 indicates that this is not likely. Migration dynamics are hard to reverse and the motives that stimulated this type of migration during the 1970s are no longer present. Inter-regional migrations throughout Brazil have diminished and stabilized. Thus it is highly improbable that successful local farming would trigger another Amazon-bound migration similar to that of the 1970s.

Although all of these issues are relevant, it is not possible to address them in this chapter. The objective here is merely to make explicit what policy instruments are needed to curb Amazonian deforestation, not to provide a blueprint for their implementation.

10.4.   RECENT GOVERNMENT INITIATIVES

After two decades without substantial investment in Amazonian infrastructure, the Brazilian government is proposing policies that will profoundly alter the regional landscape. One of the most controversial initiatives is the surfacing of the BR-163 road; this would greatly reduce transportation costs to farmers (mainly large soybean growers in Mato Grosso) and cause a population inflow as land prices rise with the development initiative. This is the single most significant development action since the beginning of the 1980s, when the BR-364, which links the state capitals of Cuiabá in Mato Grosso and Porto Velho in Rondônia, was surfaced. The surfacing of BR-163 would dramatically increase access to the Amazon's natural resources. Second, the Ministry of Environment is implementing a new forest policy based on the expansion and consolidation of national and state forests in the Legal Amazon (National Forests Program – PNF). The government's goal is to allocate 500 000 square kilometres (10 percent of the Brazilian Amazon) for the creation of national forests. And, finally, the federal government has made an international commitment to protect biodiversity in the Amazon through expanding the national protected areas system to cover a minimum of a representative 10 percent of the Brazilian territory.

These government initiatives offer both opportunities and risks. The risks stem mainly from the investment in infrastructure and from the difficulty in organizing economic forces that improved access unleashes. In many ways, these initiatives may reverse some of the perverse effects that lead farmers to deforest, such as the reduction in information gaps, creation of structured markets and reduction in transport costs in the output markets. The opportunities also derive from a heightened government commitment to confront its environmental responsibilities, in response to clearly articulated public support for more rational land use patterns in the region.

NOTES

1. The percentage of the land destined for legal reserve depends on the vegetation type. For example, in the Amazonian savannas, the size of the legal reserve is 35 percent. The 80 percent mentioned here is for areas of Amazonian forests exclusively.
2. Milaré (2004) cites more than sixteen categories of permanently peserved areas. See Milaré, Édis 2004. *Direito do Ambiente: Doutrina, Jurisprudência, Glossário*, São Paulo: Editora Revista dos Tribunais (3rd Edition).
3. Snowareski, Maurício 2003. *Permissões Negociáveis para Corte Raso em Reserva Legal: Uma Avaliação da Aplicabilidad no Arco do Desflorestamento da Amazônia*. University of Brasília, Department of Economics: Master's Thesis.
4. Proost, S. 1995. 'Public policies and externalities', in Folmer, H. and Gabel, H.L. (eds) *Principles of Environmental and Resource Economics*. Aldershot: Edward Elgar.

References

ABEP. 1998. *Gente em Movimento: Um Retrato da Migração no Brasil*. São Paulo: Associação Brasileira de Estudos Populacionais.

Alston, L.J., G.D. Libecap, and R. Schneider. 1996. 'The Determinants and Impact of Property Rights: Land Titles on the Brazilian Frontier'. *The Journal of Law, Economics and Organization*, 12(1): 26–61.

Alston, L.J., G.D. Libecap and B. Mueller. 1999. *Titles, Conflict, and Land Use: The Development of Property Rights and Land Reform on the Amazon Frontier*. Ann Arbor: The University of Michigan Press.

Alvin, P.T. 1978. 'Perspectivas de Produção Agrícola na Região Amazônica'. *Interciencia*, 3: 243–51.

Aragón, L. 1978. 'Migration to Northern Goiás'. Ph.D. dissertation, Michigan State University.

Australian Academy of Technological Sciences and Engineering. 1988. *Technology in Australia 1788–1988*, pp. 56–57. Online edition, 2000. http://www.austehc.unimelb.edu.au/tia/058.html.

Bacha, E.L. 1977. 'Issues and Evidence on Recent Brazilian Economic Growth'. *World Development*, 5(2): 47–67.

Bakx, K. 1990. 'The Shanty Town, Final Stage of Rural Development? The Case of Acre'. In Goodman, D. and A. Hall (eds). 1990. *The Future of Amazonia: Destruction or Sustainable Development?* London: Macmillan.

Belassa, B. 1979. 'Incentive Policies in Brazil'. *World Development*, 7(2): 1023–42.

Bergsman, J. 1970. *Brazil's Industrialization and Trade Policy*. New York: Oxford University Press.

Berry, R.A. and W.R. Cline. 1979. *Agrarian Structure and Productivity in Developing Countries*. Geneva: International Labor Organization.

Binswanger, H.P. 1994. 'Brazilian Policies that Encourage Deforestation in the Amazon'. *World Development*, 19(7): 821–29.

Binswanger, H.P. and J. McIntire. 1987. 'Behavioural and Material Determinants of Production Relations in Land Abundant Tropical Agriculture'. *Economic Development and Cultural Change*, 22: 75–99.

Bojanic, A. and R.G. Echeverría. 1990. *Retornos a la Inversión en Investigación Agrícola en Bolívia: El Caso de la Soya*. ISNAR Staff

Notes 90–94, The Hague: International Service for National Agricultural Research (ISNAR).

Boserup, E. 1965. *The Conditions of Agricultural Growth: The Economics of Agrarian Change under Population Pressure*. London: George Allen & Unwin.

Brandão, A.S.P. and F. Rezende. 1988. 'The Behavior of Land Prices and Land Rents in Brazil'. Paper presented at the XX International Conference of Agricultural Economists, Buenos Aires, 24–31 August.

Brito, M.A. 1987. 'Questões Associadas à Evolução Recente da Agricultura Brasileira na Região Norte na Década de 70'. *Revista Brasileira de Geografia*, **49** (January/March): 11–46.

Bunker, S.G. 1979. 'Power Structures and Exchange between Government Agencies in the Expansion of the Agricultural Sector in Pará'. *Studies in Comparative and International Development*, **14**(I): 56–76.

Bunker, S.G. 1985. *Underdeveloping the Amazon: Extraction, Unequal Exchange, and the Failure of the Modern State*. Chicago: University of Chicago Press.

Burt, O. 1981. 'Farm Level Economics of Soil Conservation in the Palouse Area of the Northwest'. *American Journal of Agricultural Economics*, **63**(1): 83–92.

Campari, J. 1996. 'The Dynamics of Deforestation in the Brazilian Amazon: The Role of Liquidity Constraints on the Optimal Allocation of Forest Resources'. Working Paper. Department of Economics, University of Texas at Austin.

Campari, J. 2002. 'The Economics of Deforestation in the Amazon: Evidence from Colonization Projects in Brazil'. Doctoral dissertation presented to the Economics Department of the University of Texas at Austin.

Chayanov, A.V. 1966. *The Theory of Peasant Economy*. In D. Thorner, B. Kerblay, and R.E.F. Smith (eds). Irwin, Illinois: Homewood.

Chomitz, K.M. and T.S. Thomas. 2001. 'Geographic Patterns of Land Use and Land Intensity in the Brazilian Amazon'. Development Research Group discussion paper. Washington, DC: World Bank.

Davis, S. 1977. *Victims of a Miracle*. Cambridge: Cambridge University Press.

De Janvry, A. 1981. *The Agrarian Question and Reformism in Latin America*. Baltimore: The Johns Hopkins University Press.

Dracon, R. 1990. 'Government Policy and Environmental Quality in Developing Countries: Complements or Substitutes?' Paper. Department of Economics, University of California, Santa Barbara.

Encarta99. *Brazil*. Microsoft Corporation. CD-ROM: 1993–98.

Evans, P. 1979. *Dependent Development: The Alliance of Multinationals, the State, and Local Capital in Brazil*. Princeton: Princeton University Press.

Faminow, M.D. 1998. *Cattle, Deforestation, and Development in the Amazon: An Economic, Agronomic and Environmental Perspective*. London: Oxford University Press.

FAO/ECLA. 1964. *Livestock in Latin America*. Rome: United Nations Food and Agricultural Organization/Economic Commission on Latin America.

FAO/UNDP. 1992. 'Principais Indicadores Sócio-Econômicos dos Assentamentos de Reforma Agrária'. FAO/PNUD/Ministério da Agricultura e Reforma Agrária. Project BRA-87/022. Brazil.

Fearnside, P. 1986. *Human Carrying Capacity of the Brazilian Rain Forest*. New York: Columbia University Press.

Fearnside, P. 2001. 'Land Tenure Issues as Factors in Environmental Destruction in Brazilian Amazonia: The Case of Southern Pará'. *World Development*, **8**(29): 1361–72.

Feder, E. 1979. 'Lean Cows, Fat Ranchers, a Study of the Mexican Beef Industry'. Manuscript. Berlin.

Feder, G. 1985. 'The Relation between Farm Size and Farm Productivity: The Role of Family Labour, Supervision, and Credit Constraints'. *Journal of Development Economics*, **18**: 297–313.

FEMA. 2002. 'Sistema de Licenciamento em Propriedades Rurais de Mato Grosso: Relatório 2000–2001' (forthcoming). Cuiabá, Brazil: Fundação Estadual de Meio Ambiente de Mato Grosso (FEMA).

Fishlow, A. 1973. 'Brazilian Size Distribution of Income'. *American Economic Review* (62): 391–402.

Foweraker, J. 1981. *The Struggle for Land: A Political Economy of the Pioneer Frontier in Brazil, 1930 to the Present*. London: Cambridge University Press.

Gasques, J.C. and C. Yakomizo. 1986. 'Resultado de Vinte Anos de Incentivos Fiscais na Agropecuária da Amazônia'. XIV Encontro Nacional de Economia, ANPEC, Brasília, December, vol. 2.

Gazeta Mercantil. 2001. *Balanço Anual*. Ano XXV(25/July 2001): 200–202.

Gentry, A. and J. López-Parodi. 1980. 'Deforestation and Increased Flooding in the Upper Amazon'. *Science*, **210**: 1354–6.

Gillis, M. and R. Repetto. 1988. *Deforestation and Government*. New York: Cambridge University Press.

Goodland, R. 1980. 'Environmental Ranking of Development Projects in Brazil'. *Environmental Conservation*, **7**: 762–65.

Goodland, R. 1985. 'Brazil's Environmental Progress in Amazonian Development'. In Hemming, J. (ed.). 1985. *Change in the Amazon Basin,*

Vol. 1: Man's Impact on Forests and Rivers. Manchester: Manchester University Press.

Goodland, R. and H. Irwin. 1975. *Amazon Jungle: Green Hell to Red Deserts?* Amsterdam: Elsevier.

Hecht, S.B. 1984. 'Cattle Ranching in Amazonia: Political and Ecological Considerations'. In Schmink, M. and C. Wood (eds). 1984. *Frontier Expansion in Amazonia*, pp. 366–98. Gainesville: University of Florida Press.

Hecht, S.B., R. Norgaard and G. Possio. 1988. 'The Economics of Cattle-Raising in Eastern Amazonia'. *Interciência*, **3**: 233–40.

Heltberg, R. 1998. 'Rural Market Imperfections and the Farm-Size Productivity Relationship: Evidence from Pakistan'. *World Development*, **26**(10): 1807–26.

Hochman, E. and D. Zilberman. 1986. 'Optimal Strategies of Development Processes of Frontier Environments'. *The Science of the Total Environment*, **55**(1): 111–20.

Holden, S.T. 1991. 'Peasants and Sustainable Development – The *Chitemene* Region of Zambia – Theory, Evidence and Models'. Ph.D. dissertation. Agricultural University of Norway, Ås.

Holden, S.T. 1993. 'Peasant Household Modelling: Farming Systems Evolution and Sustainability in Northern Zambia'. *Agricultural Economics*, **9**: 241–67.

Holden, S.T. 1997. 'Adjustment Policies, Peasant Household Resource Allocation, and Deforestation in Northern Zambia: An Overview and Some Policy Conclusions'. *Forum of Development Studies*, **1**: 117–34.

Holden, S.T. 1998. *Shifting Cultivation and Deforestation: A Farm Household Model.* Discussion Paper D-08/1998. Department of Economics and Social Sciences. Agricultural University of Norway, Ås.

Holden, S.T., B. Shiferaw and M. Wilk. 1998. 'Poverty, Market Imperfections, and Time Preferences: Of Relevance for Environmental Policy?'. *Environment and Development Economics*, **3**: 105–30.

Hunt, D. 1979. 'Chayanov's Model of Peasant Household Resource Allocation'. *Journal of Peasant Studies*, **6**(3): 247–85.

IADB. 1971–76. *Inter-American Development Bank Annual Reports.* Washington, DC: IADB.

Ianni, O. 1979. *Colonização e Reforma Agrária na Amazônia.* Petrópolis: Editora Vozes.

IBGE. 1920–85. *Agricultural Census.* Rio de Janeiro: Instituto Brasileiro de Geografia e Estatística

IBGE. 1989. *Anuário Estatístico do Brazil 1989.* Rio de Janeiro: Instituto Brasileiro de Geografia e Estatística.

IBGE. 2001. *Censo Populacional*. Rio de Janeiro: Instituto Brasileiro de Geografia e Estatística.

Jones, D.W. et al. 1992. *Farming in Rondônia*. Report for the Oak Ridge National Laboratory for the U.S. Department of Energy. Department of Regional Planning, Virginia Polytechnic Institute and State University, Blacksburg, Virginia.

Kaimowitz, D. and A. Angelsen. 1998. 'Economic Models of Tropical Deforestation – A Review'. Center for International Forestry Research (CIFOR), Indonesia.

Kaster, M. and E.R. Bonato. 1980. 'Contribuição das Ciências Agrárias para o Desenvolvimento: a Pesquisa em Soja'. *Revista de Economia Rural*, **18**(3): 415–34. Brasília, DF.

Katzman, Marvin T. 1977. 'Paradoxes of Amazonian Development in a "Resource-Starved" World'. *Journal of Development Areas*, **10**: 445–60.

Knight, P.T. 1971. *Brazilian Agriculture, Technology and Trade*. New York: Praeger.

Leff, N.H. 1967. 'Export Stagnation and Autarkik Development in Brazil'. *Quarterly Journal of Economics*. May: 286–301.

Low, A. 1986. *Agricultural Development in Southern Africa. Farm Household Economics and the Food Crisis*. London: James Currey.

Mahar, D. 1979. *Frontier Development Policy in Brazil: A Study of Amazonia*. New York: Praeger.

Mahar, D. 1989. *Government Policies and Deforestation in Brazil's Amazon Region*. Washington, DC: World Bank.

Malan, P.S. and R. Bonelli. 1977. 'The Brazilian Economy in the 70s: Old and New Development'. *World Development*, **5**(I/2): 19–37.

Margolis, M.L. 1973. *The Moving Frontier*. Gainesville: Florida University Press.

Margulis, S. 2001. 'Who are the Agents of Deforestation in the Amazon and Why do they Deforest?' Concept Paper. Brasília: World Bank.

Marques, Fabrício. 1993. 'Limite Imaginário'. *Veja*, **26**(22).

Martine, G. 1982. 'Expansão e Retração de Emprego na Fronteira Agrícola'. *Expansão da Fronteira Agrícola*. In N. Gligo and C. Muller (eds). Brasília: University of Brasília.

Martine, G. 1992. 'Processos Recentes de Concentração e Desconcentração Urbana no Brasil: Determinantes e Implicações'. Discussion Paper. Brasília, D.F.: Instituto Sociedade População e Natureza.

Martins, J. de S. 1975. *Capitalismo e Tradicionalismo: Estudos sobre as Contradições da Sociedade Agrária no Brasil*. São Paulo: Pioneira.

McConnell, K. 1983. 'An Economic Model of Soil Conservation'. *American Journal of Agricultural Economics*, **65**(1): 83–9.

Mesquita, O. and S.T. Silva. 1987a. 'A Evolução da Agricultura Brasileira na Década de 70'. *Revista Brasileira de Geografia*, **1**(49): 3–10.

Mesquita, O. and S.T. Silva. 1987b. 'A Evolução da Agricultura Brasileira na Região Sul Década de 70'. *Revista Brasileira de Geografia*, **1**(49): 159–95.

Mesquita, O. and S.T. Silva. 1987c. 'Da Policultura Regional à Hegemonia da Soja – O Oeste do Paraná em Questão'. *Revista Brasileira de Geografia*, **105**(January/June): 155–70.

Mink, S.D. 1993. *Poverty, Population, and the Environment*. Environment Discussion Paper 189. Washington, DC: World Bank.

Moliton, L.C. 1975. 'A Climate Study of the Energy and Moisture Fluxes of the Amazonas Basin with Considerations of Deforestation Effects'. Ph.D. dissertation, University of Wisconsin.

Monbeig, P. 1952. *Pionneurs et Planteurs de São Paulo*. Paris: Armand Colin.

Moore, B. 1968. *The Social Origins of Dictatorship and Democracy*. Boston: Beacon Press.

Moran, E. 1975. 'Pioneer Farmers of the Transamazon Highway'. Ph.D. dissertation, Department of Anthropology, University of Florida.

Moran, E. 1979. 'Criteria for Choosing Homesteaders in Brazil'. *Research in Economic Anthropology*, **2**: 339–59.

Moran, E. 1981. *Developing the Amazon*. Bloomington: Indiana University Press.

Moran, E. 1984. 'Colonization in the Transamazon Highway'. In M. Schmink and C. Wood. 1984. *Frontier Expansion in Amazonia*. Gainesville: University of Florida Press.

Moran, E. 1989. 'Adaptation and Maladaptation in Newly Settled Areas'. In Schumman D.A. and W.L. Partridge (eds). 1989. *The Human Ecology of Tropical Land Settlement in Latin America*. Boulder: Westview Press.

Moreira, M and H. Moura. 1997. 'Dinâmica Populacional da Região Norte'. *Seminário Desenvolvimento Econômico e Crescimento Populacional: Tendências Recentes e Cenários Futuros*. Campinas, SP: 3–4 April.

Mueller, B. 1994. 'A Dynamic Model of Frontier Settlement'. Conference Proceedings. XVI Encontro Brasileiro de Econometria. Sociedade de Econometria, Florianópolis.

Myers, N. 1980. *Conversion of Moist Tropical Forests*. Washington, DC: National Academy of Sciences.

North, D. 1990. *Institutions, Institutional Change and Economic Performance*. New York: Cambridge University Press.

O'Donnell, G. 1979. *Modernization and Bureaucratic Authoritarianism*. Berkeley: University of California Press.

Ozório de Almeida, A.L. 1985. 'Migrações Internas e Pequena Produção na Amazônia: Uma Análise da Política de Colonização do INCRA'. Internal Discussion Paper 77 (May). IPEA: Rio de Janeiro.

Ozório de Almeida, A.L. 1991. 'Colonização da Amazônia: Reforma Agrária numa Fronteira Internacional'. *Perspectivas da Economia Brasileira – 1992*. Rio de Janeiro/Brasília: IPEA.

Ozório de Almeida, A.L. 1992. *The Colonization of the Amazon*. Austin: University of Texas Press.

Ozório de Almeida, A.L. and J.S. Campari. 1996. *Sustainable Settlement in the Brazilian Amazon*. New York: Oxford University Press.

Ozório de Almeida, A.L and C.F. Velloso dos Santos. 1990. 'A Colonização Oficial na Amazônia nos Anos 80'. Texto para Discussão No. 207. Rio de Janeiro: Instituto de Pesquisa Econômica Aplicada (IPEA).

Pires, J.M. and G.T. Prance. 1977. 'The Amazon Forest: A Natural Heritage to be Preserved'. In Prance, G.T. and T. Elias (eds). *Extinction is Forever*. Bronx: New York Botanical Garden.

Pompermayer, M.J. 1979. *The State and Frontier in Brazil*. Ph.D. dissertation, Stanford University.

Repetto, R. 1989. 'Economic Incentives for Sustainable Production'. In Schramm, G. and J. Warford, (eds), *Environmental Management and Economic Development*. Baltimore, MD: John Hopkins University Press.

Rezende, G.C. 1981. 'Credito Rural Subsidiado e Preço da Terra no Brasil'. Internal Discussion Paper 41. Rio de Janeiro: IPEA/INPES.

Reydon, B.P. and L.A. Plata. 2002. 'Evolução Recente do Preço da Terra Rural no Brasil e os Impactos do Programa da Cédula da Terra'. In http://www.nead.org.br/portugues/estudos/bastiaan.php.

Roche, J. 1959. *La Colonisation Allemande e le Rio Grande do Sul*. Paris: Université de Paris, Institute des Hautes Études.

Ruthemberg, H. 1980. *Farming Systems in the Tropics*, 3rd edn. Oxford: Clarendon Press.

Salati, E., A. Dall'Olio, E. Matsui and S.R. Gat. 1979. 'Recycling of Water in the Amazon Basin: An Isotope Study'. *Water Resources Research*, 15(5): 1250–58.

Sanders, J.H. and V.W. Ruttan. 1978. 'Biased Choice of Technology in Brazilian Agriculture'. In Binswanger, H.P. and V.W. Ruttan (eds). *Induced Innovation, Technology, Institutions, and Development*. Baltimore: Johns Hopkins University Press.

Santos, R. 1979. 'Sistema de Propriedade e Relações de Trabalho no Meio Rural Paraense'. In Monteiro da Costa (ed.). *Amazônia: Desenvolvimento e Ocupação*. Rio de Janeiro: IPEA/INPES.

Sawyer, D. 1979. *Peasants and Capitalism in the Amazon Frontier*. Ph.D. dissertation, Harvard University.

Sawyer, D. 1984. 'Frontier Expansion and Retraction in Brazil'. In Schmick, M. and C. Wood. *Frontier Expansion in Amazônia*, pp. 180–203. Gainesville: University of Florida Press.

Sawyer, D. 1990. 'Migration and Urban Development in the Amazon'. Paper prepared for the World Bank as part of a critical literature review on Amazonian migrations. Washington, DC: World Bank.

Sawyer, D. 2001. 'Evolução Demográfica, Qualidade de Vida e Desmatamento na Amazônia'. *Causas e Dinâmica do Desmatamento na Amazônia*, pp. 73–90. Brasília, DF: Ministério do Meio Ambiente.

Schmink, M. 1982. 'Land Conflicts in Amazonia'. *American Ethnologist*, **9**(2): 341–57.

Schmink, M. and C. Wood (eds). 1984. *Frontier Expansion in Amazonia*. Gainesville: University of Florida Press.

Schmink, M. and C. Wood. 1992. *Contested Frontiers in Amazonia*. New York: Columbia University Press.

Schneider, R. 1995. *Government and the Economy on the Amazon Frontier*. World Bank Environment Papers 11. Washington, DC: World Bank.

Schneider, R., E. Arima, A. Veríssimo, P. Barreto and C. Souza Jr. 2000. *Sustainable Amazon: Limitations and Opportunities for Rural Development*. Brasília/Belém: World Bank/Imazon.

SEPLAN/MT. 2000. *Annual Report 2000*. Secretariat of Planning of the State of Mato Grosso, Brazil.

Serôa da Motta, R. 1991. 'Recent Evolution of Environmental Management in the Brazilian Public Sector: Issues and Recommendations'. In D. Erocal (ed.). *Environmental Management in Developing Countries*. Paris: OECD.

Serrão, E.A.S., D. Napstad and R. Walker. 1996. 'Analysis: Upland Agricultural and Forestry Development in the Amazon: Sustainability, Criticality, and Resilience'. *Ecological Economics*, **18**: 3–13.

Skole, D.L., W.H. Chomentowsky, W.A. Salas and A.D. Nobre. 1994. 'Physical and Human Dimensions of Deforestation in Amazonia'. *Bioscience*, **44**(5): 312–22.

Smith, N.J.H., E.A.S. Serrão, P.T. Alvin and I.C. Falesi. 1995. *Amazonia – Resiliency and Dynamism of the Land and its People*. Tokyo: United Nations Press.

Smith, N.J. H., I.C. Falesi, P.T. Alvin and E.A.S. Serrão. 1996. 'Agroforestry Trajectories among Small Holders in the Brazilian Amazon: Innovation and Resilience in Pioneer and Older Settled Areas'. *Ecological Economics*, **18**: 15–27.

Sombroek, W. (n.d.). 'Annual Rainfall and Dry-Season Strength in the Amazon Region and Their Environmental Consequences'.

Southgate, D. and D. Pearce. 1987. 'Natural Resources Degradation in Developing Countries: A Causal Analysis of Agricultural Colonisation'.

Discussion Paper 87-26. Department of Economics, University College London.

Southgate, D. and D. Pearce. 1988. *Agricultural Colonization and Environmental Degradation in Frontier Developing Economies.* Environment Department Working Paper 9. Washington, DC: World Bank.

Spears, J. 1988. 'Continuing Tropical Deforestation: A Review of Priority Areas for Technological and Policy Research'. Environment Department Working Paper 10. Washington, DC: World Bank.

Stedman, P.A. 1998. *Root Causes of Biodiversity Loss: Case Study of the Brazilian Cerrado.* Washington, DC: World Wildlife Fund.

Stepan, A. 1968. *The Military in Power.* Princeton: Princeton University Press.

Stepan, A. 1973. *Authoritarian Brazil.* Princeton: Princeton University Press.

Stiglitz, J.E. and A. Weiss. 1981. 'Credit Rationing in Markets with Imperfect Information'. *American Economic Review*, **71**(3): 393–410.

Toni, F. and D. Kaimowitz. 2003. 'Municípios e Gestão Florestal na Amazônia: Introdução e Marco Teórico', pp. 23–63. In *Municípios e Gestão Florestal na Amazônia.* Natal (Brazil): A.S. Editores.

Waibel, L. 1979. 'As Zonas Pioneiras do Brazil'. *Capítulos de Geografia Tropical e do Brasil*, 2nd edn, pp. 279–312. Rio de Janeiro: IBGE.

Waino, J. 1998. 'Brazil's Agricultural Sector Benefits from Economic Reform'. *Agricultural Outlook* AO-251, May. Economic Research Service, United States Department of Agriculture: 37–43.

Walker, R. and A.K.O. Homma. 1996. 'Land Use and Land Cover Dynamics in the Brazilian Amazon: An Overview'. *Ecological Economics*, **18**: 67–80.

Wilkinson, J. and B. Sorj. 1992. *Structural Adjustment and the Institutional Dimensions of Agricultural Research and Development in Brazil: Soybeans, Wheat and Sugar Cane.* OECD/GD (92). Paris: OECD Development Centre.

Williams, G.W. and R.L. Thompson. 1984. 'The Brazilian Soybean Policy: The International Effects of Intervention'. *American Journal of Agricultural Economics*, **66**(4): 488–98.

Wood, C. and Marianne Schmink. 1979. 'Blaming the Victim: Small Farmer Production in an Amazon Colonization Project'. *Study in Third World Societies*, **7**: 77–93.

World Bank. 1999. *Brazil: Country Brief.* 10 September 1999. http://wbln0018.worldbank.org.

Young, C.E.F. and J.R.B. Fausto. 1998. 'Valoração de Recursos Naturais como Instrumento de Análise da Expansão da Fronteira Agrícola'. *A Economia Brasileira em Perspectiva.* Rio de Janeiro: IPEA.

Index